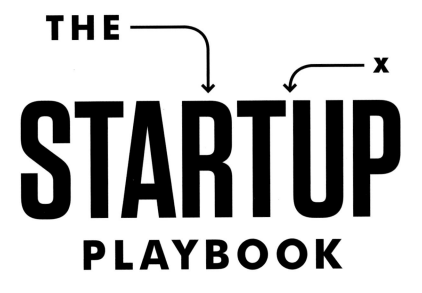

THE STARTUP PLAYBOOK

THE

STARTUP X

PLAYBOOK

Secrets *of the* Fastest-Growing Startups
from Their Founding Entrepreneurs

David S. Kidder

New York Times **Bestselling Author**

With Hanny Hindi

Foreword by LinkedIn founder Reid Hoffman

CHRONICLE BOOKS
SAN FRANCISCO

LIBRARY OF CONGRESS CATALOGING-IN-PUBLICATION DATA:

KIDDER, DAVID S.

  THE STARTUP PLAYBOOK : SECRETS OF THE FASTEST-GROWING STARTUPS FROM THEIR FOUNDING ENTREPRENEURS
/ DAVID S. KIDDER.

      P. CM.

  ISBN 978-1-4521-0504-8

 1. NEW BUSINESS ENTERPRISES—MANAGEMENT. 2. ENTREPRENEURSHIP. I. TITLE.

  HD62.5.K522 2013

  658.1'1—DC23

                                2012019684

MANUFACTURED IN CHINA

DESIGNED BY MINE™

10 9 8 7 6 5 4 3 2 1

CHRONICLE BOOKS LLC

680 SECOND STREET

SAN FRANCISCO, CALIFORNIA 94107

WWW.CHRONICLEBOOKS.COM

DEDICATION

This book is for my most important "startup" and the center of my life and heart, my family: Johanna and my three sons, Jack, Stephen, and Lucas.

I hope this book inspires and serves you as it has me in living out the purpose of our family; to utilize our God-given gifts to make an extraordinary, positive impact on people and the world.

CONTENTS

9 **FOREWORD**
REID HOFFMAN

11 **INTRODUCTION**

20 **CHRIS ANDERSON**
FUTURE PUBLISHING

26 **CHARLES BEST**
DONORSCHOOSE.ORG

32 **SARA BLAKELY**
SPANX

38 **STEVE BLANK**
E.PIPHANY

44 **MATT BLUMBERG**
RETURN PATH

50 **RODNEY BROOKS**
IROBOT,
HEARTLAND ROBOTICS

56 **JEFF BUSSGANG**
OPEN MARKET, UPROMISE,
FLYBRIDGE CAPITAL PARTNERS

62 **STEVE CASE**
AMERICA ONLINE (AOL)

68 **MARC CENEDELLA**
THELADDERS

74 **ROBIN CHASE**
ZIPCAR

80 **CHIP CONLEY**
JOIE DE VIVRE HOSPITALITY

86 **JEFF DACHIS**
RAZORFISH, THE DACHIS GROUP

92 **MICHAEL & ELLEN DIAMANT**
SKIP HOP

100 **CHRIS DIXON**
SITEADVISOR, FOUNDER COLLECTIVE,
HUNCH

106 **MARC ECKŌ**
MARK ECKŌ ENTERPRISES

112 **KEVIN EFRUSY**
IRONPLANET, CORIO

118 **CATERINA FAKE**
FLICKR, HUNCH, FINDERY

124 **MITCH FREE**
MFG.COM

130 **LISA GANSKY**
OFOTO

136 **TOM GARDNER**
THE MOTLEY FOOL

142 **EILEEN GITTINS**
BLURB

148 **SETH GOLDMAN**
HONEST TEA

154 **JOE GREEN**
CAUSES

160 **SCOTT HARRISON**
CHARITY: WATER

166 **SCOTT HEIFERMAN**
I-TRAFFIC, FOTOLOG,
MEETUP

172 **REID HOFFMAN**
LINKEDIN

178 **JEFFREY HOLLENDER**
SEVENTH GENERATION, AMERICAN
SUSTAINABLE BUSINESS COUNCIL

184 **BEN HOROWITZ**
OPSWARE

190 **TONY HSIEH**
LINKEXCHANGE, VENTURE FROGS

196 **CYRUS MASSOUMI**
ZOCDOC

202 **JIM MCCANN**
1-800-FLOWERS.COM

208 **STEPHEN & HEIDI MESSER**
LINKSHARE

214 **ELON MUSK**
PAYPAL, SPACEX, TESLA MOTORS

220 **JACQUELINE NOVOGRATZ**
ACUMEN FUND

228 **HOSAIN RAHMAN**
JAWBONE

234 **ADEO RESSI**
THEFUNDED.COM,
THE FOUNDER INSTITUTE

240 **LINDA ROTTENBERG**
ENDEAVOR GLOBAL

246 **KEVIN RYAN**
ALLEYCORP

252 **KIRILL SHEYNKMAN**
STANFORD TECHNOLOGY GROUP,
PLUMTREE SOFTWARE,
ELASTRA CORPORATION

258 **JEFF STEWART**
MIMEO, URGENT CAREER, LENDDO

264 **JAY WALKER**
WALKER DIGITAL, PRICELINE

270 **THE BEST ADVICE**

290 **INDEX**

292 **ACKNOWLEDGMENTS**

FOREWORD
REID HOFFMAN

Entrepreneurs are pioneers. In creating new businesses, they venture out across the market-scape to discover and build new products and services. Like pioneers, these journeys are frequently long, lonely, and risky. But, also like pioneers, these journeys are essential for the growth of our society—to build new economies, new ecosystems of work and life.

This book offers lessons in pioneering from key entrepreneurs. Pioneers needed to know locations, weather, supply logistics, travel, and various technologies like maps, navigation, and transport. Entrepreneurs need to understand markets, industry transformations, finance, business operations, and various technologies involved in products, services, and modern business. Pioneers and entrepreneurs have to assemble networks of support: teams, finance, and expertise. When successful, both set up new lives and work opportunities for people. Pioneers establish towns and territories; entrepreneurs establish companies and other institutions.

Both leave the established order to build something new. They have many reasons: a vision, a mission, love of a product, or are simply compelled. But leaving the established order is hard. You leave significant infrastructure and support behind. And, you take real risks journeying into the unknown.

We are all familiar with heroic stories of entrepreneurs. These stories tell of easy, quick, or inevitable success. In reality, there are almost always massive challenges, delays, setbacks, risks, and uncertainties. Indeed, entrepreneurs and pioneers have to believe that their journeys will be successful; they would never have set out without that belief. But the journey is almost always hard. Here, entrepreneurs share key lessons—in the hope that those who set out on their own will make new mistakes rather than their old ones. They also hope to make the journey somewhat less lonely by sharing their experiences. I frequently describe entrepreneurship as jumping off a cliff and assembling an airplane on the way down. This book is about airplane assembly, weather patterns, and flying intelligently.

Good Luck.

INTRODUCTION

Starting a company is a staggering journey into the unknown. It is simultaneously thrilling and terrifying. You are setting yourself up for a spectacular challenge and the likelihood of failure is high. It is essential to prepare, and to have a sober respect for the experience. In *Outliers*, Malcom Gladwell estimates that it takes over 10,000 hours of dedicated training to develop expertise in any field. This is the commitment you are making when you start a company; become an expert startup founder.

Developing one's company-creation thesis requires a never-ending and humbling commitment. The simple mission is to truthfully reflect and understand, persistenty press on, and perfect. "It's the shift from defining ourselves as who we think we are to who we are *becoming*." This book is the latest chapter in my own journey of *becoming* the best entrepreneur I am capable of being.

In building my last two companies, I created what I've come to define as a "startup playbook": an evolving collection of the core ideologies, beliefs,

"Building a startup will be the home-ownership of the next century."

tools, and methods that reveal a model of building companies, from concept to—hopefully—thriving reality. I promise all my team members that they will have the chance to become complete startup executives; that they will know and experience the successes and failures of the entire startup journey; and that our startup playbook will remain the company's operating system and the foundation that we will all build on year after year. However, these past few years, I realized that I needed to upgrade my playbook, largely because my most recent company was rapidly scaling in complexity, people, partners, products, culture, and many other dimensions. The playbook I began with simply wasn't robust enough to capture all the extremes of taking a company from its fledgling roots, when you are solving five to ten challenges at a time, to a much larger company, where you are suddenly required to juggle hundreds of problems simultaneously, often instantaneously. I decided it was time to hit the reset button and pull in as much knowledge as quickly as I could. I reached out to my most admired friends and contacts, many of whom are considered among the best entrepreneurs in their fields. Some I have known for most of my career, while others I was meeting for the first time. I wanted their startup playbooks in order to rebuild mine. Now, I am sharing their playbooks with you.

The entrepreneurs I turned to have experience in as many varied sectors as I could gain access to in both the nonprofit and for-profit worlds—from technology and finance to flowers, drinks, shoes, spaceships, and pantyhose. All of them are game-changers; many are billionaires, whether in the realm of ideas, publishing, media, or philanthropy. When we spoke, I tried to get them to answer two central, burning questions:

1. What are your most vital theses for creating successful, scaling startups?

2. What are the key practices, behaviors, and ideas that power a startup's growth in its first five years?

These questions were designed to be tight enough to focus the conversations into straightforward, iconic ideas, while also being loose enough to let the interviews touch on topics ranging from product development to team building and HR; from investors to culture, design, marketing, finance, crisis management, and more. I sought to discover the critical competitive behaviors that helped these respected (often legendary) founders and visionaries create the leading companies in their markets.

In the end, for the purposes of the book, we focused on some forty of the nearly fifty interviews we completed either in person or via remote video. In each interview, we followed a scripted set of questions devised to tease out the entrepreneurs' guiding theses. Throughout the interviews, I took detailed notes and probed for the living ideas that their playbooks comprise, highlighting their best advice across a broad set of startup challenges and personal journeys. We wanted these entrepreneurs to tell us "how it really is"; boy, did they deliver.

In the process, we came upon too many remarkable ideas to summarize here, but there were several that stood out. One in particular came from my friend, talented technology entrepreneur and blogger Chris Dixon, who observed: "Building a startup will be the homeownership of the next century." He's exactly right. The idea of the American Dream is rooted in our national ethos, in the belief that we have the freedom and self-directed power to create prosperity. But in the past, we have been led to believe that our single biggest asset is equity in our homes, when in fact, our best asset is ourselves: our gifts, our goals, our efforts. You are your best investment. The new American Dream is creating and building your own startup. The equity is you.

DEFINING A STARTUP

What is a startup? Most define it as any company with a limited operating history, new, and usually in a phase of product and market discovery. During this phase, founders are typically roaming around in the darkness, looking for intellectual light switches to illuminate how their ideas stand up to customer needs and competitive offerings. The actual term *startup* became popular during the dot-com boom as a way of describing venture-backed technology companies. But for the purposes of this book, I'm expanding the definition to include any original new business initiative by a founding team that is focused on a high-growth, risk/reward profile, scalability, and market leadership. These startups often attract seed-stage, or angel, investor interest, then graduate to venture capital, though not all require or seek outside capital. The startup phase often ends when a company crosses certain growth milestones, most often when it hits profitability, is publicly traded, or is acquired.

While the failure rates are very high, the ones that survive and thrive often produce outsized economic returns. One of the main goals of this book is to reset or optimize the focus of entrepreneurs' efforts so they choose the right idea to build on from the beginning. We hope that by learning about the "prisms" the founders use to focus their ideas you will be able to select or refine your business idea and strategy to capture the qualities and attributes of other high-growth companies. In many cases, it's as important to choose what to focus on as what to quit, and when. If your startup idea does not have credible parallels to those offered in *The Startup Playbook*, you might consider retuning your business thesis, pivoting (changing the direction of your goal), or even deciding to stop altogether, as the opportunity costs and risks may outweigh the commercial potential.

Determining if you are right for the startup experience can involve a complex personal evaluation. The good news is that entrepreneurship can be taught. It's a journey, not an outcome, and you simply need to be doggedly committed to personally growing until you unlock your playbook, and pursue and execute on your greatest idea.

CUT TO THE CHASE!

By now, I hope you are saying to yourself, "Just give me the answers!" And I will. But first it's important that I point out that for some, the ideas provided here will seem obvious, self-evident. In fact, they may already be part of your own company's lexicon—the company you started that failed; the one that's already succeeded, but for which you are seeking a refresher course; or the one you intend to start someday. But as you read the origin of these ideas in the stories of the founders that forged and shaped them, you'll realize they are actually very deeply rooted concepts. In most cases, the entire outcome of your ambitions rests on your ability to process the art and science of these ideas—that is, to execute a vision. These are not box-checking ideas; they are the ones that the market will value your company against, so it's important to take time to test your business in a profoundly unbiased way against them. I personally believe it's fatal not to do so.

Here are the biggest and most critical ideas from *The Startup Playbook*:

1. *Know Thyself*
One of the most fundamental conclusions I came to after spending time with the entrepreneurial royalty whose advice formulates this book is that nearly all of the founders know how to play to their own strengths—they rarely, if ever, chase market "whitespaces." Few, if any, revealed a desire to

work in an area where they did not hold an unfair advantage, from a gifted-ness or passion perspective. Moreover, their companies fully reflected these strengths. A company's market reputation is anchored in its founder's—often in a very public way. If you consider how difficult and improbable breakout success is in any given market, you can begin to understand why it is so critical to use a battering ram of proprietary assets—beginning with the heart and mind of the founder—to break through. Your startup company must be rooted and flow from the founder's innate gifts.

2. Ruthlessly Focus on Your Biggest Ideas

People often underappreciate how effective great entrepreneurs are at tim-ing a market play. Great entrepreneurs have a sixth sense about a broad range of trends and data. This active and passive knowledge collects in their minds in ways that inform the timing and arc of the execution plans. And when they identify a real trend, often born out of a contrarian per-spective on markets, they lock on the One Big Idea. You might think this is a natural part of an alpha entrepreneur's mind, but it's not. In fact, choos-ing a maniacally focused path and betting it all is one of the hardest parts of the job and it requires the most courage. But it is often what's required to truly win a market. Entrepreneurs love options. This has been my great-est area of weakness as an entrepreneur. While you might think keeping your options open creates added opportunity and paths to fortune, it actu-ally does the reverse. Having too many options serves to dilute the atten-tion, resources, focus, and discipline it takes to learn how to prosper in a market. The successful founder's job is to get to the answer as quickly as possible. It's a widely held belief in the tech valleys that you must fail fast. Ultimately, you are trying to unlock your product-to-market fit equation as quickly as your talent and capitalization will allow. It is critical to select your problem well, focus intensely, and crack the code.

3. Build Painkillers, Not Vitamins

This is an old mantra from the venture-capital world, but it is always a bit startling to me when I meet incredibly talented people chasing ideas that are simply features, or partial services, that couldn't compete in mature markets. In the minds of the customers, these types of offerings are elective, like deciding whether or not to take a vitamin. Yet, there is an oasis in the entrepreneur's mind, encouraged by the small audience of family and friends, where optimism will translate into dreams of a large, scaling company. This rarely happens. On the other hand, if there is a large market of potential customers who can describe their specific pain to you, your job is to create the painkiller that will take away the hurt forever. Once customers start on your service or product, they never go off it. It becomes a necessity. Vitamins address problems in a holistic way, but they don't take away pain. If you can't describe your company's value as a painkiller, then I recommend you redefine and refine your business thesis.

4. Be Ten Times Better

It's hard not to be enthralled and drawn into a great entrepreneur's near-pathological optimism about his or her business (I can hear my former board groaning—particularly my friend Albert Wenger of Union Square Ventures). But it is critical that this optimism not cross over into wishful-thinking territory, which is the enemy of forming great companies. The reality is that while optimism is a critical attribute of any great entrepreneur, it cannot overcome the market friction of existing incumbents. The statistical obstacles to moving dollars or time from your competitor's offerings to your startup are staggering, making the challenge nearly impossible. The reality is that you need an atomic-grade weapon in your arsenal that can destroy the military-grade protections the incumbents have erected to keep you away from their customers. If you are wondering why customers are not flocking to your startup, it is likely because you have not figured out how to defeat those defense systems.

Luckily, there is a simple way to win. And by simple, I mean it is absolutely the most difficult thing you have to accomplish in order for your startup to survive: be ten times better than your competitors. You cannot be incrementally better. Incrementalism kills companies. Your entire organization must focus on an area of strength where you can defeat your competitors and radically differentiate your company by being ten times better than anyone else in the world. This is the bar you set for your team; you must own and be known for this value. It must define your product and/or services roadmap. Only from this winning position can you gain the leverage to dramatically force yourself into new market opportunities and scale your company.

5. Be a Monopolist

This was a surprising theme I took away from many conversations with the founders profiled in this book. From the very beginning of their startup years, most of them planned to create a company with monopolistic characteristics. Their intentions were not predatory or abusive; in fact, almost all believed in open markets. For them, thinking "monopolistically" was simply a way to focus on building market-dominating companies. This was revealing in terms of their ambition. Few entrepreneurs think as boldly as they need to from the very beginning. Yet, this type of thinking needs to be woven into the fabric of a company's psyche from Day One. The early period is critical for teaching yourself and your team that we are only limited by the scope of our vision. Embracing this principle will force you to see past the day-to-day, hand-to-hand combat it takes to build a company and aim for total market-domination.

GOING BEYOND YOUR PLAYBOOK

I want to be as completely transparent with the readers of this book as I am with my teams, going beyond the usual "executive summary" type of business wisdom. When you come right down to it, companies are really about people, starting with you. As the axiom goes, if you cannot lead yourself, you cannot lead others. This is a gritty and uncomfortable truth. Building companies exposes you; it tears you down and often forces you to rebuild. The entire company and its ultimate outcome are a reflection of your ability to set the foundational purpose, beliefs, and focus that contribute to a lasting organization that effectively solves a major market problem, which is why you have to dig so very deeply into your personal and professional operating system. In this spirit, I wanted to take the opportunity to share with you the core beliefs I've learned from my own life experience:

You've Won Humanity's Lottery; Be Grateful. Take Risks.
Over the years, I've been fortunate to have the opportunity to travel to some of the most remote places on the planet. Whenever my worldview intersects with the stark reality of the harsh world outside of the bubble many of us are lucky to inhabit, I almost always return home thinking, "I am more them than I am myself." Put another way: of the billions of people who have ever lived, it is highly improbable that I would end up being fortunate enough to inhabit a sliver of history, humanity, and geography that offers all the experiences of life as I know it. The fact is, we have a responsibility to take great risks because in truth, we have few true risks at all. I believe a life fully lived should be lived boldly, loaded with chances to push yourself to the greatest extremes of your abilities. We should be grateful that we have those kinds of opportunities. Seize them.

"When you come right down to it, companies are really about people, starting with you."

Don't Suffer from the Sin of Comparison. Follow Your Own Path.

When asked about the top people or ideas that have influenced their lives, many people generate an ideal list that likely includes parents, faith, community, and personal ambitions. But I would argue that these overlook a profound influence at the top of almost everyone's list: comparison. People are, by nature, social creatures. Companies must be rooted in trust, which means that leaders who compare their company's progress against the market's daily news cycle; competitive, blowhard, screaming CEOs; and rumor-mill press releases will drive their companies into the ground and their people straight into panic and oblivion. You need to trust your gut, focus on the voice of your customers, and move forward on a committed, decisive path.

Quit Weaknesses, Focus Only on Strengths.

This is not a complex or even original idea, but depending on how far you commit to quitting weaknesses, you can profoundly alter the course your life. How confidently do you value your focus, your most passionate efforts (not simply your passion), your time? If you value them highly, quit every activity that steals time without contributing to the important goals that grow and enrich your life. The physical and intellectual time recovered will be repurposed into your greatest gifts and efforts, leading to dramatic personal and economic returns. This can be as simple as outsourcing regular chores and activities (bill-paying, home maintenance, errands) that impede your complete physical and intellectual focus on your most important efforts (including rest). If you value your core talents and ideas in this light, they are your greatest assets, your equity, and your true net worth. You cannot afford to steal energy and focus away from them.

Love and Forgive People. Contempt Kills.

Few things can kill a relationship or a company faster than contempt. The negative inner monologue of criticism ultimately seeps into our stature and communication with our partners and collaborators. Contempt needs an antidote. In this spirit, I feel one of my most important jobs at my companies is to give my teams the ability to take great risks without fear of failure or peer contempt. I want to create a culture that celebrates risk without fear. Then, when we fail—which everyone does—we can learn from and address those mistakes, even with fearless directness, yet ultimately forgive each other and move forward. This idea is captured in our iconic idea the 7:1 Rule. We've actually trademarked it. We try to do seven times as much good as we do bad. It's an impossible ratio, which is the point. The bar is very high. As hard as you must push yourself, you are simply not going to be perfect, so don't hide failure. Admit it, address it, learn from it, and then forgive it and move forward. This is the antidote for contempt that transcends culture, religion, and law. The 7:1 Rule is a basic precept you can adopt to protect your company from the deadly threat of contempt. Within this same emphasis, I want to *overcommunicate* how important it is to remove people and investors from your team who are not in concert with this idea. They will ultimately destroy more value than they create. Startups and relationships are simply too hard. You need to have the wind at your back, not in your face.

Ben Horowitz is one of my favorite technology entrepreneurs and investors. He shared with me this observation: startups are stupidly hard. In fact, he told me, the decision to pursue them is irrational because the experience can be such a torturous one. I can personally guarantee that at some point you will experience exactly what Ben is describing. I would go so far as to say that until you have "blinked at death" your company has not fully matured. So unless you are completely, irrationally committed to solving a major market problem or opportunity, don't do it. Only the most passionate and irrational people ultimately arrive at the best ideas to solve major market needs. One of the most critical ways to survive the startup experience is to feed your unbreakable desire to see and touch a future that you feel you are uniquely created to invent.

It's also worth recognizing that while this book is overweighted with technology entrepreneurs, this is not meant to be a "how-to" book for the "tech valleys." It is intended to transcend markets, lifting the startup wisdom and journey from great entrepreneurs to instill in you a profound sense of confidence; the feeling that, "I could do this!"; that you are not alone and that it can be done—by you.

Putting together *The Startup Playbook* has been a fantastic personal experience, as important and redefining an experience as any emotional or physical journey I've ever taken. Creating this book has been a gift to me, and to my team. I hope it's also a gift to you.

CHRIS ANDERSON

FOUNDER:
FUTURE PUBLISHING

CEO:
TED TALKS

INTRODUCING CHRIS ANDERSON

Chris Anderson has a unique gift. In addition to possessing the forward-thinking sixth sense that has allowed him to predict and capitalize on movements and products that are positioned to change the word, Chris is an accomplished curator of human nature. He gathers the passions of some of the most gifted people on the planet with his TED conference, moderating a complex engagement of experts in politics, scientific research, economics, and popular culture. By broadcasting the TED talks to millions via the Internet, he has revolutionized the way ordinary people access and interact with the world of "big ideas" that directly or indirectly shape their lives.

TED was once a small but beloved, invitation-only conference limited to the privileged few who could attend in person. When Chris himself first participated in 1998, the total number of people in the audience was about eight hundred. Today, a decade after acquiring TED, Chris has dramatically expanded the conference's format and brand, building it into one of modern media's most important digital platforms and reaching millions of passionate followers.

Any up-and-coming entrepreneur could learn a lot from Chris's playbook. His pioneering innovation behind TED's success is that he redefined distribution and accessibility by figuring out how to make the medium multiply both the message and the bottom line.

CHRIS'S STORY

Chris Anderson is a true global citizen, one who has also had a complete experience as a startup entrepreneur. He was raised in Pakistan, India, and Afghanistan until the age of thirteen, when he entered boarding school in England. From there he attended Oxford University, where he first studied physics but graduated with a degree in philosophy. Eventually, he combined his passions by becoming a science journalist.

In 1984, Chris became excited by the arrival of home computing. "People just laughed when I said, I really would like to start my own magazine," he told a TED audience. "Fifteen years later I was somehow publishing more than a hundred of them." Chris's good fortune was that his interests in the publishing world, technology, science, and computing were converging, and he was at the forefront of creating one of the first technology publishing empires.

Chris Anderson: In the mid-'80s, home computers were just coming around and I was completely consumed by them. There had just never been anything more exciting to me. There was the thrill of being able to write your own programs right in your living room, plus you could play a bunch of games. It was just mind-bogglingly cool, this invention that had come into our arms. Some people didn't feel it at all, but the people who did really felt it deep.

It was clear that there was going to be a lot of growth and progress in computing. Producing magazines that tapped into that passion was a start for me. Our early strategy was to launch magazines that were focused on one type of computer. There were a handful of general computer magazines, but those weren't useful to most readers. At the time, people only had one computer and programs written for one computer didn't work on another. If you were reading a magazine about an Amiga when you had a Commodore 64, you were wasting your time. So if you could have a magazine that was all about your computer, that was a big deal. To me, there's all the difference in the world between someone casually paging through something and someone feeling like they have to run out on publication day to buy it. Wherever you see real engaged passion, that means there's something worth investigating.

In many ways, this business I was running was boring to a lot of people. These were hobbyist magazines, not *Time* or *Life* or *Vogue*. They were deeply boring for everyone except the people they were aimed at, and for them they were gold. Our company's slogan was "media with passion." Rather

---

THE TED TALKS STORY

TED was launched in 1984 as a conference dedicated to three things: technology, entertainment, and design. Since it became a regular event in 1990, it has been held every year, first in Monterey and now in Long Beach, California. Speakers have included political luminaries like Bill Clinton and Al Gore, pioneering scientists like Jane Goodall and Richard Dawkins, media and technology mavericks like Julian Assange and Arianna Huffington, and business visionaries like Bill Gates and Larry Page.

In 2002, Chris purchased TED through The Sapling Foundation, a nonprofit he founded in 1996 to "foster the spread of great ideas." The most significant advancement to TED occurred in 2006, when the conference's entire recorded archive was distributed online for free. Since then, more than 300 million people have watched the videos, making TED the most popular conference in the world.

than trying to gain as wide a readership as possible with every property, we wanted to flip the model on its head and create a number of properties that were each interesting to a specific group. The key was to make the magazines a *must-buy* for those people. That allowed us to charge high cover price, high advertising rates, and so forth.

Chris scaled his first publishing startup, Future Publishing, and sold it to Pearson seven years after founding it. He then moved to the United States, where he founded a second startup, Imagine Media. The flagship property of his new company was the magazine Business 2.0. *Today, Chris looks back on the magazine as part of the larger hysteria overtaking the tech world at the time.* Business 2.0, *he told TED, was "as thick as a telephone book, pumping hot air into the tech bubble." At the height of that bubble, his company (which re-merged with Future Publishing) reached a market cap of more than $2 billion. Then the bubble burst. In February 2001, Chris laid off 350 people in one day. He managed to save the balance of the company, but still was ready to move on to the next big challenge. In search of a new endeavor, he thought back to an insipring conference he had attended a few years earlier.*

I first came to the TED conference in 1998 and kind of fell in love with it, like a lot of people do. But to a media person and an entrepreneur, what was striking about what was happening there was the audience. First of all, the audience was tiny, maybe only 800 people. But this was a very influential group of people who were normally very hard for the media companies to get to. Second, they were absolutely obsessed with this event. They would say things like, "It's the highlight of my year!" or "This thing has changed my life!" These were the kinds of statements you normally wouldn't expect to hear about a conference. That really got my attention, seeing that level of passion from those types of people.

Through his nonprofit Sapling Foundation, Chris purchased TED in 2002. In 2006, he and his team took the prescient step of digitizing and distributing the TED archive for free, which unleashed extraordinary new momentum for the conference.

The people who regularly attended TED cared so much about it that I wondered if other people who weren't there would also care if they were given exposure to it. We actually didn't know the answer to that question for many years because we couldn't get external distribution of TED content. Television wasn't interested, and there just wasn't a way of distributing the content of the talks on a mass scale that made any sort of economic sense.

Then, online video came along, and we tried a couple of experiments. The numbers didn't explode straight away, but it was crystal clear from the first responses to putting those talks out that they evoked a passionate reaction. One woman wrote to us and said, "I'm sitting at my computer with tears running down my cheeks watching this person tell their story." Another said, "Watching this talk together prompted the best conversation my fifteen-year-old and I have had in five years."

After seeing the responses to a lot of launches, you get a sense of the temperature. With TED, the temperature was sizzling. There was something really exciting and enthusiastic there. At that point, it felt like it was worth flipping our whole business focus to the distribution of the [conference] talks. Done the right way, it could be really huge.

Chris was right. Hundreds of millions of people have watched TED Talks online. Now, he is looking at ways to engage that audience even further.

We've only scratched the surface on quite a number of issues. When people watch a talk, they want more; they want to understand more, get involved, or delve deeper into the issue. Our goal now is find ways that allow them to do that.

THE CHRIS ANDERSON PLAYBOOK

Passion Is a Proxy for Potential

The traditional advice is "follow your passions"; I'm not saying that at all. From a business-opportunity point of view, tracking other people's passions is even more important. There are often situations where something hasn't necessarily taken off yet, but you see that gleam in someone's eye and you can feel how much they care about something. That probably represents an opportunity. That kind of passion is a proxy for potential.

Leverage Communities for an Upward Spiral

The secret to a successful startup is that it won't work until you can persuade other people to do your work for you, to engage in passionate evangelism for your product or service. In some businesses, you can get something even better: a network effect that takes your little idea to a much bigger place in quite a short period of time. It can be based on many different things, including your reputation. The better you get, the more great people will want to come and work for you or simply promote you. The result is an upward spiral that brings you to a still better place.

Build for a Niche While Maintaining Broad Appeal

Winning ideas have to connect across a broad array of areas. They have to engage technology in an intelligent way, but they also have to tap into market psychology, human psychology, and customer psychology. It's not enough for something to be superficially "cool." It has to be presented in a particular way so that a small number of people will get excited about it. Then those people will tell others, and that's how it will spread.

BUSINESS OPERATIONS

Engage the Whole Process

Founders have to be part of the whole startup process. You have to smell and taste and absorb and feel every part of it, and keep rearranging the pieces until you suddenly feel it go "Snap!" Do that, and you'll reach a point where you know that the elements are there so that if you go in this or that direction, it's actually going to work. Although some founders are very technology focused and others are much more marketing focused, I would argue that you need to embrace a broader view of the world.

CUSTOMER DEVELOPMENT

Understand Your Audience's Interests

Even if you have an audience that's passionately committed to your offer, it can easily go away. A lot of things might bring that about: arrogance, technological shifts, or someone else coming along with a better proposition. Consider what happened to the magazine business when the Internet came along. Suddenly, people who were passionately committed to video-game magazines started to get their information online. It was there, on demand, for free, and their passion for the video-game magazines leaked away. To avoid being surprised by those shifts, you have to constantly pay attention to your community's center of interest and adapt your product to keep it.

FAILURE

The Threat of Failure Drives Determination

When you experience an actual failure, you learn from it and move on. But when you're threatened with the prospect of failure, that is a massive motivator. It basically drives determination, and nothing is a better predictor of your prospects than how hard you're prepared to fight when it really looks like you're done.

LEADERSHIP

Don't Make Big Decisions at a Time of Weakness

When you're under extreme stress, you'll be tempted to say, "We'll have to close this whole thing down" or "We'll have to make this big gamble." But you're not mentally equipped to make smart decisions when you're feeling weak and beaten up. The right strategy is to get through it; get yourself to a place, psychologically, where you have some perspective and make the big decisions when you're strong.

MARKETING

Define Your Brand in Eight Words or Less

You need to be sure that the people your product is targeting are able to "get" it very quickly. If you can't define your brand in three to eight words, you're doomed. For instance, we had the idea in 1998 of launching a new magazine for business in the Internet age. It was exciting and we got good feedback, but I just didn't have the right name for it. Then, I was talking about it with [Amazon founder] Jeff Bezos at TED, throwing out ideas like *Business 2000* or *New Business*. He came up with *Business 2.0*, and in a flash, I knew that was exactly right.

PRODUCT DEVELOPMENT

Don't Be Afraid to Give It Away

As I mentioned, the rules about what you can keep and what you should give away have shifted. If something can be shared digitally, in many cases it should be. Consider what has happened in the music industry. Twenty years ago, there were CDs and there were concerts, and they both cost roughly the same thing. Today, the cost of digital music has been slashed to zero and the concert is $100. That's a really radical shift in the value proposition. Though it seemed to be destroying value, giving away digital content actually created demand.

PUBLIC RELATIONS

Build Your Reputation Through Transparency

Billions of people are now instantly connected to one another online, which means that a reputation can fly around the world in the blink of an eye. Whether it's a reputation for generosity or a poor reputation, it will move really quickly. Spreading a *positive* reputation might require giving away something that, traditionally, you would have treasured for yourself. It might have been worth protecting ten years ago, but it's not worth protecting now. Your reputation spreads faster than the ability of your competitors to exploit the information you've released. In our case, we do a big, expensive event, and it turns out that giving away all the content of that event, far from destroying it, increases the demand for it.

VISION & MISSION

Vision Is a Team Thing

Everyone knows that hiring the right people is critical to an organization's success. But you won't get the best out of them unless you let them help shape your vision. All the best strategic decisions at TED over the last ten years have emerged as a result of animated conversations with the amazing people who work with me. Ideas are not light-bulbs that switch on out of nowhere. They come when creative people spark off each other. You have to give that process every chance. You not only get better ideas that way, you also get buy-in.

CHRIS'S VISION FOR THE FUTURE

One of the most ambitious expansions of TED's mission was the creation of TEDx, a licensing program that allows third parties to hold TEDx conferences anywhere in the world. "There's always the danger that you'll spoil your brand by giving it away. But the whole point of expanding was people wanted to organize TED events. So by having the brand 'TED' with a huge 'x' on it to indicate that these events were independently organized, we found the right fit.

"Every day, we're surprised by and learn from things that TEDx organizers are doing. One of the great differences between running a for-profit company and an organization like TED is that it's much more possible now to focus on the radical openness strategy and let the community do its thing. Let the tiger leap where it will; maintain just the lightest touch on the tail to stop it from going completely over the cliff. Usually, the tiger will find exciting new terrain and bring you along with it."

CHARLES BEST

FOUNDER:
DONORSCHOOSE.ORG

INTRODUCING CHARLES BEST

Flowing directly from the very meaning of his last name are the extraordinary intentions that inspired Charles Best to found DonorsChoose.org. This online platform has created a community that marries personal philanthropy and the opportunity to support the dream projects of dedicated public-school teachers. Thanks to DonorsChoose, donors in Albuquerque can sponsor an educational field trip to the museum for students in Chicago. A teacher in St. Louis can purchase books for her class with the help of Californians. Every teacher that raises a hand in this unique forum now has a chance to find resources for students that are otherwise unavailable in his or her own community.

In a particular classroom, the impact of a DonorsChoose.org project could boil down to a single moment in a child's life. A fifth-grade art project might be the early first step of a great graphic designer. A field trip to a factory might plant a seed in the mind of a future inventor or business leader. To facilitate these learning moments, a child's education needs to be filled with a variety and volume of stimulating experiences, the cost of which is prohibitively high. But as Charles understands so clearly, the social cost of not developing all of our children to their fullest potentials is much, much higher.

With DonorsChoose.org, Charles is guiding resources into the hands that need them and facilitating millions of life-changing moments. It is impossible to overstate the meteoric impact of that vision.

CHARLES'S STORY

From the moment he began his career, Charles was committed to service. As a senior in college, he considered two options: becoming a police officer or becoming a teacher. He chose the latter. It was when he began teaching history at Wings Academy, a high school in the South Bronx, that he realized how the chronic underfunding of public education was hindering teachers and students alike. DonorsChoose.org grew out of this realization.

Charles Best: The first thing I did, which is now almost cliché, was endeavor to scratch an itch I was feeling. I was a teacher in the Bronx, talking with my colleagues about books we wanted our students to read and a field trip we wanted to take them on, and we were getting frustrated that we couldn't bring those ideas to life. We sensed that there were people out there who wanted to help improve our public schools, but they just couldn't do so with confidence or accountability.

To address this problem, Charles founded DonorsChoose.org in 2000. For the first three years, Charles ran the site while continuing to teach full-time. It was an immediate success, thanks to the groundwork Charles had been doing behind the scenes.

DonorsChoose.org was launched in the teachers' room at my school on the good old-fashioned principle of free food. I walked in with my mom's pear torte and offered to share with everybody on the condition that if they wanted a piece, they had to visit this new website I'd built and post a project representing what they wanted most for their students. That's how we got the first eleven projects on our site. I anonymously funded those first requests myself. It gave my colleagues the misimpression that the website actually worked and that there were all these donors just waiting to support teachers' dreams. That false rumor spread across the Bronx, and we got hundreds of teachers posting requests.

Then, to get actual donors to the site, my students volunteered every day after school for about three months. They handwrote and addressed letters, pulling names from my high school and college alumnae directories. We sent out 2,000 letters telling people about this website where somebody with $10 could actually become a philanthropist; they could pick a project that spoke to them, see where the money was going, and hear back from the recipients. My students' letters generated the first $30,000 in donations.

THE DONORSCHOOSE.ORG STORY

Founded in 2000, DonorsChoose.org is an Internet-based, nonprofit organization that facilitates donations to the specific educational projects of public-school teachers. When teachers post their requests on the site, donors can pick which ones they want to support. DonorsChoose.org then purchases necessary supplies, provides them to the schools, and generates a line-item budget for the donor, who also receives a thank-you note from the class he or she has assisted. To date, 93,000 teachers have used DonorsChoose.org to secure more than $55 million for 115,000 public-school classrooms—nearly all of them in low-income communities—and "citizen philanthropists" have helped more than two million students around the country.

It took that offline, hand-to-hand hustling to generate some liquidity in this new philanthropic marketplace. Bit by bit, we brought it to a place where it could begin to develop a life of its own.

With growth came the temptation to expand into new markets. The first real opportunity to do so came from the New York Police Department.

A couple of years after we launched the organization, the NYPD approached us about allowing police officers to post project requests. I was really into that idea. I had taken the police officer exam my senior year in college and had been choosing between being a teacher and a police officer, so the idea that teachers and cops from New York City could post projects on our site was really meaningful to me.

We were all ready to go. Our board chairman was ready to fund the project, and making adjustments to the site wouldn't be difficult. At that point, the police department realized that donating to an officer's project request was going to be an easy way to bribe a cop. It should have been obvious, but it wasn't because everybody's intentions were good. If we wanted to implement this program, we would have to do a warrant check on every donor to see if they had outstanding parking tickets or anything else on their records! That taught us that there were serious logistical scalability issues hidden behind what had seemed like an intuitive extension of our program. Reality smacked us on the face, but it gave us focus. We realized we needed to stick with public school projects and focus our expansion efforts on a geographic extension of that.

The turning point came in 2003, when Oprah Winfrey featured DonorsChoose.org on her show; but the celebrity booster most closely associated with the program is Stephen Colbert, who has promoted the site since 2007. That year, he filed for the Democratic primary in his native state of South Carolina and asked viewers to support his bid by contributing to DonorsChoose.org. In 2009, he gave up his birthday, asking friends, family, and fans to contribute in lieu of sending gifts. "DonorsChoose.org makes me feel like every day is my birthday," Colbert said, "that, and my 364 counterfeit driver's licenses."

In 2010, we saw more than a million dollars in donations come from what can only be described as lucky, unforeseeable happenings. One of these was Stephen Colbert and Jon Stewart's rally in Washington D.C.—what eventually became the "Rally to Restore Sanity and/or Fear." Colbert's fans decided that the way to get Colbert and Stewart to commit to that rally would be to bum rush DonorsChoose.org and fund hundreds and hundreds of classroom projects. At one point, they were making donations every ten minutes. They called it "blackmailing Stephen with kindness," and it raised $600,000 for the projects on our site.

A little while into the campaign, Stephen started acknowledging and encouraging what his fans were doing. But it was completely user initiated and bottom up. Stephen did not come up with the idea to do this, nor did we initiate it. It couldn't have been farther away from any strategic decision by us. We were just very lucky. And yet, to show the intersection of luck and working for your luck: we had built a platform where anybody can set up a giving page, can be part of a leader board, and the leader boards can be in competition with each other. So the technology was there, waiting, for this kind of luck to come our way.

THE
CHARLES BEST
PLAYBOOK

Scratch a Personal Itch

The first rule is to pay attention to the intuitive "itches" that accompany certain ideas. But VC-blogger Mark Suster pointed out a new twist on this formula: "scratch your own itch" makes sense, but it's also led to the marketplace being overcrowded with bar and music apps. The end-goal shouldn't be to scratch a personal itch that leads you to launch another bar app. The goal has to be to do something that you can imagine yourself being passionate about for at least six years.

Get Out of the Way

Find colleagues who are every bit as imaginative as you are, and every bit as prolific in implementing process improvements. Every one of our great scalability victories came when I pulled out of process engineering, including my decision to crowdsource the screening and vetting of classroom projects on our site. Get out of the way and good things will follow.

Create Transparent Choice

Users will reward you for being transparent and giving them choices. It's now becoming commonplace, especially among online non-profits, to invite the donor to contribute toward operating costs. To appreciate this kind of transparency, it's helpful to think about the corollary in the for-profit world. Imagine if they exposed their operating margins on the price tags of the products they sold. For example, the tag on a $12.00 T-shirt would list $4.00 in variable costs like buying the T-shirt wholesale, and $8.00 in fixed costs like paying the rent. Each consumer would then have the option of supporting those fixed costs. When we give donors the power to allocate their dollars, that's exactly what we do.

CHARLES'S BEST ADVICE

BUSINESS OPERATIONS

Crowdsource, Front to Back

Crowdsourcing is not original, but we've pushed it across multiple dimensions. We crowdsource the labor of classroom teachers designing microsolutions for the students they serve, and we crowdsource to donors the labor of deciding which microsolutions should be brought to life. Of course, front-end crowdsourcing isn't revolutionary. With organizations like Kiva or Kickstarter, peer-to-peer philanthropy has become a movement. But we also implement crowdsourcing at the back end, behind the scenes: teacher-users volunteer time to review other teachers' requests and vet them for integrity and quality. We're now pushing crowdsourcing even further by deploying an API and asking the developer community to share the labor of making the DonorsChoose.org website an even richer experience.

CUSTOMER DEVELOPMENT

Crank the Pump

If you look at our growth curve over the last eleven years, it's not a step function. It's a pretty clean hockey stick. That gives the impression that our site has a life of its own, but my job is to *not* think that and to keep cranking the pump. In fact, we could even scientifically demonstrate the need to actively build growth because our virality coefficient is a lot less than one: every ten donors who support a project on our site bring in between one and three additional donors. But if you're using a true virality coefficient greater than one, like Hotmail-standard, then even some great companies don't qualify for having a life of their own yet.

HIRING

Check References in Person

When you need to check a reference for an important hire, suck it up and motivate yourself to conduct the reference check in person. Even if you only have time for a ten-minute conversation, go see the person you're speaking with physically. It's just about the only way you can hope to get honest signals (if not honest words) from somebody who's worked with your candidate before.

MARKET DEVELOPMENT

Expand Across Locations, Not Sectors

With very few exceptions, microgiving websites experience growth and success when they focus on a particular sector. In our case, focusing on U.S. public schools serving low-income communities has enabled us to attract more donations than we would have gotten by being a totally open-ended philanthropic marketplace. We've expanded from our original focus in New York City, but we've stuck with our core sector.

MARKETING

Leverage Good Luck

There was no planning for the degree of promotion Stephen Colbert has given us, but we've looked for all opportunities to build on that exposure. As a nonprofit you don't have a big marketing budget, so it has to be focused, but you do have the advantage of having a great mission that people want to hear about. We made sure to get links to our site on websites and social networks that would be frequented by people who might have heard of us through Stephen.

METRICS

Track Nonprofit Performance with For-Profit Precision

Nonprofits should be every bit as data driven, technologically agile, and performance minded as for-profit companies. DonorsChoose.org is not the first nonprofit to feel that way; Teach for America has been a pioneer in that respect, and there are many others for us to learn from. A major turning point in our organization was to begin operating, thinking, and performing more like a consumer Web company than a traditional nonprofit.

TALENT

Support Managerial Hiring Decisions

Participate in hiring second-degree reports, but don't blackball candidates that the real manager is excited about. In those situations, your role in the interview should be to sell the candidate on joining your team. In doing so, you'll get a feel for culture fit, and you'll have insights to share with the manager. Don't be the decider in somebody else's hiring process.

VISION & MISSION

Purpose Is Central to Motivation

The motivation for founding a company should be the fun of constructing and building something, and the feeling that you're making an impact. For me, the goal is to help kids from low-income families get the materials and experiences they need for a great education. Making a social impact in the world is a metric of personal worth that is as important, or more important, than the money you've made.

CHARLES'S VISION FOR THE FUTURE

During a 2010 interview with Adrian Bye of MeetInnovators, Charles told the outrageous story of a Chicago principal who threatened to fire a teacher for making a request on DonorsChoose.org. "Just by virtue of requesting a class set of dictionaries, this teacher was revealing that the school didn't have dictionaries and that was incredibly embarrassing." Charles wants to prompt more revelations of this kind, but he doesn't want them to cause embarrassment. He wants them to cause systemic change.

"We would love to kind of expose and prod the broader system into putting us out of business at least on 50 percent of the current classroom projects, which are for essential materials that this system ought to be providing. I think there would be a continued role for DonorsChoose.org in innovation. Where a teacher who has a really experimental idea, a way of teaching that might go beyond the typical curriculum, a field trip that will bring learning to life could get funded. Any project that involves resources or ideas that go beyond the standard, mandated curriculum, where private philanthropy really is the appropriate way to fund innovation and experiment, I think we would have a continued role there. Ultimately, though, we'd like to be put out of business on all the projects on our site that are for essential resources."

SARA BLAKELY

FOUNDER:

SPANX

INTRODUCING SARA BLAKELY

When I spoke with Sara Blakely, she told me something that's going to change the way that I parent. When she was a little girl, her father would ask, "What did you fail at today?" He made it clear that failure was an indication that you *tried* something. It was a good thing. That's a profound idea, and it speaks against many of the assumptions of our success-based culture. If you celebrate a child's gift rather than her effort, you do her a disservice. In exactly the same way, it does no good to celebrate an entrepreneur's idea. The important thing is being able to execute on it.

Sara came upon the initial idea for Spanx when she cut the feet out of her pantyhose in 2000. But this inspiration wasn't just a lucky accident; it was part of her innate commitment to thinking outside the box . . . and thinking in general. "I think!" she says, "I think recreationally! I have periods of time where I turn off my TV and sit on my couch and I think." This habit has bred a confidence in her own ideas, and is a clear indication of the independent spirit that powers Sara's work. She doesn't need others to validate what she knows to be true; she just does it, knowing that any failures will eventually improve her efforts in a way that encouragement never could. That perspective is unique, and it feeds her characteristic momentum and drive.

SARA'S STORY

Sara's commitment to improving women's lives predates her own memories.

Sara Blakely: From a very early age, I felt extremely blessed and lucky to be a woman in the United States. Nothing significant happened in my childhood to cause this; I grew up in an upper-middle-class family. My father was a lawyer, my mother was a stay-at-home mom and artist. But for as long as my parents can remember, they tell me, I was driven by a recognition that women were being held back from their potential in a lot of places around the world, even in America.

When Sara was a teenager, she was traumatized first by the death of a close friend, then by her parents' divorce. It was, in part, those events that inspired her immense drive.

When I was sixteen years old, some very traumatic things happened in my life. In one year, my very good friend was run over by a car and killed, my dad left, and my parents got divorced. But when my dad left the house, he handed me the CD set *How to Be a No-Limit Person*, by a motivational speaker named Dr. Wayne Dyer, and that had a profound impact on me. I was so passionate about it that I even took it to my principal and asked why they weren't teaching this in school!

In every obstacle there's an opportunity. In those traumatic events, I was blessed by being introduced to this very effective and productive way of thinking. I feel like I was given training in how to think and harness inspiration at a very young age.

After college, Sara supported herself as a salesperson while pursuing a career in stand-up comedy. That career didn't take off, but Sara didn't give up on thinking big.

When I graduated from college, I went straight into selling fax machines. I was door-to-door for seven years. Then I cut the feet out of my pantyhose and I've been off promoting Spanx ever since. Now, women have been cutting the feet out of their pantyhose for a variety of reasons for twenty years, but no one took the idea and ran with it. I think the difference was the amount of mental preparation I had been doing prior to that day—a lot of thinking, a lot of visualizing, and a lot of goal-setting. I was very clear in asking the universe to show me an opportunity and give me my own idea. I had assessed my strengths and weaknesses as a sales rep. I knew I could sell and I knew I liked people, *and* I was selling a product I didn't understand or even particularly like. If I could create my own product that I actually really liked, I felt I could do better.

The very first time I cut the feet out of my pantyhose, I knew that was my opportunity. This was what I had been manifesting and thinking about. I thought, "Thanks! Got it; gonna run with it."

Sara was excited, but she remained discreet.

I think that one of the biggest reasons that Spanx exists is that I didn't tell anyone my idea early on. I kept it to myself for one year and pursued it at night and on the weekends. All anybody knew was that Sara was working on some crazy idea. No one told me to do that; it was a completely intuitive feeling. After a year of this, I sat my friends and family down and said, "It's footless pantyhose." They looked horrified. "*That's* what you've been working on?!" It wasn't malicious; there was a lot of love and concern: "Sweetie, if it's such a good idea, why doesn't it already exist? And even if it *is* a good idea, those big guys are going to blow you out of the water in the first couple of months." If I'd heard those things on the day I first cut the feet out of my pantyhose, I think I'd probably still be selling fax machines today.

With $5,000 of her own money, Sara produced and aggressively promoted the first prototypes of her slimming, footless pantyhose.

> "I could tell customers why they needed my product in thirty seconds."

I could tell customers why they needed my product in thirty seconds. "I've invented footless pantyhose so you can wear white pants with no panty lines, look thinner, and wear any style shoe. You've got clothes that have been hanging in your closet for years because you can't figure out what to wear under them. You need this."

Then I realized that I could add another layer of impact by making this visual. So I took pictures of my own rear end: me in white pants with Spanx, and me in white pants without Spanx. I brought them to Kinko's and laminated them, and I would stand at the entrance of stores to hook people in. If after thirty seconds of explaining "why you need this product" I still didn't get them, I held up my laminated pictures and they would say, "Oh, I see . . . I'll take two!" Talk about putting your butt on the line!

That wasn't Sara's only marketing innovation. The other was to apply for a patent.

A lot of people get extremely consumed in the patent process. A patent is only as good as your ability to defend it, but a lot of entrepreneurs don't realize that. If you have nothing left after spending a lot of money on a patent lawyer, you won't get any protection.

I didn't hire a patent lawyer. I wrote the application myself and had a lawyer do the claims part for about $700 because I realized that a patent would only benefit me as a marketing tool. By having the phrase "patent pending" on the package, I could call myself an "inventor." I felt that that stood out more and created a lot of buzz: people in the media are more eager to talk about a new "invention" than they are to talk about a new "designer."

Spanx has been an incredible success for Sara, but she has never lost sight of her original passions.

For me, Spanx is about empowering women and giving them confidence, a stepping-stone to my ultimate manifestation: helping women globally. Income is power in our society and can generate things in big ways. God must have a sense of humor, I am getting to my goal of helping women by helping their rear ends first. I never saw that one coming!

THE
SARA BLAKELY
PLAYBOOK

Think for Recreation

One of my favorite things to do is to recreationally think. I could be sitting on my couch, feeding my baby, or taking one of my fake "commutes." (I live three minutes from my office, but sometimes take a forty-five-minute drive on the way to give myself uninterrupted thinking time.) When you focus in that way and pay attention to all of your surroundings, it brings opportunities to the surface that you may have only seen in a vague and unclear way before. Every single person every day probably either sees a need or an opportunity for how a product could be better.

Cultivate a Limitless Vision

Whatever you can think, you can create; just have a very clear vision. I take mental snapshots of things that I want to manifest in my life, and they're as clear as Polaroid pictures. I'm not clear on how I'm going to get there, but I'm 100 percent clear that I will get there. In high school,

to take one very specific example, I told people that I was going to be on *The Oprah Winfrey Show*. It was clear as day. Once you have your snapshot, work on filling in the blanks to get to that place.

Seek the Right Kind of Feedback

Ideas—even million-dollar ones—are most vulnerable in their infancy; don't share them with too many people. However, don't hide your plan from people who can help you move it forward. When I came up with the idea for Spanx, I spoke with potential investors and people at the hosiery mills. If someone can help you in a specific way, don't be paranoid: ideas are almost never stolen until they're already thriving in the marketplace. Just don't approach friends and family for validation or feedback, because then your ego gets involved too early on in the process. Instead of pursuing your idea, you'll spend all of your time defending and explaining it, and that can be discouraging.

FAILURE

Don't Be Afraid to Fail

When I was growing up, my dad would encourage my brother and me to fail. We would be sitting at the dinner table and he would ask, "So what did you guys fail at this week?" If we didn't have something to contribute, he would be disappointed. When I did fail at something, he'd high-five me. What I didn't realize at the time was that he was completely reframing my definition of failure at a young age. To me, *failure* means not trying; failure isn't the outcome. If I have to look at myself in the mirror and say, "I didn't try that because I was scared," that is failure.

FOCUSING TIME & ENERGY

Improve Your Offer, and Revenues Will Follow

I never spend my time thinking about how to make more money. My mind is always on moving the company forward by focusing on the excitement around creating something that either doesn't exist or making something that does exist better. I'm always asking, "What is the next product I can give to women?" I met a woman at the airport who explained why her bras didn't work for her, so I made a bra to fix the problem. Those kinds of conversations are where I get my inspiration and then the money follows.

HUMAN RESOURCES

Identify Areas for Improvement

In every employee review, whether it's for a receptionist job or the head of product development, I always ask, "What are three things that you can do better in your job, and what are three things that you think the company could do better?" It's so fascinating to hear some of the ideas that come out of people's mouths. This not only makes employees feel like their voice matters in the company, regardless of their position, but it forces people to get out of the box and find ways to do things besides what's been shown to them.

LEADERSHIP

Courage Is Acting Despite Fear

I don't want anyone to think that somebody who's achieved what I have achieved did it because of an absence of fear. I'm afraid of a lot of things. Sometimes it's a purely physical reaction: I've flown every four or five days for I don't know how many years and I still get sweaty palms each time. But courage is doing something despite the fear, and I've worked hard on being a courageous person. I feel like life is short, and today isn't a dress rehearsal. I never want to miss an opportunity because I was afraid. There is always going to be a degree of stress and anxiety going through this life process, but I've learned to channel them in a way that has fueled me and continues to fuel me.

PRODUCT DEVELOPMENT

Don't Make It Cheaper; Make It Better

I broke into an industry that was completely money-focused. Nobody was paying attention to women and thinking about how these undergarments felt, or how they fit. All the competition was just trying to make these commodities cheaper and cheaper, thinking that was the way to go. All of a sudden, I show up and charge more for one pair than anybody can comprehend, and women lined up in droves to buy them. I think I left the industry in shock, but I really believed that we needed to make it better, not cheaper.

PUBLIC RELATIONS

Be Your Own Publicist

When I first started out, I debated spending a bunch of money on a PR company to promote Spanx. Then I imagined myself as the person on the other end of the phone. If I were at the *Wall Street Journal* or *People* magazine, what would be more impressive: getting a call from someone who represents fifteen products or getting a call from someone who's passionately telling me about something she invented? I promoted Spanx myself, along with friends who liked the product, and it was much more effective.

TALENT

Hire Your Weaknesses

Like most entrepreneurs, I couldn't afford to hire anybody else when I first launched the product. I was the inventor, I had $5,000, and that was it; I had to be every department. But after two years, I could afford to hire people into roles that I didn't enjoy. In particular, I gave a ton of power and strength to my CEO, Laurie Ann Goldman, who's been with me for nine years. She's a strategic leader. Most important, she's *consistent*. To be an effective manager on a day-to-day basis, you have to be consistent. I'm more of a creative person. I recognize that about myself, which is why I hired my weaknesses early on. I think if most founders don't relinquish some control, then we hold back the development of our companies.

WORKING FOR YOURSELF

Money Is a Magnifying Glass

Money makes you more of who you already are. If you are a jerk, it will make you a bigger jerk; if you're insecure, you become even more insecure; if you are generous, you become even more generous; if you are nice, you become even nicer. Making money is like holding up a magnifying glass to who you are, personally and professionally. It creates a lot of energy and power, and it's up to you to use that in a really good way.

SARA'S VISION FOR THE FUTURE

Because she has built an outstanding team to manage Spanx on a day-to-day basis, Sara can focus on her true passion: inventing products. "I still love to dream up products. I'll be on a plane or in the shower, and then I'll excitedly call the team with a new challenge. 'I want to create a bra made out of pantyhose. I want it to be super-comfortable, and I don't want there to be any back fat for women in T-shirts.' The team will get excited and inspired, and then they'll call the manufacturer, who will insist that it can't be done. I always say, 'That's never true. We put a man on the moon; I know we can create control-top fishnets.'

In both cases, Sara was right. The bra "without back fat" is on the market as "Bra-llelujah," and the control-top fishnets are "Tight-End Tights." Branching into completely new territory, Sara recently launched Spanx for men. This is just another example of how this successful entrepreneur manifests her vision through a combination of inspiration and her own unshakable confidence. As Sara herself says, "You've got to have the inner confidence to believe in yourself when everyone else is telling you no."

STEVE BLANK

FOUNDER:

E.PIPHANY

AUTHOR:

THE FOUR STEPS TO THE EPIPHANY

THE STARTUP OWNER'S MANUAL

INTRODUCING STEVE BLANK

Every startup has a defining moment: a crisis that will either carry it to the next phase or kill it. There is no way to build a company without going through this ugly adolescence. Like adolescence, however, the experience still manages to feel entirely unique to the person undergoing it. I myself have lived through this phase four times in my career. The first three times, I felt completely alone. But the last time, I had a new resource to draw on: Steve Blank's *The Four Steps to the Epiphany*.*

I've read Steve's book many, many times—in the office, at home, on the beach. My copy is dog-eared and marked-up for good reason: it places our deepest fears and concerns into a wider perspective by illuminating these "unique" challenges as stages in a universal journey. For startup founders, his book is The Catcher in the Rye.

Not only is Steve one of the founding fathers of Silicon Valley entepreneurship, but he is a true Renaissance man, having done everything from repairing fighter planes during the Vietnam War to building eight companies. Even better, speaking with him is like having a conversation with your favorite uncle. He's seen everything, and he has an uncanny ability to defuse "end-of-the-world" anxieties. "It's going to be OK," he'll say reassuringly, "as long as you do this."

Along with the book you are holding, The Four Steps to the Epiphany should be essential reading for every startup founder.

*Since this interview, Steve released a second book, The Startup Owner's Manual. This step-by-step guide to getting startups right has quickly become an indispensible resource for entrepreneurs of all stripes and a key text in business school entrepreneurship programs around the globe.

STEVE'S STORY

Steve took the occasion of our interview to go all the way back to the founding of the first corporation and the launch of the first MBA program. After all, he is a professor.

Steve Blank: When I think about entrepreneurship, I always go back to Joseph Campbell and his book *The Hero With a Thousand Faces.* Campbell recognized a pattern thousands of years old that recurs in mythologies across every culture: the heroic quest. Whether it's Moses, Luke Skywalker, or Jesus—the quest begins when the hero hears a call. It could be the voice of God or a burning bush, or a hologram of Princess Leia pleading, "Help me, Obi-Wan Kenobi." The hero puts together a motley team to heed the call (think about Jesus and his disciples) and sets out on his quest, undergoing trials, then a death and a rebirth.

The point I'm making is not about Joseph Campbell and myths, it's about how we're mentally wired. I will contend that the startup story follows a similar, universal pattern because it is also about mental wiring.

Steve is referring to the tale he's seen unfold dozens of times in his career as an entrepreneur and an investor. Call it, "The Founder's Quest."

Imagine you're a first-time entrepreneur and you are lucky enough to get a Series A from a senior partner at Sequoia. A traditional VC sits on anywhere from eight to twelve boards at a time. In their lifetime, they'll go through four, five, six cycles of that. Could be that they've seen the entire life cycle of a company forty to fifty times. You get two of those VCs, and they might have had the experience fifty to a hundred times of not just sitting on the board of a company, but of seeing its entire life cycle, and they've seen thousands of pitches. Now, they might look like just another guy sitting at the table, but if you get the right VCs—they'd have to be deaf, blind, stupid, and on drugs not to have something that you need to know. They have seen companies mess up in four hundred ways. They've lived through this stuff.

Let me give you an example of what I mean. One VC at a board meeting once turned to me and said, "Steve, let me tell you what's going to happen." And he proceeded to describe how things would unfold over the next months. I thought he was nuts. Six months later, I realized he'd accurately predicted the entire series of events. I thought, "This guy must be

---

THE E.PIPHANY STORY

Before becoming a Silicon Valley guru, Steve founded eight startups. His most recent was E.piphany, a customer-relationship management (CRM) provider he launched in 1997. As Steve explains on his blog, an initial setback became the company's turning point. In search of early clients, Steve met with Silicon Graphics' head of marketing, Joe DiNucci. DiNucci told him that he'd hit on a big CRM problem. In fact, it was so big that Silicon Graphics had already built a custom, in-house solution; they would not be an E.piphany customer.

Discouraged at first, Steve later saw an opportunity and seized it: he brought DiNucci onboard as E.piphany's VP of sales and licensed Silicon Graphics' CRM code for $1. By 2004, E.piphany's revenues exceeded $70 million. The following year, SSA Global acquired the company for $329 million.

channeling God." Now thirty years later, I look back at that guy and say, "Yeah, he was a pretty good pattern recognizer." He's lived through it. Companies and startups don't have an incalculable number of ways to screw up.

> "When you run a startup, you're breaking every rule, shattering every piece of glass."

One of the myths of Silicon Valley is that startups follow some kind of regular plan. Think about venture capital in the last fifty years in Silicon Valley: you wrote a business plan, they funded your plan, they looked at that creative writing exercise in the appendix called your "revenue plan," then they managed you in board meetings to that revenue plan. And by the way, no plan ever had a hockey stick and said "zero" for five years—it was all increasing revenue. I joke with my students that there must be a secret key code in Excel that will generate $100 million in five years. It's kind of funny when you think about it, but when you're in a formal VC-driven board meeting it's not funny if you don't make the plan. When you don't make the plan, there's lots of screaming and gnashing of teeth.

It's almost like a Japanese Noh play. Stuff unfolds like clockwork. VP of sales gets fired. A new VP of sales comes in. They're not stupid, so they change the strategy. That doesn't work. They fire the VP of marketing. The CEO, if he's the founder, becomes the chief strategy officer. But no one ever asked, is this an anomaly that's just occurring at my startup and I'm a failure as an entrepreneur? What you don't have as a first-time entrepreneur is any perspective on the fact that this is the common mode—most startups fail. But the management pattern was to treat that like an exception and cause a crisis. There was no wisdom from venture capitalists that said we're trying to impose an execution model on what is really a learning-and-discovery model. We're just wasting executives, resources, and angst by trying to overlay what large companies do onto startups, which are doing something very different. Large companies execute known models. Startups are all about the quest. They're searching, in the first year or two, for a repeatable and scalable business model. VCs were the ones who didn't get that, because they went to business school.

Without disparaging the potential value of business school programs, Steve is very clear about the fact that their curricula aren't suited to the realities of creating new companies, which is what startups do.

The modern corporation can be traced back to the East India Company, founded in 1600. Harvard didn't come up with the first MBA until 1908. The first question is, how did we do without MBAs for three hundred years? And second, what did Harvard do? They looked at three hundred years of business experience and said, "Hey, why don't we put in one place a course on how to run a company? You need to know about strategy, about finance, about HR, etc." And they came up with a degree called the master of business administration. It was about how to execute and run companies—not about business creation. But it was perfect timing because this was the start of the expansion of the American empire. We needed a cadre of trained, professional managers. So there's a "B" school that fit that particular time, but I'm now advocating for an "E" school: Entrepreneur school.

THE STEVE BLANK PLAYBOOK

Build from Your Core Expertise

Ideas come from a lot of places. Many of the best ideas come from domain experts. For example, you've been in an oil company doing reservoir simulations for years, and you realize that there's a much smarter way to do this but they just won't listen. Not only that, but you keep hearing customers say that they would kill to have an improved option, so you found a company to execute that smarter solution. That's the ultimate company; you know there's a better way and you know there are customers for it.

Convince Yourself; Convince Your Team; Convince an Evangelist

What's really important to you can be measured by what you spend your time thinking about in the shower versus what you do not get to until you're driving home from work. When you're taking notes about your idea at three in the morning; when you wake up every day and think, "Now I can work on my startup!"—that's when you know you're really committed. The next step is to recruit your team; that process is the earliest test of your idea's power. You want somebody selling your idea as enthusiastically as you are. Once that early evangelist is in place, your initial team is complete.

Entrepreneurship Is Teachable

We're finally beginning to understand that entrepreneurship might be teachable. I don't think you can teach "Winning Startups," but not teaching entrepreneurship would be like saying that we shouldn't teach art because we're not guaranteed to produce the next Michelangelo. If Michelangelo had taken classes, he would've learned how to mix paints, how to use perspective—all of the basics he had to teach himself. He might have gotten to the *Pietà* or the Sistine Chapel four or five years earlier. Learning the principles of entrepreneurship could make the process of founding a startup much more efficient.

STEVE'S BEST ADVICE

BOARDS

Populate Your Board with "Dinosaurs"

In addition to entrepreneurs who leverage domain expertise, there are entrepreneurs whom I'd call "domain un-experts." They're the outsiders who see things and say, "This is stupid. How come they're not using *X* or *Y* to solve this problem?" As I've found out, there's often a very *good* reason why they're not using *X* or *Y*. You might be a genius, but you still have a lot to learn from people who've worked in a domain for decades. If your board of advisers doesn't include the dinosaurs that you're trying to kill, you're screwed.

BUSINESS OPERATIONS

Make "Good Enough" Daily Decisions

Startup founders need to make very fast decisions. If someone comes into your office with a question, they should leave with an answer. I call it "good enough" decision-making. You have to be comfortable with the fact that there are no right answers to the questions you get all day, but you still have to answer them in real time. There are rare cases where this isn't true, and they're easy to spot. Is this a revocable decision, or is it an irrevocable decision? If it's a revocable decision, just do it. You'll unwind the architecture or the feature later. Deciding whether to fire ten people or sign a five-year lease; those are irrevocable decisions. They can't be "good enough."

COMPETITION

Re-Segment the Marketplace

In some markets, the incumbents seem so entrenched that taking them on seems impossible. But, you might understand the needs of a certain segment of customers that nobody else is serving. Instead of attacking Microsoft on the entire OS business, you'll tackle them on service, or something else. You re-segment the marketplace and take the niche that you've newly defined. This is the insight behind the "Blue Ocean Strategy" that W. Chan Kim and Renée Mauborgne have popularized in the past few years.

CUSTOMER DEVELOPMENT

No Business Plan Survives First Contact with Customers

The minute someone uses *business plan* and *startup* in the same sentence, I know they don't get it. In a large corporation, business plans make a lot of sense. You write them for the second, third, fourth, or *n*th product. There are a lot of knowns in a large corporation. That's not true in a startup. You're dealing with a marketplace that has never encountered an offer like yours. No startup business plan survives first contact with customers.

LEADERSHIP

Ask for Forgiveness, Not Permission

When you run a startup, you're breaking every rule, shattering every piece of glass, punching through walls, and leaving rubble along the way. It's like being a platoon commander in Afghanistan or Fallujah. You're operating in chaos and you need sharp elbows to get in front of the line. If you're not comfortable operating in that way, get out of the job. Otherwise, you'll be removed, or you'll kill your company.

MARKET DEVELOPMENT

Make Investment Decisions Within a Market Context

Consider an executive who decides to target 15 percent of the PDA market. The marketing head will say, "I need a $15 million budget." The head of manufacturing will say, "I need to build three factories in China." Those are huge investments, but they might be worthwhile. Fifteen percent of the PDA marketplace is hundreds of millions of dollars. Twenty years earlier, it would have been absurd. The budgets would have been the same, but 15 percent of a nonexistent marketplace is "zero." A decision that would amount to burning loads of money in one era would be considered using it effectively in another. The only thing that changes is the market context.

METRICS

Identify Metrics That Test Your Hypotheses

Startup founders can't focus on income statements, balance sheets, cash flow—all of the metrics that fuel large corporations. When you don't have revenue, those metrics are irrelevant. You need to identify the metrics that test the hypothesis your business is built to prove. If you're in a Web business, it might be the number of clicks, the number of page views, the number of sign-ups or form submissions. After optimizing those metrics for a time, you need to determine whether they're the right ones. When you start, you don't even know what your metrics should be.

VISION & MISSION

Know Your History

Whether you are a domain insider or an outsider, you need to really achieve an understanding of how your sector has evolved into being what it is today, when your new company is entering it. Not only does looking backward provide you with an understanding of what segments want most for innovation, but it will give you a perspective on how to grow and overtake a greater share of your market in the future.

STEVE'S VISION FOR THE FUTURE

Steve shares valuable lessons that every startup founder needs to learn in *The Four Steps to the Epiphany*. Additionally, he has spent years teaching undergraduate and graduate business students at the University of California, Berkeley's Haas School of Business, Stanford's Graduate School of Engineering, and the Columbia Business School.

Given the current makeup of universities, Steve's classes occupy a space that leaves much to be desired. "There's 'B' school, but I'm advocating for the 'E' school," he says. "The real question is, what should go in that bucket?" In January 2011, Steve began answering his own question when he began teaching The Lean LaunchPad at Stanford. "It turned out to be a perfect combination of business-model design, customer development, and design thinking. It was a home run." The National Science Foundation adopted the course for its groundbreaking Innovation Corps in 2011 and is using it to teach hand-picked teams of the U.S.'s top scientists and engineers how to commercialize their tech ideas. Hopefully, it will soon form the foundation of the "Entrepreneur School" that Steve envisions.

MATT BLUMBERG

FOUNDER:
RETURN PATH

INTRODUCING MATT BLUMBERG

Matt Blumberg is the startup scientist. In everything he does, he's conducting research: studying, testing, recording, validating. He collects data and allows it to speak for itself. When he reaches a conclusion, he becomes very resolved in his thinking; his ideas have the power of proofs. But Matt is humble enough to realize that every scientific proof is amenable to revision. A voracious reader and a careful listener, Matt is always open to hearing new arguments and considering new findings. Most strikingly, though, he's a prodigious contributor to his own discoveries.

In the years since he started Return Path, an email scoring and certification solution, Matt has meticulously honed a machine that produces successful companies. On his blog, Only Once, which he's maintained since 2004, he has produced an encyclopedia of the insights and lessons he's derived from that process.

Matt uses his writing to think through problems and reaffirm his beliefs. He digs deeply into every issue he considers, and he considers everything: boards and managers, fundraising and spending, sales and marketing. To take just one example, Matt's Human Resources department is considered one of the best in the country, and he often visits other companies with Return Path's vice president of people, Angela Baldonero, to share HR best practices. This openness is unique; I can't think of another CEO who releases all of his business thinking into the marketplace.

Matt is in the business of building companies; he could succeed in any number of fields. His deliberation and thoughtfulness could fill out any CEO's skill set. Given how gracious he is in sharing his ideas, there's no reason why we can't all learn from him.

MATT'S STORY

Matt Blumberg has spent a large part of his career dealing with the ways in which people communicate. Sometimes, this has meant building new tools for old devices. Before it was acquired by AOL, Matt ran marketing and online services for MovieFone/777-FILM. Later, MovieFone became www.moviefone.com, which gave Matt his first exposure to online business. While many of his colleagues were looking for ways to profit from the Internet, Matt decided to spend his time focusing on what remains the largest source of online traffic: email.

Matt's initial business was Email Change of Address, an online equivalent to the postal service's Change of Address service.

Matt Blumberg: Email Change of Address (ECOA) is a very simple idea—that people who change email addresses need help updating their personal and business contacts, and also their most trusted commercial email newsletter relationships. It's a free service for consumers, and a paid service for opt-in email marketers and publishers who use our service to reacquire their customers with renewed permission and a shiny new email address.

Very early on, Return Path ventured into a number of other businesses. These included email market research (Authentic Response) and an "email deliverability" business. The latter is best explained with a metric that Matt has introduced to the industry: "Inbox Placement Rate," or IPR. What percentage of emails sent by a company land in a user's inbox?

I think this better explains what marketers mean when they say "delivered"—in other words, an email delivered anywhere other than the inbox is not going to generate the kind of response marketers need. The problem with the term "delivered" is that it usually means "didn't bounce." While that is a good metric to track, it doesn't tell you where the email lands. It could have landed in the spam folder and still registered as "delivered." Inbox placement rate, by contrast, is pretty straightforward: how much of the email you sent landed in the inbox of your customers and prospects?

In a dramatic transformation, the deliverability business quickly became Return Path's focus. This was made official when the company sold their Email Change of Address business to their major competitor, Fresh Address, in 2008.

When we created ECOA in 1999, we were sure it was the proverbial $100 million idea. (What idea wasn't in 1999?) More than six years later, though, while the product was a success and profitable, it never took off

THE RETURN PATH STORY

Spam accounts for between 78 and 92 percent of all emails sent—that's trillions of messages. Return Path works to certify and score emails so that real businesses can reach their audiences and email recipients can avoid thousands of irrelevant messages. According to their research, 20 percent of legitimate emails don't reach their recipients. Return Path's certification tools help businesses reduce that number. In the twelve years since Return Path was founded, the company has entered a number of subsidiary businesses, including Email Change of Address (ECOA), a market-research business (Authentic Response), and a consultancy (Strategic Solutions). In 2008, Matt and his board folded those businesses into their core competency: email deliverability.

with that explosive growth we'd imagined early on. Return Path, on the other hand, had grown a lot, both organically and through mergers and acquisitions. So since about 2002 or early 2003, we basically put the ECOA business on autopilot, tending to it as needed, making sure it still worked well and was adequately competitive in the market, but no longer investing meaningfully in its growth.

In addition to growing more slowly than Matt and his team had hoped, Return Path's numerous business lines were often at odds with one another. Despite maintaining a strict separation between their deliverability and bulk-sender businesses, Return Path's management team knew they were facing an ethical dilemma.

"Be picky about your VCs . . . they are your inner circle."

Being a bulk sender of email had both advantages and disadvantages for us as a company. On the one hand, it was good for us to see firsthand some of the issues that impact our clients. We were, in fact, our own client, one business unit to another. On the other hand, being a bulk sender carried a real business risk of compromising our position as a trusted intermediary between senders and receivers. It was always a fine line to walk, and while we never got in trouble for it, we were always concerned—to the point where for a long time we didn't allow our other business units to apply for our customer whitelist.

His willingness to make drastic changes has been a key to Matt's success. It's something many entrepreneurs find extremely difficult.

I never said to myself, "I've got to solve everyone's email-changeover problem or I'm not going to make it in life." I was actually much more passionate about creating a company—bringing extra growth to the economy and building a unique and compelling place where people could spend a chunk of their careers. I'd argue that it's actually better to be passionate about building great companies than it is to be passionate about solving one particular problem. If you're only passionate about solving a single problem, you're going to have a much harder time when things aren't working and you need to make a change. Pivoting is much harder if you're emotionally wedded to a single idea.

Running a startup is all about flexibility. Unless you are that one-in-a-hundred entrepreneur whose original idea turns out to be exactly the wonderful, high-growth, high-margin business that you thought it was going to be on the back of that cocktail napkin, you need to be nimble and to shift as you spot new opportunities. Our company, for example, has been completely transformed over the years, first into a broad-based provider of multiple email-marketing and market-research services, and more recently into a pure player in email deliverability and whitelisting.

All the while, Matt has documented the process of building Return Path on Only Once (the title of his blog refers to the fact that being a first-time CEO is an experience you have "only once"). The blog is an important way for Matt to communicate with his team and network in and out of his industry, but it is also the repository of his findings on a wide variety of issues.

One of the best things about publishing a blog is that it has forced me to spend a few minutes here and there thinking about issues in a more structured way and crystallizing my point of view on them. That crystallization is invaluable.

THE
MATT BLUMBERG
PLAYBOOK

Pretend Your Company Is a Party and You Are the Host

I always spend a huge amount of my time making sure people feel welcome; that they have a good time, that there's plenty to eat and drink, that they are mingling and getting along with the other guests, that they get enough time with you as the host. Then they want to invite their friends to join and feel appreciated for having spent the time with you.

Don't Shy Away from Mergers and Acquisitions

We have done something like nine successful acquisitions (plus two failed ones), two divestitures, and a spin-out (the corporate equivalent of a TV-series "spin-off"). Yes, all of that has taken time and energy and money. But it has helped us shape a great business over the years. Sometimes it's just easier and faster in terms of go-to-market to buy up a team, a piece of technology, a piece of IP, than it is to start from scratch yourself.

Cultivate a Killer Board, and Run It like
You Run Your Management Team

Be picky about your VCs: they aren't just your source of capital, they are your inner circle. Similarly, use the opportunity of the "CEO calling card" to find fantastic directors who will be committed to you and to the company. Then manage the group. Send them all-important news (good and bad) early and often. Send clear and consistent reporting materials well in advance of meetings. Run your board meetings as strategy sessions, not as boring, reporting-oriented, 120-page, read-the-slides summits!

CULTURE

Include a Combination of Optimists and Pessimists in Your Management Team

One of the challenges of being a CEO is that you have to be the most optimistic person in the company and the most pessimistic person in the company at the same time. You celebrate when things go well, but you also worry that things are never going to be so good again. That same balance needs to inform your executive team. It should include people who are paranoid and others who are native optimists. The pessimism part especially has to be baked into your company's operating system.

HIRING

Hire Good Cultural Fits

Hiring a new person into an organization is a bit like doing an organ transplant. You can do all the scientific work up front to see if there's a match, but you never know until the organ is in the new body—often after some months have gone by—whether the body will take or reject the organ. Why are some people just not a good match? It could be a few things, but in my experience it's usually one of three. Sometimes the execution isn't there. Other times, specifically in cases where the person is coming into a new job that didn't exist before, it turns out the job was poorly specified or didn't need to exist. But in most cases, I think the cultural fit just isn't there. That's not really anyone's fault, although it *should* be something you can interview for to a large extent.

HUMAN RESOURCES

Involve Innovative People with a High Tolerance for Risk

Your first employees can't be afraid of high-risk environments. In a startup, you need people who are comfortable trying things out and seeing what sticks. My VP of product management always says, "Nothing interesting happens in the office," and that's become our watchword. For instance, in the early days of our business, all five of us on the team went downstairs to the Starbucks and handed out $5 gift cards to people who were willing to fill out a questionnaire about their email usage patterns. As the CEO, you're constantly figuring out your place in the market, and your entire company *should* be doing the same thing.

LEADERSHIP

Be Radically Transparent, but Appreciate the Limits of Transparency

People do their best work when you trust them and give them all of the information they need to make good decisions. Moreover, most people will go beyond the scope of their own jobs when they have information about what's going on around them. To encourage that level of trust and engagement, you should be radically transparent, but also be mindful of what people can and cannot handle. (You want your company to be aware of dangers, but not freaked out by them. You want your executive team to be aware *and* freaked out.) Ultimately, there are very few things that you *shouldn't* be transparent about.

METRICS

Know When You're Being Boiled

Every consultant tells the story of the frog in the pot of boiling water: change the temperature gradually enough, and the frog stays in the water until it dies. As CEO, you have to learn to smell smoke and realize there's fire. Otherwise, you'll get to a point where you've been soaking in boiling water and you're too limp to climb out.

PUBLIC RELATIONS

Never Make the Same Pitch Twice

No two pitches for your company should sound alike. You should always try new material and see what sticks with the audience you're addressing; you have to try things on for size. When you go to the store, you try on six blazers before you settle on the one you like. Defining your business is complex; a continual process of discovery is critical.

TALENT

Don't Collect Outstanding Individuals; Field a Great Team

You want people who are very flexible in their thinking and can survive in an atmosphere of change. You also need to field the best overall team. People who can get work done together effectively are "functional experts," and these are more valuable than "rock stars." They're not self-promoters. They're members of a group that puts the business first and has an understanding of people, the market, internal dependencies, and the broader implications of any and all decisions.

WORKING FOR YOURSELF

Track Your Time Religiously

I am meticulous about keeping an accurate calendar, including travel time. I even go back to my calendar and clean up meetings after they've happened to make the calendar an accurate record of what transpired. At the end of each quarter, my assistant and I download the prior three months' worth of meetings, categorize them, and see where my time went. For me, the big ones are: Internal, External/Client, Board/Investor, Free, Travel, and Non-Return-Path business. I feel like the time-ratio of the important categories should be 40 percent Internal, 40 percent External, 10 percent Board/Investors, and 10 percent Non-Return Path. Then we make changes to the upcoming quarter's calendar to match my targets. This exercise has been really helpful in keeping me proactive and on track.

MATT'S VISION FOR THE FUTURE

Matt's plans for the future involve refining his machine for building companies. At Return Path, that is a collaborative process that culminates in an annual "360 Review." Reviews are compiled through self-assessment, the person's manager, any subordinates, and a handful of other people who work with the person. They're done anonymously, and they're used to craft employees' development plans for the next year.

Matt's recent review sharpened his focus for the next two years. With characteristic precision, he outlined his plans on his blog, leading off with "Institutionalize impatience and lessen the dependency dynamic on me. Make others in the organization as impatient as I am for progress, success, reinvention, streamlining, and overcoming/minimizing operational realities."

Further self-assessment comes in the form of three essential questions he asks at the end of the year: *Am I having fun at work? Am I learning and growing as a professional? Is my work financially rewarding enough, either in the short term or in the long term?*

While three "yes" answers are ideal, two means you're in good shape and know what to work on. One "yes" might indicate that you should think about if your job is right for you. This kind of assesment can be productive for anyone who cares about his or her practice.

RODNEY BROOKS

FOUNDER:

IROBOT

HEARTLAND ROBOTICS

INTRODUCING RODNEY BROOKS

All of us have sci-fi fantasies about what the future will look like. "Flying cars" make frequent appearances, and much of the rest is also a variation on *The Jetsons*. High on the wish list, of course, is Rosie, the robotic maid. Push the time frame out far enough—fifty years, a hundred years, two hundred years—and most people will say that this kind of progress is inevitable. But Rodney Brooks, creator of the Roomba robotic vacuum cleaner, reminds us that nothing is "inevitable." Somebody with a concrete vision of the future has to *build* it.

Rodney began his career at MIT, where he eventually became director of the Artificial Intelligence Laboratory. His approach to robotics was radical: rather than building robots that thought, Rodney built robots that responded to stimuli. He summed up his new approach with the phrase "fast, cheap, and out of control,"* which poked fun at the old dictum that manufacterers should strive for two-thirds of "fast," "cheap," and "reliable." The phrase paradigm shift is overused, but Rodney really did bring one about in the field of artificial intelligence.

Rodney wasn't satisfied with this accomplishment, however. While still at MIT, he founded a series of companies to convert his ideas into realities. He quickly realized that doing so would require making some hard decisions about compromising his passions. To illustrate the revolutionary balance he has achieved between business and science, he says, "I'd rather have half of my idea change the world than my whole idea be a few papers in a journal."

* In 1997, Academy Award–winning director Errol Morris featured Rodney in a film of that name.

RODNEY'S STORY

At a time when nearly all entrepreneurs were trying to capitalize on the Internet revolution, Rodney Brooks kept his lifelong commitment to making things.

Rodney Brooks: Ever since I was seven or eight years old, I loved it when I switched a thing on, the lights flashed, and it did something. That's what fascinates me: getting something to happen in the world.

Soon after receiving his PhD, Rodney joined the faculty at MIT. While he was there, he got training in a crucial entrepreneurial skill: raising capital.

I ran the biggest lab at MIT—the computer science and artificial intelligence lab, which had more than 800 people. I was constantly out trying to raise research money. And when MIT and other nonprofit and governmental institutions started backing off from computer science, I had to raise that money from private companies. I had to figure out what their pain points were and talk about how computer science research could help them. That's also where I first started focusing on megatrends, or problems people were concerned about on a global scale.

While still at MIT, Rodney began his career as a startup founder. After some early failures, he cofounded iRobot in 1990 with Colin Angle and Helen Grenier.

Around 1999, Colin, Helen, and I were trudging the streets of New York going from VC to VC. One firm sent a college junior who was interning for them to come talk with us. We started our pitch, and he interrupted us about ten minutes in with a question. "You mean you build stuff? No one builds stuff anymore!" He wasn't interested.

We continued anyway, but iRobot was a long push. What we really didn't take to heart early on was that we needed something we could easily convince people they *wanted*. We were too focused on developing things we thought were important, but they were too far-out. One of the things we tried was nuclear power plant–inspection robots, but we couldn't get any traction in the market. Nobody really felt like they needed a robot to do that. Well now, iRobot has a number of PackBots in Japan's Fukushima Daiichi nuclear plant (which was compromised during the 2011 earthquake), going into places where no people should go.

THE IROBOT STORY

Rodney cofounded iRobot in 1990. The company's purpose was to introduce simple and inexpensive robots in areas where they had not been used before, but it was a decade before iRobot had their first major success with the release of PackBot, a series of military robots, 2,000 of which are today deployed in Iraq and Afghanistan. Two years later, iRobot released their most popular product: the Roomba, a robotic vacuum cleaner. iRobot's other home products include Scooba (a floor washer), Looj (a gutter cleaner), and Create, a customizable robot for hobbyists. At the end of 2010, iRobot had sold more than six million home units.

At one point, I really shook everyone up. I got everybody together and told them we'd lost our way, that as of today, things were going to be totally different. At the time, the company was called I.S. Robotics, and I had a number of mugs printed up that said, "I.S. Robotics: Phase Two." That meant this is where we are *right* now. It's a new phase; we've left the old one behind.

It wasn't until nearly our fifteenth and sixteenth tries that we finally stumbled upon two items that were a good product–to-market fit: PackBot and Roomba. The PackBot was our line of military robots with defensive

"If we're not doing something that's game-changing, then frankly I'm not interested in doing it."

capabilities. It wasn't too hard to convince people in the military that sending a robot out to defuse a roadside bomb was better than sending a nineteen-year-old kid in a bombsuit. And though the application seems radically different, selling the Roomba was a similar no-brainer for our customers: who wouldn't prefer an automatic vacuum cleaner to a manual one?

Eventually, Rodney decided that it really was time for a new phase. He left iRobot and founded Heartland Robotics. In 2012, Heartland rebranded as Rethink Robotics to better represent the scope of their business.

I've learned some things over the last few years, and my current process is very different from my previous companies. It's not just about going to the customers. It's about identifying major trends and having a vision of how you can participate in and affect them. My role is trying to make sure that everybody sticks with our vision enough that we don't end up doing something that's easy, but isn't game-changing. If we're not doing something that's game-changing, then frankly I'm not interested in doing it.

Investors are often wary of visionaries without very clearly defined plans. But those concerns quickly dissolve in the face of the great predictor of future performance: past success.

It doesn't hurt to have success. With my later endeavor, the investors have seen that I was willing to make compromises before and that I know what it takes to actually get something to market and get something to work. This makes the investors a lot more willing to give us the benefit of the doubt and trust us a bit. Of course, they're still VCs, so they occasionally wonder how we can make our company a social networking company.

Rodney and his team have not disclosed their plans publicly, but are close to making a major launch. As the company moves to this new phase, Rodney's priorities are shifting accordingly.

Today, we're gearing up to manufacture a new product and distribute it worldwide. So my role is starting to transition from communicating the vision to my team to communicating it to the outside world. I have to go out, find lots of customers, and infect them with the belief that what we're building is going to change their lives.

THE
RODNEY BROOKS
PLAYBOOK

Capitalize On Your Talents to Change the World

My strength is building systems that interface between computation and physicality. The question that guides me is how I can use that strength to change the world in a positive way. There are many ways that I can imagine the world being a better place, but only a few of them intersect with my particular talents. You have to determine exactly how you can be useful or big in the world by capitalizing on your talents.

Identify and Participate in Megatrends

My process today is much more focused than it was at my previous companies. I begin by looking for megatrends—changes in the world that will create major new demands. My goal is to create a company that can be there to meet those demands. You can't address every megatrend you identify. But given how significant these changes are, there is some niche you can work in that addresses at least one of them.

Accelerate Progress

When proposing a major new project, I always ask VCs, "Can you imagine X not being true in fifty years?" If they say, "Of course X is going to be true in fifty years," then I know I've got them. The next question is why we shouldn't make it true in *two* years instead of waiting for fifty. My talent is getting things to work that people think are many decades in the future. I say we can make them happen now.

CUSTOMER DEVELOPMENT

Find a Match Between Your Talents and Your Customers' Needs

If you're not bringing value to customers, you're not going to succeed. That doesn't mean you should identify potential customers and do whatever it takes to give them value. It means that you should identify what you have that's of value, find the right customers, and tweak things accordingly. It's not just about going after customers, but finding a match between what you're good at and what will provide value.

FINANCE

Don't Outsource Your Happiness to the Stock Market

Jeff Bezos taught me to never outsource my happiness to the stock market. You have to concentrate on what you're doing and on being internally successful. Don't worry what the stock market thinks of you—about your valuation in Series B or at an IPO. Worry about delivering more than the direct monetary valuation.

FIRING

Fire People When They Lose Faith in Your Ideas

When people lose faith in the idea, you have to let them go, because they start to undermine it for everyone else. Sometimes they will hide the fact that they've lost faith, because, of course, they've got expenses and responsibilities and they don't want to be out looking for another job. But superficial commitment is not necessarily going to get you where you need to go.

HIRING

Find Producers Who Are Also Visionaries

One of the tricky things about being an entrepreneur is finding people who can engineer and deliver on schedule, but who are also willing to take intellectual risks. If you're doing something radically new, you need a team that's willing to go on a ride that's very different from anything they've encountered before. It's hard to find people who can both deliver and try something quite radical and stay with the vision.

LEADERSHIP

Be an Unreasonable Man

George Bernard Shaw said, "All progress depends on the unreasonable man." One of my jobs is to be the "unreasonable man" at my company. I have to pull people just a bit beyond their comfort zones so we can truly make an impact. The trick is to get really good people, empower them, listen to their ideas about what's actually practical, and then push them beyond that.

METRICS

Let Your Metrics Evolve as Your Market Evolves

Engineers like to have a number and work toward that number. But in robotics, things are complex, and putting a straight number on things is very hard. You have to stick to your metrics, but you also have to know when to relax those metrics as you begin to understand your customers better. It's rather tricky, and it infuriates engineers when you change the numbers on them, but flexibility is a necessity.

PRODUCT DEVELOPMENT

Compromise on Features to Keep Your Team Invested

Sometimes you have to be willing to give things up because your team isn't ready to go as far as you are. You push, but you have to concede to them when you're about to take them over the edge. There are some features that you leave aside for version two or three, and some that you might never get to at this particular company. It's a practical reality, a trade-off that my academic friends have a hard time understanding.

TALENT

Promote Employees Who Contribute Beyond Their Immediate Jobs

There are certain employees who can't help contributing all over. Of course, some people are bubbling over with lousy ideas, but sometimes someone bubbles over and *helps* in many different areas. When that happens, you clearly know that you want to develop that person further because they get what you're trying to do and will move heaven and earth to make it happen. Wander around the cubicles now and then. Look for people who see the bigger picture beyond their particular team and contribute across a broad spectrum. They're the ones that you want to raise higher and higher up in your organization.

RODNEY'S VISION FOR THE FUTURE

When he discusses the megatrend that Rethink Robotics will participate in, Rodney tends not to talk about human labor. American jobs were lost with the shift overseas, and rising overseas costs are putting multinational corporations in a bind. Rodney's answer, of course, is robots. As he wrote in *Discover* magazine in 2010, "The Robot Invasion Is Coming—and That's a Good Thing." He believes robots will replace many human tasks. "There will be many more robots in our houses, in our hospitals, in our factories, and in the military." Does this mean people won't have anything to do? Rodney is emphatic that it does not. In the revolutions of labor of the past, he says, "We found things that were a lot easier than backbreaking labor in the sun and the fields. Let people rise to better things."

JEFF BUSSGANG

FOUNDER:

OPEN MARKET

UPROMISE

FLYBRIDGE CAPITAL PARTNERS

INTRODUCING JEFF BUSSGANG

Jeff Bussgang brings the methodical passion of an architect or an engineer to the practice of building companies. Like an engineer, he wants to build perfect objects—the watch that's beautifully designed and tells time correctly. And like other practical-minded artisans, Jeff wants his creations to have an economic impact.

When he's deciding whether to build or invest in a company, Jeff is clinical in the measurement of business opportunities. Of course, there are dangers to that approach, namely missed opportunities. Many businesspeople with an academic turn of mind (and most MBAs) are uncomfortable making decisions unless they have all the information. Jeff isn't like that. He'll synthesize all the data available to him, however limited it might be, and if he is satisfied, he'll take a risk.

The willingness to place large bets despite limited knowledge requires a strong core of confidence in your abilities and beliefs. If it weren't already obvious from his investment portfolio or his experiences at Open Market and Upromise, Jeff's confidence would still be evident in his willingness to hazard bold opinions. He recognizes that business claims aren't provable assertions, but he's not paralyzed by that fact. Whether he's blogging, participating in a board meeting, or laying out his plan for "mastering the VC game" (also the title of his book), he's willing to say, authoritatively, "This is the right way to do that." More often than not, he's right.

JEFF'S STORY

Throughout his career, Jeff has been careful to balance his passion for ideas with an "intellectual engine" committed to rigorous analysis. As he's the first to point out, the intellectual side is the dominant one.

Jeff Bussgang: For better or for worse, I was always an MBA-founder. My first job was in product management even though I had a background in computer science, and at my core I was always thinking about system structure and building permanent, sustainable organizations.

After earning an MBA from Harvard and working as a management consultant at the Boston Consulting Group, Jeff had his first major startup experience at Open Market, an early Internet commerce firm.

We went through a lot of ups and downs at Open Market. We grew very quickly and then we hit a wall. Early on, we had a terrific IPO. In 1996, we had a billion-dollar market cap with $1.8 million of trailing revenue. Then we stumbled. Our growth slowed: we had gone from $1.8 million to $22.5 million to $61.3 million, and then the next year we did $61 million again. A ridiculous set of expectations built up around the company, and then we went flat the next year. Our stock price dropped and we lost a lot of people.

That's when you do the gut check. "Are people here because they're mercenaries, or are people here because they want to be part of something special and because they have loyalty and affection for the team?" When you hit a speed bump, some people become deer in the headlights, some people finger-point, and some people go political. But some people take ownership, accept accountability, and rally. It's obvious which of those you want on your team.

When you go through tough times like that, you have to live by the Navy Seals' motto: "No man left behind." No matter what, you have to bring everyone along—intellectually and financially.

At Open Market, Jeff served as the VP of Worldwide Marketing, Product Management, and Business Development. Yet he willingly gave up this significant role when his gut instinct told him he had found the perfect opportunity to create a company of his own.

THE UPROMISE STORY

Upromise provides two services: a college-savings program for consumers and a data-driven loyalty program for enterprise partners. Consumers who join Upromise have the option of making purchases through their accounts—either online or at affiliated restaurants, grocery stores, and drug stores—with a registered credit or debit card. A percentage of these purchases is placed in their Upromise savings funds. In 2006, Upromise was acquired by Sallie Mae, the largest provider of federally guaranteed student loans in the United States for more than $300 million.

Upromise was my partner Michael Bronner's idea. He had identified a huge pain for the American household: paying for college. Outside of buying a home, it's the largest purchase a family is ever going to make. On the flip side, there's the pain businesses have, which is attracting and retaining loyal customers. We met over breakfast to discuss the idea. I went home and told my wife that I was going to leave my officer job at a big public company, with eight figures of unvested stock options left on the table, and start a company with a guy I'd never met before that day. But then again, I've always been someone who embraces risk. Sometimes you want to take more risk if you think there's going to be more reward at the other end.

Despite the risk of leaving Open Market, Jeff knew to trust his and Michael's analysis.

We identified tens of millions of households that wanted, more than anything else, to save enough money for their kids to go to college. Harmonizing those two pieces, the consumer and the business, and figuring out a system that would generate profits underneath—that was the magic of Upromise.

With nothing but twenty-five PowerPoint slides, we raised $34 million in our Series A in March 2000. It was an extraordinary financing. We couldn't have had more interest and more enthusiasm for the business. Before we'd generated a single nickel of revenue, we raised another $55 million in a Series B.

After that experience of receiving a flood of investment, I feel like I'm in Alcoholics Anonymous as a recovering "fat" entrepreneur. It was almost bad that we raised that much money because we had so much room for error, and, as a result, I made some sloppy decisions. Now, I'm actually coteaching a course at the Harvard Business School on lean startups.

In addition to teaching students to run lean, Jeff makes a direct impact on startups through the venture-capital firm he helped found in 2003: Flybridge Capital Partners.

I'm general partner at Flybridge Capital. My partners are folks who have previously invested in me. When we set up our firm, we could have chosen to be investors at any stage of the startup process, but we decided to focus on the very earliest stages. We did that because we would have the most fun. We all are passionate about entrepreneurship and love building companies and embracing risk.

The culture we've tried to build at Flybridge emphasizes being humble and respectful. If you emphasize those old-fashioned values, then you're always going to have that humility that leads to being open to making mistakes. No one at your organization will think they are always right, or that they need to be. I want my employees to have that; I want my kids to have that. I think it's an essential set of traits to have.

Jeff is an active investor who serves on the boards of many companies, including Cartera Commerce, Click Tactics, DataXu, i4cp, Plastiq, SimpleTuition, and Tracx.

The challenge I often put forward on the boards I sit on is to say to CEOs, "Draw the org chart of what you want to look like twelve months from now. Then think about all the things you're doing today—communication, people, processes, decision-making—and compare that to where it needs to be in a year. If you're not building toward that, it's going to be all wrong."

THE
JEFF BUSSGANG
PLAYBOOK

Hope Is Not a Strategy

A fatal mistake that some people make is either to ignore data or actually deny what the facts are presenting. It's easy to fall into that trap at a startup because you're constantly getting barraged with imperfect information. You shouldn't let that paralyze you, but you can't turn your analytical filter off. Always take in information and make adjustments along the way. That's not the same thing as needing to know everything. You have to be comfortable making decisions with very few data points. But you should always strive to be very data-driven and know the truth. Now, you may still decide to do something with a low-probability outcome because the risks are low and the end result is so incredibly nirvana-like. But at least do the math and think it through before you leap into that situation.

Focus on Customer Pain

Sometimes, founders come up with their own great ideas and then try to project those ideas onto customers. I prefer the opposite approach. I like to interview customers and find out what their problems are. In particular, I really focus on what I call "customer pain." Where are customers, or big groups of customers, feeling pain? How high a priority would it be for them to find a solution? Only when I find something really high-priority do I try figuring out a solution to that pain point.

Envision Solutions with Obvious Benefits

While it's important to synthesize what you've heard from customers, vendors, and other participants in the industry, you have to apply your own judgment to figure out a "wow!" solution. You also need to be sure that whatever you're delivering has an immediate and obvious benefit. People are busy, if they don't immediately see the benefit of what you're giving them, they'll move on. When I can think of something that solves a pain and has immediate and obvious benefits, then I get really excited.

CULTURE

Build a Love-Driven Culture

Some organizations are fear-driven, but I prefer to get involved with companies that have love-driven cultures, and by that I mean love for what they're doing. It could be making search more efficient for small to midsize enterprises; it could be helping millions of families save for college. It could be a whole range of missions and purposes. People really have to believe in what they're doing because creating companies is impossible. If you do the expected value math on company creation, then any rational human being would turn away. The probabilities are too negative, and the odds are stacked too high. But the reason that people make this irrational decision anyway is that they have passion. If you make sure that your first ten employees are really focused on that mission, you'll lay the groundwork for a love-driven culture.

FAILURE

Conduct Brutal Postmortems

Postmortems are incredibly valuable tools for exploring how mistakes occurred and how they can be prevented in the future. At Open Market, every time we lost a customer account or had a flawed product release, we would get all the constituents in the room and do a brutally honest postmortem. It's an incredibly powerful and valuable way of probing experiences and really learning from them. It's OK to make a mistake, but don't let the same mistake happen twice or, God forbid, allow *the same team* to make the same mistake twice.

FOCUSING TIME & ENERGY

Address Problems That Nobody Else Can Solve

I learned an important coaching lesson from a peer who took me aside and said, "You need to hang back and let your people come up with the solutions themselves. If you don't, you're going to get sucked into their problems as opposed to focusing on things that are really going to move the needle on the business." If you're obsessed with problems that other people should be dealing with, you're not using your time well.

HUMAN RESOURCES

Read Body Language

When things get tough, great people turn it up a notch. They may be quiet, but you can see them getting in a little earlier and working a little later; being a little faster with their deliverables and a little more rigorous in what they're trying to accomplish. They push and give you 110 percent. You can actually see it in their body language. But when people are demoralized, their energy level goes down. It's like LeBron James in the fourth quarter when he's down. In the last couple of playoff sequences, we've seen him shut down. Other athletes, like Kobe Bryant, turn it up in the final moments of the fourth quarter. Their eyes light up and they're begging for the ball. Michael Jordan was the same way. You've got to look out for that kind of behavior. Body language speaks volumes.

LEADERSHIP

Seek Out Criticism

I actually want people to tell me where I'm wrong and, in turn, I want to tell other people where they're wrong. Some people don't appreciate that, but others find it very valuable. It's a component of having a data-driven, fact-driven view and not being afraid of the truth. Seek out criticism, and take it as well as you can.

MARKET DEVELOPMENT

Consider Market Dynamics Alongside Market Size

It's tempting to look at an industry and say, "Boy, that could be a really big market." But the airline industry is a really big market, and the net profitability of that industry is negative. It's not just how big the market opportunity is. You need to know whether the dynamics in that market could yield a profitable and valuable company.

RAISING CAPITAL

Only Raise as Much Capital as You Need

At Upromise, we raised nearly $90 million prelaunch. Because we had that much capital, it caused us to make some really bad decisions and waste a lot of money. Capital efficiency is very difficult to maintain when you have a lot of it. As a result of that experience, I'm an advocate of lean startups. People are raising a lot of money right now with concept sales, but founders need to think hard about building lean startups and being great, efficient project managers.

TALENT

Be a Mentor

All the people in this book have had fantastic mentors who have guided them. I've had incredible mentors in my life, and I've tried to be a mentor to others to the extent that I can. If you're not mentoring someone, you're missing out on something important. Leadership in the community and mentorship of young people are both crucial to what we do as entrepreneurs, and that's something that I really enjoy focusing on.

WORKING FOR YOURSELF

Don't Neglect the Contract with Your Family

The best advice I received early in my career is not to forget about the contract that I made with my spouse when starting a company. As I've said earlier, building companies is impossible. Everything is working against you. Unless you have an agreement with your life partner about the roller-coaster ride ahead, you can really get into trouble. You're strongest as a professional and as a person when you have a strong family foundation to rest on; you'll be able to handle criticism and all the setbacks that you'll have to face.

JEFF'S VISION FOR THE FUTURE

In the past fifteen years, Jeff has helped build two successful companies, written a book (*Mastering the VC Game*), and built a major venture-capital firm. But ask him if he's successful, and he'll say no. More than $100 million in revenues and an IPO (Open Market) and a sale to Sallie Mae (Upromise) might seem like cause for celebration, but Jeff doesn't allow himself to dwell on success. "I fail a lot as an investor, and I've got to keep picking myself up and reminding myself not to be afraid to make the next set of mistakes, but to keep taking the shots."

However, he's definitely a player who will always be looking forward. "When I think back on the things I've done that look successful on paper, I get caught up in it. I can tell you the ten things that were terrible and bad and awful much faster than I can tell you all the great things that I did. I still have so much more to strive for and achieve. But I know there are great opportunities and adventures ahead."

With Flybridge Capital's portfolio of more than fifty companies today, Jeff is clearly still that superstar player who is going to keep on making shots.

STEVE CASE

FOUNDER:
AMERICA ONLINE (AOL)

CHAIRMAN AND CEO:
REVOLUTION LLC

INTRODUCING STEVE CASE

Everything that we take for granted today is the result of a dream someone dared to pursue in the past. Steve Case can legitimately claim that he was one of the first to imagine what we now call the commercial Internet.

Throughout the 1990s, Steve and the AOL team were expanding the reach of email and online access—and literally getting America online. While it is nearly impossible to believe today, they were doing this at a time when the majority of Americans did not yet own computers, much less modems. When Steve cofounded America Online in 1985, 3 percent of Americans were online. Steve was a man ahead of his time, and he was ahead of his time for a long time.

AOL was not an overnight success, building the company took ten years. Over that entire period, Steve had to convince a skeptical marketplace that the Internet would achieve its much-vaunted potential. He was right, of course, but neither he nor his employees nor his investors could have been sure of that in real time. Americans did not simply appear online automatically; we are online today because Steve and visionaries like him brought us there.

STEVE'S STORY

In June 1983, at the age of twenty-four, Steve joined a company called Control Video Corporation as director of marketing. That effort failed but, in 1985, Steve cofounded Quantum Computer Services, with himself as the executive vice president being groomed to become the company's CEO. Six years later, in 1991, Steve was finally promoted to that role. By then, the company had become America Online.

Steve Case: When AOL first started out, only 3 percent of American households were connected. Most people didn't even have PCs, and the few who had PCs didn't have modems, it really was a peripheral part of the computing experience. So AOL really was an example of believing that someday everybody would be connected, Internet activity would be ubiquitous, and you could build a significant medium around that.

We weren't the only ones who had that vision, and our competitors were much bigger. Prodigy was a joint venture of CBS, IBM, and Sears; GEnie was a division of GE; and CompuServe was a division of H&R Block. By contrast, we raised less than $10 million in our first five years, a pittance compared to what Prodigy and CompuServe had at their disposal. We knew we couldn't win a round in hand-to-hand combat; it required more of a guerrilla marketing strategy. For us, that meant great products, including a consumer-friendly interface application.

Rather than allowing themselves to be distracted by their formidable competitors, Steve and his team focused on their core mission: providing consumers with low-cost, reliable Internet access.

We really believed in the power of the Internet, and that everybody would benefit if they had access. For us, the challenge was to lower the barriers and improve those benefits so that everybody would want to get online. The software had to be simple to use, and the service had to be affordable. Initially, it cost consumers $6.00 per hour to be online, or 10¢ per minute. That was too high, and we eventually wanted to migrate our pricing to unlimited access. It was a populist notion of building this medium, and we were very driven by that.

Today, AOL is remembered as a company that experienced nearly unprecedented growth, though in the early years, it nearly failed a number of times.

**THE
AOL
STORY**

When Quantum Computer Services was founded in 1985, the majority of Americans had not yet purchased a computer. In 1991, however, Quantum changed its name in order to boldly declare an outrageous goal: "America Online." The following year, the company raised $10 million in an IPO valuing the company at $70 million and began its amazing ascent. At its peak, less than a decade later, AOL was valued at more than $150 billion.

We went through three rounds of layoffs in the first five years. There were times when we thought a new partnership would help us expand, only to see it fail. We would run out of money and have to retrench. It was a classic situation, right down to friends and family suggesting that I find a different path. But we were not willing to give up; we were really passionate about our idea of getting everybody online.

After ten years of company building, Steve was poised to lead AOL through a decade of extraordinary growth.

> "I'm only interested in big ideas that aren't easy to execute."

AOL was an almost-twenty-year journey. The first ten years were the building phase. We were rolling up our sleeves and figuring out what was really going to be critical to our success. The goal at that stage was to create the simplest, friendliest product on the marketplace, and to form strategic partnerships that would help us expand and lower the cost of the service. I focused on everything from the language of our press releases and ads to the way our welcome screens looked.

In the next ten years, my role was very different. I was in my thirties during AOL's growth phase, and I was managing about 100 employees. By the time I turned forty, we had upward of 10,000 employees. These were the years of expansion and hypergrowth. I realized I needed to stop meddling, set direction, and delegate goals to my team.

Not only had the new medium Steve helped define caught up to the major incumbents; it surpassed them. In 2000, the ascendency of digital media was confirmed when AOL acquired Time Warner for $164 billion. To this day, this was the largest merger in business history. It was also widely regarded as having been a mistake. However, Steve timed the market well, orchestrating a merger at the peak of the dot-com boom that enabled AOL shareholders to own 55 percent of a much larger, more profitable, and diversified company. Steve stepped down as CEO to enable the merger to go forward, and resigned as chairman, as well, two years after the merger, frustrated with the company's inability to drive synergies and innovate in new markets. Indeed, after resigning, he advocated that AOL and Time Warner should be restored to separate companies. That split took place in December 2009.

When AOL experienced its initial growth, we were attackers disrupting the marketplace. In post–Time Warner decline, the politics of a large company with diverse interests and agendas made things difficult as well. AOL lost that attacker edge and became more of a defender.

In 2005, Steve founded investment firm Revolution LLC with Donn Davis and Tige Savage. Their major investments include the car-sharing service Zipcar and the social-commerce company LivingSocial.

Whether it's AOL creating the concept of the Internet as a medium, or Zipcar transforming the concept of car-ownership and urban living, or LivingSocial transforming commerce and communities, I'm only interested in big ideas that aren't easy to execute. These take a long time to get going, but when they do, you can see the light at the end of the tunnel showing you how they could become big, game-changing businesses, and therefore good investments. More important, they could become transformative forces in terms of improving people's lives.

THE STEVE CASE PLAYBOOK

Change the World

The key driver for me is finding businesses that change the world. These are businesses that empower consumers in new ways: giving them more choice, giving them more control, giving them more convenience in important aspects of their lives. I'm much more interested in built-to-last companies that are ten years in the making than built-to-flip companies that the founders hope to sell in two to three years. The risk of our current business climate is that we've created a generation of entrepreneurs with a form of attention-deficit disorder. Some think long term, but many have a short-term horizon of cycling through products and few have the patience to see a long-term vision through. Everybody is going to die eventually; what's going to be on your tombstone? "I created seven companies that I sold" or "I changed the world by doing . . . " Why not try to change the world?

Focus on People, Perseverance, and Passion

These "Three P's" are the keys to successful entrepreneurship. People are the most important, particularly in the first year of a venture. To maximize their value, spend as much time as you can assembling the best possible team that really complements your skill set and can

lead a little bit into where you're heading, not just where you are. Creating the right kind of dynamic in terms of culture and commitment is really critical. Perseverance: never underestimate the value of really caring about your idea and being unwilling to drop it. If you have a big idea, and you know in your heart it's going to happen (Passion), but know there will be roadblocks and challenges along the way. In this regard, a high degree of passion and commitment is extremely important. In my experience, really big ideas often take a decade to reach fruition.

Sign Up for an Important Battle

One of the by-products of the Internet is that the barriers to starting a company have gone down significantly. As a result, many entrepreneurs simply want to build a product, create some momentum in the marketplace, and sell their company. There's nothing wrong with that, but I wish we had less of it. We have a great need for people focused on the bigger ideas about fundamentally reshaping education, or reshaping healthcare, or reshaping energy. Entrepreneurs are the change agents and need to take the lead in building iconic, lasting companies that will improve people's lives. We need them to sign up for the important battles, not just the easy ones.

COMPETITION

Be an Attacker, Not a Defender

Entrepreneurship is inherently risky because you're taking paths that haven't been tested before. What people underestimate is how risky it is to operate in a "stable" business as a defender rather than an attacker. The reason America has had such success over the past two centuries is that we have been the attacker. We need to make sure that we continue to have that urgency and passion, and that we don't become complacent and rest on our laurels.

CULTURE

Be Loyal to Your Team, but Make Changes as You Scale

In the early days of AOL, most people didn't know what we were doing and didn't want to join our company. It wasn't obvious back then that the Internet would be a big deal. The people we did attract were true believers. They knew what would happen with the medium and they wanted to be part of this company. As a result, those people ended up getting a lot of responsibility a lot sooner than they imagined. Most of them rose to the occasion, but some didn't so we had to make some course corrections. But we really believed in that passion and loyalty aspect, and so we weren't too quick to replace people. That's not to say that we didn't hire people over them or change their positions if we needed a different skill set. In general, we erred on the side of giving people more responsibility than they might have otherwise had.

CUSTOMER DEVELOPMENT

Build for a Mass Audience

In our first five years, our goal was to create a mass market for what was then called "consumer online services" (now known as "the Internet"). To achieve that goal, we had to create something that everybody would be comfortable using and that didn't require a great deal of technical skill. Some people teased us at the time, calling it "the Internet on training wheels," but we were proud of that. That was exactly what we were trying to do; we really wanted to get everybody online in a way that was so easy and affordable that it became almost irresistible.

DEPLOYING CAPITAL

Persist and Survive

Once you have found the revolutionary idea that you are ready to start a company in pursuit of, you need to be sure you survive to see it through. You need to be smart about survival in the beginning; this means experimenting as much as it means being conservative with cash flow. Occasionally there's an overnight success, but more often it is a marathon, not a sprint.

LEADERSHIP

Set Direction and Step Aside

If you really are a great CEO, you should wake up in the morning and have nothing to do. That would mean that you have set a clear vision, assembled a great team you could trust to move that vision forward, and given them the flexibility to operate. Of course, you'll never achieve that level of perfection, but you should organize with that goal in mind.

MARKET DEVELOPMENT

Don't Build Companies. Build Industries.

One way to identify entrepreneurs or companies that will change the world is by finding startups that are trying to create an entire industry rather than just build a company. At AOL, we felt that we were creating the Internet industry. At Genentech, they felt that they were creating the biotech industry. That ambition is the foundation of lasting, iconic, platform companies.

PRODUCT DEVELOPMENT

Experiment and Adjust

In the first year or two, you don't know exactly what your product is going to be or how your company is going to play out. Discovering that requires some degree of experimentation. You have to try things quickly and make adjustments, then do more of what's working and less of what isn't. With the speed of the IT development cycle in particular, this approach has become increasingly important.

TALENT

Build a Team That Can Scale with Your Business

As your business scales and expands, the skill sets you need on your team will change. Part of your job as the founder is to recruit talent and people who have the new skills you need, but you also have to look for opportunities to leverage your existing talent. Inevitably, you might have to drop some people, but you can move others to positions that didn't exist when they first joined. To use a sports analogy, it really is like constantly trying to get the best possible team on the field; you can never settle. A CEO must be constantly focused on talent—making sure that the people you have are playing well as a team and constantly being on the lookout for new talent to add to the mix.

STEVE'S VISION FOR THE FUTURE

In early 2011, President Obama named Steve the chairman of the Startup America Partnership. The organization is charged with encouraging new startups and existing entrepreneurs with high-growth potential, which they call "speedups." When we spoke, Steve explained the larger context. "If you look at our history over the last 235 years, you'll find that America was built by entrepreneurs. We don't have the largest economy in the world by accident. Cities were built by entrepreneurs, industries were built by entrepreneurs, the economy was built by entrepreneurs."

Also in 2011, President Obama appointed Steve to the President's Council on Jobs and Competitiveness. Steve clearly understands the connection between his two new roles. "If you look at the net job creation in the last thirty years, you'll find that forty million jobs have come from high-growth companies under five years old. If we're going to get our economy moving, create new jobs, and ensure competitiveness, we have to do it by instilling entrepreneurship and startups in the next generation. Recognizing these as a core part of the American story is important; we can't afford to take either for granted."

MARC CENEDELLA

FOUNDER:

THELADDERS

INTRODUCING MARC CENEDELLA

In the early days on TheLadders, Marc Cenedella could not have been a more hands-on entrepreneur. Frustrated with the costs and pace of professional software development, Marc taught himself to code and built the first version of TheLadders. Confident that nobody was better than he was at *finding* high-quality job listings, he assembled all of the early data that fueled the site. Marc never allows himself to get lost in the details of product development, or any other aspect of his business. He always has his eye on the next milestone and the path toward it.

As companies scale, their founders become significantly less influential on a day-to-day basis. This is one of the hardest things for hands-on entrepreneurs to accept, but Marc Cenedella has made this reality the basis of his long-term vision for TheLadders. He was a one-man development team at a company of three, but he never expected to remain in that role in a company of thirty or three hundred. His time horizon isn't month to month or quarter to quarter; it's year to year. At every stage, he is asking himself two questions: "How do I make myself obsolete?" and "What should I be doing next?" With five million members and growing, it would seem that Marc found the right answers.

MARC'S STORY

Marc founded TheLadders by leveraging a unique expertise. In general, this is true of many entrepreneurs. But Marc's expertise was an uncommon one: he was an expert "Googler."

Marc Cenedella: I come from a big family, with thirty-six first cousins. Back in the early days of the Web, when most people really weren't comfortable on the Internet, I was the "Google Guy." My cousins would actually call and ask me to do Google searches for them because I was better at it than they were.

By 2003, a couple of my cousins were looking for jobs and asked for my help searching online. I told them it was really easy: "Just go here, here, and here." They were still confused, so I just went and did it for them. I'd find jobs, put them in an email, and send it to them. They loved it. "This is amazing! Where did you find these jobs?!"

Eventually, I was getting weekly calls asking for my "jobs email." I'd been a senior executive at HotJobs for two years at that point, so I knew more about how the whole ecosystem of jobs was coming online than anybody else did. That's when I came up with the idea for TheLadders. When we first started out, we would find all the jobs online that paid $100,000 and up, put them into an email newsletter, and send it out.

I brought in two partners: Alexandre Douzet, who's now our COO, and Andrew Koch. We met regularly at the Starbucks on Union Square in New York City to work out the idea. Starbucks is an amazing place to start a business.

At the end of 2001, Marc helped facilitate the sale of HotJobs to Yahoo, which freed him up to focus on building TheLadders full-time. One thing that was immediately clear was the need for TheLadders to differentiate itself in the marketplace.

There are other job sites, and many of them are good businesses. For example, Indeed.com has taken the approach of building a strong algorithmic model and trying to capture the entire online-job ecosystem. There were also opportunities on the other side of the business, with Internet-assisted recruiting. We took a different approach: find the top 10 percent of jobs being offered and focus on those. As of September 2011, we have expanded to include all professionals.

THE THELADDERS STORY

When Marc founded TheLadders in 2003, established sites like HotJobs and Monster were unlikely places to find six-figure salaries. Recruiters didn't want to be inundated with unqualified applicants throwing Hail Marys, so they didn't post their highest-paying positions. TheLadders changed that. They prescreened résumés and, eventually, charged a monthly subscription fee. Both decisions filtered applicants and helped guarantee "a high-quality, engaged, and responsive talent pool." In 2008, a Research Now recruiter-usage study ranked TheLadders first in overall satisfaction among recruiters with a focus on six-figure talent. Today, the site has more than five million active readers.

As the company expanded, Marc tried to maintain a long-term perspective and remain focused on the next crucial milestone.

The first thing we needed was a live site that people could use to sign up for a free newsletter. I approached a group of software developers I knew from HotJobs and asked them what it would take to build that site. They basically said it was going to take three months and $30,000 to build a prototype. I didn't want to wait and I didn't want to write a check for $30,000. Instead, I went out and bought $359 worth of books, taught myself programming, and built the site over the course of three weeks in August 2003.

The next step was to get 10,000 subscribers to the free newsletter. That would be one milestone. When we got to 25,000, we could turn on a paid version, but in the meantime, we'd have to build a paid version. That meant hiring e-commerce and security experts to work on that architecture while still building our audience.

At every stage, it was about figuring out what is critical and cutting away everything else. Sometimes, that means you're going to do things horribly wrong. If you go back on Archive.org or the Wayback Machine and look at the first version of the site, it's very, very easy to believe that I coded it myself in three weeks. The important thing, though, was that it was live.

In 2008, TheLadders' growth was halted by the prospect of a global economic recession. At first, it had looked like growing unemployment might be a boon for Marc's business, but in this instance, increased traffic did not end up producing increased revenues.

In the early months of the financial downturn, more people were unemployed and looking for jobs, and they came to our site, so we were actually doing great. At the time, a subscription to TheLadders cost between $25 and $30 each month and customers paid by credit cards. We were getting more signups, but then we were blindsided by a completely different problem. Over the course of eight weeks in 2008, credit-card default rates went from 3 percent to 9 percent. That ends up being a huge difference in your business, about a 35 to 40 percent decline in revenues. So we ended up having to lay off nearly a quarter of our staff.

TheLadders recovered very quickly. As a result of Marc's efforts, they were even able to reacquire employees they had lost during their cuts.

Obviously, this was about the worst thing you can go through. But at moments like these, character isn't formed; it's revealed. Rather than try to hide from my team at the time, I personally became the customer services rep for the employees we had to let go. We rewrote all of their résumés; we offered everybody who had been making more than $100,000 free access to the system. I sent out a daily email and made it clear that anybody who had a question could contact me directly.

One woman who had just joined us out of college contacted me on Facebook. "I joined three months ago, and now you're letting me go. That's the wrong thing to do. It's awful." I asked to speak with her on the phone, and I did my best to explain why we had to make the cuts. I didn't expect her to agree, but I was hoping I could make her understand our position. I feel it's important to be empathetic and treat others as you'd want to be treated. Four months later, we were in a better financial position and had new job openings in the company. She came back and reapplied, and now she's a manager here.

THE
MARC CENEDELLA
PLAYBOOK

Use Passion as Your Filter

Realistically, there won't be a hundred things or a thousand things that you could execute on as an entrepreneur. It's probably closer to a dozen, at most. In the beginning, you can try a bunch of different ideas and see what works, but you can only do that for a very short amount of time. At some point, you have to pick one and go, and it *has* to be something that you have a passion for.

Find Something Nobody Else Can Do

Selection is critical. When you launch a venture, you have to be comfortable with the idea that this is what you're going to do for the rest of your professional life. It has to be awesome; it has to be ten times better than anything in the marketplace. Also, it can't just be better because nobody else *is* doing it currently. It has to be something that nobody other than you *can* do, especially once you're up to scale.

Show Up and Don't Quit

Some entrepreneurs say they're successful because they're so smart and have this strategic advantage; that's bull. The ones who say, "You know what? I didn't quit," there's really deep wisdom in that. Showing up and not quitting is a remarkably important part of life. It's not enough to start something. You have to push through the early challenges, and you can't let the early successes make you complacent.

═══ MARC'S BEST ADVICE ═══

COMPETITION

Build a Multiyear Barrier to Entry

Every business will have a lot of competition in the early days, so it's important to select a marketplace where you can differentiate yourself significantly. When you reach a certain scale, competitors can copy your offer, but they can't do it as well as you. You want to find a business where the initial barrier to entry prevents competition for a few years. That allows you to build a position that's very defensible. Ultimately, there are no real barriers to entry expressed in terms of decades; they are expressed in terms of years.

CULTURE

Overcommunicate in a Crisis

People can never feel good about a negative experience like layoffs, but they can be comforted. That's why it's important to overcommunicate, particularly in a crisis. If people aren't on the verge of saying, "Please stop. It's a little much," then you're not communicating enough. Keep going until people cry uncle.

FIRING

Cut Twice as Deep as You Want To

When you have to make cuts, go twice as deep as you want to. Some people try to cut "just the right amount," but you never know that amount for sure. (Invariably, it's higher than you think.) If you make the very hard-nosed decision to cut twice as deep once, you won't have to go through the trauma of a second round.

FOCUSING TIME & ENERGY

Allocate Time to Milestones

Hundreds of factors go into making a startup successful. Should you spend an hour coding, an hour talking to sources of capital, an hour marketing, or an hour convincing an NYU freshman to be an unpaid intern? There's no spreadsheet you can run that against; it's all relying on intuition. To decide, you need to be clear about the critical path you're taking to your next milestone and which steps you need to take to get you there.

HIRING

Trust Instinct over Credentials

Never hire someone if you have a twinkling in your gut telling you it's the wrong decision. Something in their background or résumé suggests that they're "The Right Guy," but you have a feeling that they're wrong. Go with your gut.

LEADERSHIP

Don't Execute Specific Tasks

One of the frustrations of being a CEO is that it's impossible to get things done when you grow and there are more people involved. You have to realize, "Well, we're much more powerful now, so when we swing, we have to swing together to make that same wallop." The important point you should realize is that you *shouldn't* be trying to get anything specific done. By "specific" I mean accidental to the nature of the business: "I want the homepage to look this way." When you have fifty to sixty hands working on your business, you need to step back from tactical issues and focus on strategic life-or-death decisions.

MARKETING

Paint Word Pictures

Einstein was brilliant and saw things that other people didn't see. Maybe others may have had the same thoughts before him, or simultaneously, but Einstein was the best at painting word pictures. Explaining relativity, he asked people to imagine two passengers on opposite ends of a train and think about what it would mean for them to do something "simultaneously." Suddenly, a complex idea made sense to everyone. Not just in proof, but in argument, he saw the value of word experiments, like Schrödinger's Cat, that could reveal logical absurdity. That kind of storytelling is powerful; it comes up with analogies that help people understand what you're trying to express.

RAISING CAPITAL

Pick a Valuation and a Closing Date, and Stick to Them

When you're raising angel money, pick a valuation, pick a closing date, and stick to them. There's always a range for angel funding. At the time I was raising money, the range was $3 million to $5 million, so I picked $4 million. If you don't pick a closing date, things will drag on and on. People will be in and then they'll be out, but suddenly they'll be back in, come the day you choose.

TALENT

Great Athletes Don't Make Great Coaches

People who are instinctively good at something often have trouble describing how they do it. If something comes naturally to you and you didn't have to struggle to learn it, it's much more difficult to teach it. There are very few cases where the best players in sports became the best coaches.

MARC'S VISION FOR THE FUTURE

When Marc launched TheLadders in 2003, he decided to target a very specific niche: jobs paying $100,000 and above. After eight years of growth in that sector, Marc and his team have decided to expand the scope of their offering. In September 2011, they announced an initiative to help "every career-driven individual." "It's not just jobs that pay $100,000 plus," Marc told me. "It's jobs that pay $40,000 plus. "We're going from one-sixth of the market to the whole market." Given how years of economic uncertainty have upped the ante in the current job market, this decision is a civic one as much as a business one. It also reflects TheLadders' core company mission: "Love the Customer."

ROBIN CHASE

FOUNDER:

ZIPCAR

INTRODUCING ROBIN CHASE

At the most basic level, every business is about finding and remedying a market inefficiency. Robin Chase has a *visceral* aversion to inefficiency.

As far as she's concerned, Zipcar is a data company; the cars are almost incidental. Zipcar exists to bring collaborative consumption to the problem of solving inefficient resource allocation. As Robin points out, most people only use their cars about 5 percent of the time; she just can't tolerate that level of waste.

Robin's mastery of data and her belief in the importance of applying it to decision making is one of the most impressive things about her. She's not interested in gut feelings or emotionally driven opinions. She only wants to deal in a reality that is completely and utterly defensible on every level. Describing her experience at Zipcar, she says, "I understood the ins and outs of every single aspect of that business. I understood the ebbs and flows." That depth of comprehension is only possible if you allow yourself to see your business as a whole—even the parts that aren't working. In Robin's commitment to intellectual honesty, she manifests that truth every day.

ROBIN'S STORY

Superficially, Zipcar is a car-rental company. But from its very first moments, Robin recognized that Zipcar was actually the synthesis of a variety of industries and innovations.

Robin Chase: My cofounder, Antje Danielson, came up with the idea for Zipcar. Antje is German, and she based the idea on existing European models like Mobility CarSharing. In the fall of 1999, she told me about a shared-car service she had seen in Germany and asked what I thought. I said, "Wow! This is what the Internet and wireless data transmission were made for. If we put those two things together, we've got something." That's the key to new and good ideas; they come from having a very broad and multidisciplinary range of interests.

In addition to finding a new opportunity to leverage information technology, Robin was excited by the promising angle of attack presented by what she refers to as "the promise of excess capacity."

When you play with excess capacity, you change the economics of an industry. It's a sweet spot for building a company. It means that people own an asset, for instance, a car, and they're not getting as much out of it as they could. Some people drive their cars as little as 5 percent of the time, and city dwellers even less. The only way excess capacity is handled today is when somebody you know owns a car and you mooch off of them, which you can't do very often.

It might seem that traditional car-rental companies exist to solve precisely this problem, but Robin saw that their twentieth-century business model needed a radical, twenty-first-century overhaul.

Part of my skill as a leader is to present a clear and appealing vision that people can understand and repeat. But it's not something that I usually get right away. With Zipcar, for example, it took me about six months to get the message right. People were always trying to compare it with something else, like cell-phone plans. That wasn't it.

Eventually, I figured out that the goal behind Zipcar was to make renting a car as easy and convenient as getting cash from an ATM. That captured people's imaginations because they could picture the cars distributed

---

THE ZIPCAR STORY

When Robin Chase founded Zipcar in 2000, she and her partner, Antje Danielson, were bringing a proven European model to U.S. consumers. Rather than forcing drivers to go through the complex process of renting cars at daily or weekly rates, Zipcar provides a simple reservation system, hourly rates, and self-service cars parked throughout the city. Zipcar is available in fifty cities across the United States and United Kingdom. In its 2011 IPO, the company raised $174 million, exceeding expectations.

throughout the environment. They understood that you could use them twenty-four hours a day; they were fast, convenient, and easy to use like an ATM.

Zipcar initially launched in Boston in June 2000. By the end of September, Robin and her team had collected enough data to crunch the numbers and review their initial assumptions. When they analyzed their data they discovered something very troubling: their twenty-four-hour rental rate was too low.

Before we launched, we had spent months and months fiddling with the pricing model—the days, the hours, the utilization. We pored over the numbers, but with the 4,000 details to keep in mind when launching a startup, we managed to miss an obvious fact: 24 one-hour rentals didn't equal a one-day rental because you don't have 24 one-hour day rentals. We had come out with a daily rate of $40, which was too low by a lot.

About three months in, about two weeks before I was supposed to close on my Series A, I finally had a big enough data set—we had 435 Zipcar members at that point—that I could analyze the numbers. There we were, just two weeks away from closing our Series A, and I figured out that I was off by half of what I expected we would get out of it. I went into my room for two hours and just wept. I thought I'd built a house of cards and it would all come crashing down at that moment. My staff pulled me out, we talked it over, and I decided that either we could just bleed a slow financial death, or I would have to email all our customers and tell them we'd made a big mistake and had to raise the daily rate by 25 percent.

The next morning, I was just dreading what the customer response was going to be. But surprisingly, when I walked in the office door, one of my staff people said, "Robin: nineteen for you; two against." We got nineteen emails saying, "We love the service; we always thought it was way too cheap. Don't worry about it." Two wrote to say they were quitting, but I emailed them and turned them around. One of them eventually became one of our biggest champions.

We were focused on the data, intellectually honest, and willing to be transparent with our customers. If we'd stuck our heads in the sand, it could have killed the company. But because we quickly identified and fixed things that weren't working, Zipcar worked beautifully.

Zipcar owes its success to more than Robin's rigorous, intellectual analysis. The company's branding needed to make the right emotional appeal.

Marketing is everything. I can frame things in a way that makes people want to participate. So many car-sharing companies have started and failed because of branding. With Zipcar, I didn't say, "We're this environmental do-gooder company, and we have an idea. Forty percent of you sell your cars, and the rest of you share this car we're parking down the block.... It's going to be this 'dirty Birkenstock' kind of thing; good luck!" We positioned it as: "Are you cool? Are you urban? Are you financially smart?" Not only did we have these environmentally efficient cars but—I hate to use the word *hip*—our branding was cool, fun, innovative, urban, and smart. Environmental reasons for using our company were number four, and most people might never get to that.

A decade later, Robin can proudly claim a kind of success that's nearly unheard of in the startup world:

Eleven years later, Zipcar is exactly as we had originally conceived it in every aspect. I would say that is unusual.

It is.

THE ROBIN CHASE PLAYBOOK

Take Advantage of Excess Capacity

If you think about the idea of "excess capacity" broadly enough, it's very exciting. A marketplace is full of inefficiencies that you can tap into. The key is to identify things that used to be thought of as closed, single-purpose devices and discover other ways to leverage them. The great example of the past three years has been the explosive innovation in smartphone technology. Phones used to be devices that we used for one purpose, making calls, during a small percentage of our time. Now we use our smartphones many hours a day because the existence of "apps" has transformed them into multiuse devices. Find excess capacity, and you can fill it.

Enable Collaborative Consumption

In the past, it was too expensive to minimize excess capacity by sharing things. Finding the assets was too difficult; the transaction costs were too high. Today, we have access to the Internet twenty-four hours a day. Dividing things into small parts and selling those parts off has become viable for the first time. Information technology enables you to fill excess capacity by enabling "collaborative consumption." Without that technological jump, collaborative consumption would be impossible as a business strategy.

Have a Passion for Solving Problems

Every founder needs to ask him- or herself two questions: "What are you good at?" and "What is your market?" The market part is secondary. You begin with an idea and look for ways to implement it. As your thoughts become more tangible, you'll come up against obstacles. A passion for solving problems will drive you to learn more about your idea, and think more deeply about how to overcome those obstacles. In the end, you'll knock them down one by one. (Pay attention: some obstacles *can't* be knocked down. Not all ideas are good ones.) The more you look into an idea, the more mind space it starts to take up. Pretty soon, you're thinking about it all the time. That's when the train has left the station and you can start bringing your idea to market.

BUSINESS OPERATIONS

Devote Time to Small Operational Details

As CEOs, we feel like we have to focus on big projects: fundraising, major partnerships, etc. But when you stop to look at very specific operational details in your company, you'll get some really good insights. It can be a particular marketing campaign, or the way you're spending money, or an analysis of how people are using one of your services. By and large, you need deputies whom you trust to manage those areas. But when you stop to look at them yourself, even if you don't enact major changes, you learn a lot about your business.

DEPLOYING CAPITAL

Be Frugal, Personally and Professionally

In startups, every penny counts: you can't squander money when you don't have a lot of it. You'll still make mistakes, but the learning experiences won't be as costly if you're doing things as cheaply as possible. I'm very hard on my staff about costs. I insist that we spend as little money as possible, and it sometimes drives them crazy. But I hold myself to the exact same standards. I don't have a fancy car, take taxis everywhere, or go out for expensive dinners. I model the behavior that I expect. Frugality has to be a pervasive value.

HIRING

Hire People Whose Judgment You Respect

If you only hire people whose judgment you resepect, you'll avoid a great deal of second-guessing. It's much easier to tell someone they did a crummy job when you have clearly established your respect for their skills. You can avoid the implication that the person is stupid or unqualified. It's simply the fact that a specific task was done wrong. With respect in place, you can be just as blunt about yourself. I'm happy to come into a meeting and say, "I completely screwed something up." Because these cultural values permeate the company, we can be open and move together in one direction.

LEADERSHIP

Cultivate a Broad Range of Interests

It takes a broad and curious mind to come up with new combinations. To cultivate one, you need to spend time reading, attending conferences, looking at Twitter feeds—constantly engaging the outside world. When you have a very multidisciplinary range of interests, you can find ideas in other fields that apply to yours. But when you're pressed for time, it's tempting to completely shut all of that stuff out. Your world and what you're doing in it become everything. You allow yourself to be encircled in a tiny spot where there's no joy, no breath, no life, and no new ideas. You can't be very creative in that space; it's too inbred and hot. It's important to emerge from there and spend some percentage of your time looking outward.

MARKETING

Leverage Existing Networks

Marketing is an important place where excess capacity can be leveraged in your favor. When we first started Zipcar, we talked to MIT [Robin's alma mater] and asked if we could use their email lists to reach their 35,000 students, faculty, and staff. For them, it cost nothing. For me, it was a huge value. It's important to cultivate relationships with people who have those types of resources. They have access; they have volume. There are lots of different ways you can use that.

METRICS

Conduct Small Experiments and Measure the Results

I despise the sales saying that you have to touch people seven to ten times before they'll convert. Forget that. You should collect and analyze data right away. You should pilot new approaches. Experiment; think of people as consultants before you hire them full-time. "Try before you buy." Take a small bite and see if it works. There may be some things that you can only do in a really big way, but for most, you can always conduct tests first.

PUBLIC RELATIONS

Clarify Your Vision Out Loud

I talk; I write; I give interviews. The more times I do it, the better I get and my staff always overhears the conversation. It teaches them how to think about the company, the values we share, the stories we think are important—even what we think is funny. I try to manifest openness and honesty in how I treat my peers, how I treat customers, and how I approach the market. By modeling these things, I set expectations for everybody else.

VISION & MISSION

Never Hold "Immutable" Principles

A lot of entrepreneurs fail because they hold something in their minds as an immutable principle. The idea that your values should never change in the face of data is nonsensical. You have to recognize failure wherever it happens and look it straight on. When the evidence says that you're wrong, you have to be willing to relinquish even your most deeply held beliefs.

ROBIN'S VISION FOR THE FUTURE

Having presented a solution to the problem of inefficient automotive usage, Robin has applied her passion for efficiency to one of the world's largest problems: the power grid. In 2009, she explained her views to *Wired* magazine. "Our electric infrastructure is designed for the rare peak of usage. That's expensive and wasteful." Robin wants to introduce "mesh" networks to the electric grid. "Wi-Fi is like a bridge that connects the highways on either side of the stream. You build it wide enough to handle the maximum traffic you expect. If too much comes, it gets congested. When not enough arrives, you've got excess capacity. Mesh takes a different approach: Each person who wants to cross throws in a flat rock that's above the water line. The more people who do that, the more ways there are to get across the river." Users of the same network offer each other "cooperative gain" instead of competing for bandwidth.

In other words, electric networks must be turned into "information" networks. This collaborative concept belongs to a paradigm that Robin understands particularly well, and she is uniquely suited to help develop it as a solution to the challenge of more efficient energy usage in the twenty-first century.

CHIP CONLEY

FOUNDER:

JOIE DE VIVRE HOSPITALITY

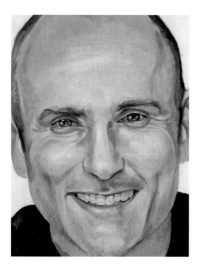

INTRODUCING CHIP CONLEY

The most profound ideas are the most obvious, and Chip Conley's idea is so profound that it can be stated in two words. Businesses, he teaches us, should "create joy."

After abandoning the world of corporate real estate, Chip set out on his life-long mission when he bought the Phoenix Hotel in San Francisco. Within a few months, he transformed a run-down, pay-by-the-hour motel into the hippest spot in the city. The hotel's restaurant, Miss Pearl's Jam House, became an institution. Rock stars like David Bowie and movie stars like Johnny Depp were frequent guests. Most twenty-six-year-olds would have been more than satisfied with that lifestyle, and Chip could very well have stopped right there. He didn't.

Chip's idea was too big. One door into the "joy" he was creating wouldn't be enough; he had the responsibility to open thousands more. We can see them today. From the Citizen's Hotel in Sacramento to the Pacific Edge Hotel on Laguna Beach, every Joie de Vivre hotel room is an entry point into the company's purpose. Chip is no longer the CEO of Joie de Vivre, but he recognizes that creating joy is a very important calling. He'll never abandon it.

CHIP'S STORY

Chip Conley is the creator of an entire vertical industry: the boutique hotel business. It's a distinction he shares with two illustrious colleagues.

Chip Conley: The boutique hotel business was started by three people: Bill Kimpton, Ian Schrager, and myself. Schrager was the Studio 54 guy; Kimpton was a former investment banker; I came along four years later. I was the youngster—a real estate developer at twenty-six. Between the three of us, we've created about 120 boutique hotels over the course of twenty-five, thirty years, and none of us had any background in the field. Over and over again, creative thinking comes from outside the core of an industry. It's the reason Steve Jobs remade the music industry, or Reed Hastings of Netflix remade video on demand.

What Chip shared with Kimpton and Schrager was a willingness to question the industry's dogmas and arrive at something completely new.

The boutique hotel said, "What if we created a really great hotel restaurant that the locals fell in love with? When they had friends come into town for business or pleasure, they'd actually recommend that hotel."

When we told this to people at the major chains, they'd say, "No one wants to go eat in a hotel restaurant." And we'd say, "Well, yes, because the product you created is so bad!" Their guests had gotten used to the situation, but that didn't mean they actually *wanted* bad restaurants in four-star hotels.

While the traditional hotel chains were reaffirming the status quo, the innovators who created the boutique hotel were identifying an unrecognized need that was ready to be satisfied.

Great business leaders are cultural anthropologists, the Margaret Meads of modern consumerism. They're able to understand how people work, how they think, how they feel. There's a bit of mind reading going on.

This is the core idea that Chip articulates in his book, Peak: How Great Companies Get Their Mojo from Maslow. *Great businesses don't exist to take advantage of some minor market inefficiency. They exist in order to serve customer needs.*

A really important question you have to ask is "Why do we matter? What do we do that actually makes a difference?" Joie de Vivre's mission is creating opportunities to create joy, to enjoy life. That mission is embedded in the DNA of the organization; it's even embedded in the organization's name.

THE JOIE DE VIVRE STORY

The flagship of Joie de Vivre's hotel empire was the Phoenix Hotel in the Tenderloin district of San Francisco, which Chip purchased in 1987. In contrast to what an earlier reviewer called "San Francisco's buttoned-up hotel establishments," the Phoenix offered "a funky, tongue-in-cheek urban resort" that catered to rock stars and filmmakers. Since that time, Joie de Vivre has built or acquired more than thirty other boutique hotels. In 2010, Geolo Capital (owned by Hyatt heir John Pritzker) purchased a majority stake in the company and announced plans to invest $300 million to $500 million in hotel acquisitions over the next three to five years.

For the first decade of Joie de Vivre's existence, Chip was a completely hands-on CEO, personally traveling to and managing all of the company's hotels. But as the prospect of a twentieth or thirtieth or fortieth hotel became more likely, Chip realized that the company needed a broader culture to ensure success.

When it became clear that I wasn't in a position to directly manage all of our hotels, we looked to create a strong culture that could sustain growth while remaining true to our values. As a model, we studied Southwest Airlines.

Southwest is one of the few companies that developed a stronger culture as they got bigger. Usually the opposite occurs. We immersed ourselves in what made Southwest Airlines successful. We read the book *Nuts!*, which is about Southwest's culture. We brought together our top thirty-five managers and invited a couple of Southwest's senior executives to talk with them. The key to Southwest's success, we discovered, was that they democratized their culture. They saw that a thriving organization could not remain centralized indefinitely.

One of our first steps toward decentralization was to create "cultural ambassadors" from each of our hotels, who are elected by their fellow employees for a one-year period. They're in charge of having ongoing conversations with cultural ambassadors from other hotels in order to keep our culture fresh. Their second job is to create a culture of recognition. That doesn't just mean recognition coming from the central office, but recognition on a person-to-person, peer-to-peer basis. Finally, they look for ways that we can engage in philanthropy as an organization—active and effective things we can all participate in every quarter and every year.

Investing in culture was crucial to our growth. It helped us create a great company that drives enthusiastic employees, who drive loyal customers, which drives a profitable business. Using another company as a model for this was very helpful.

Over the next ten years, Joie de Vivre grew from a dozen hotels to more than thirty. But Chip's path wasn't entirely free of challenges.

In 1987, we began work on a project called Costanoa, a luxury campground in California between Half Moon Bay and Santa Cruz. It was a spectacular idea, but we didn't execute correctly. It needed to be in a different location that had a warmer climate with less wind and less fog and more indoor structures. It was that simple. But because I'm such an idea guy, I was relentless in trying to make it work. I just wasn't able to see the writing on the wall from a financial perspective. I had lost all objectivity. I needed a capital partner to slap me around and say, "We're selling!"

After Geolo Capital purchased a majority share of Joie de Vivre in 2010, Chip stepped down as CEO.

I'm no longer as involved in the day-to-day operations of Joie de Vivre, but I'm still the executive chairman, and I have a very distinct idea of what we should be doing and where we should be going. It's an ongoing conversation, and I'm very open to hearing other voices.

THE CHIP CONLEY PLAYBOOK

Create Joy

The most neglected fact in business is that we're all human. It's obvious, and yet it is often forgotten in the world of spreadsheets and strategic plans and organizational charts. Customers have *expectations*, which form the baseline of what they want. Then, they have *desires*, which are a step above expectations. Then, they have unrecognized *needs*. To steal a phrase from Abraham Maslow, this "hierarchy of needs" gets lost in the business process. In my interpretation of Maslow's hierarchy, the workplace and the customer experience are meant to be joyful. That's why I named my company Joie de Vivre. How a company creates and sustains joy has a lot to do with creating a vibrant, successful, long-term venture.

Be an Outsider

Change happens on the margins. It's usually outsiders who identify the unrecognized need that customers and competitors within the industry have not been able to see. They come in and ask, "Why do you do it this way? Why couldn't you do it that way?" Now, outsiders are often new players, but they can also be existing players who put on a fresh pair of glasses once a month. If you started as a rebel, your goal should be to sustain that rebellious spirit. This is a major challenge for large organizations, but if you don't think like an outsider and a rebel, you're going to die.

Start Cheap, Small, and Local

When you start, you have no idea what you don't know. It's not even on your radar. If you keep your business small in the beginning, your initial mistakes are going to be small and you can use them to create a better product. If you scale too quickly, you won't learn lessons first-hand. You may learn them from profit-and-loss reports or customer-satisfaction reports, but you won't see them in your customers' eyes. Start small, and be open to the idea that the beta test may take two or three years. In some industries, that's hard to do. But if you can do it, you'll see the concrete reality of your business every day.

BOARDS

Leverage Boards for Objective Feedback

It's very hard to be objective about something that you love deeply. Too often, we get so attached to our businesses and our ideas that they become like our children. Asking somebody to be objective about their business is like asking them which of their children they love the most, or which is the most beautiful. This is the role of a board of advisers; you need other voices at the table. They remain at your side and provide objective feedback when your gut instinct is to deny the facts.

BUSINESS OPERATIONS

Minimize the Number of Operating Partners

It's a lot of fun for people to sit down and say, "I'm going to get three of my best friends together, and we're going to build a startup." But a business shouldn't have four operating partners. It should have two. One should be doing a collection of things that they're good at; the other should be doing another collection of things. If you have more than two partners, the two who are essential to the business start feeling resentful and take more power. The other ones feel less powerful and try to seize the power back. It happens all of the time. Therefore, you need to keep the initial core of operating partners to an efficient level. Others can come on as investors or advisors, but they can't be operators of the business.

CULTURE

Maintain a Healthy Level of Fear and Paranoia

A certain amount of fear and paranoia is healthy. But while fear and paranoia will help you run a great 100-yard dash, they'll never help you finish a marathon. At some point, small companies move from being sprinters to being marathon runners. The trick is to make the shift without losing that healthy dose of worry to create that provocative nature of innovation.

CUSTOMER DEVELOPMENT

Track the Evolution of Your Customers' Needs

Fred Smith of FedEx once said, "I thought I was in the business of transporting goods; it turns out, I was in the business of peace of mind." His customers needed to know exactly where their packages were at each particular moment, twenty-four hours a day. Their question wasn't, "Will I get it overnight?" but rather, "At what exact time will it arrive?" The key is understanding that evolution of customer desires by constantly taking yourself back to the moment when things were new and unexpected.

HIRING

Probe for Self-Awareness

My favorite interview question is, "What is the most common way that you're misperceived in the workplace as a leader?" It's a trick question: the biggest problem with leaders is their lack of self-awareness. It's not that they don't have a good skill set. They're just a bit clueless about what they do and don't do well, and how others perceive them. Asking people how they're misperceived forces them to ask, "Who is it that people see when they look at me?" That leads to the next question: "Why don't you see that?" People who aren't self-aware aren't comfortable answering that question. They'll be confused by it, or defensive about it.

LEADERSHIP

Be a Transformational Leader

There are "transactional" leaders and there are "transformational" leaders. Transactional leaders are great at making the trains run on time. They're great at being able to answer questions. They're great at being able to operate businesses that are up and going. But small businesses that are trying to get off the ground, or really grow, need transformational leaders. These people are looking for ways to transform their industries, transform the nature of the competition, transform their organizations, and transform the way their employees and customers interact. That's how entrepreneurs think and act.

MARKET DEVELOPMENT

Be Your Own Competitor

Creating an organization of provocateurs means creating an organization that contains its own competition. You need people who are open to failure and willing to rewrite the industry rules if they feel that the marketplace is moving in a different direction. If those ideas aren't being generated within your organization, they're being generated outside of it. I'd rather compete with myself than with someone else in the marketplace.

TALENT

Cultivate Provocateurs

Each day, you should call upon a handful of people to be "product provocateurs." When you're the provocateur, your job is to piss people off—not to be disrespectful, but to ask really hard questions and not be satisfied with the status quo. Initially, there will be people in your organization who take on that role automatically. They're the critical, creative thinkers in the group. But you should also assign that role to others, essentially giving them license to ask "stupid" questions. Because a great provocateur isn't there to hit people over the head with their own best ideas. Their job is to ask big, broad, fundamental, existential questions and foment debate.

CHIP'S VISION FOR THE FUTURE

In a piece he wrote for The Huffington Post a few months after stepping down as CEO of Joie de Vivre, Chip labeled 2011 "The Year of Curiosity." Always generous in crediting his mentors and inspirations, Chip attributed the notion (and a new practice he adopted that year) to the late management theorist Peter Drucker:

"For more than sixty years, Peter Drucker studied one subject at a time, from Japanese art to Civil War history, with the intent of mastering the subject. Curiosity may have killed the cat, but it helped Mr. Drucker keep a facile mind and a youthful spirit into his mid-nineties. So, starting in 2011, I am going to take one subject per year and devour it—both mentally and experientially. This first year I'm going to tackle the sublime and geological magic of natural hot springs. Why and how were these created? Why do some smell so different than others? What are the health benefits or risks associated with using them? And, what's the history of public bathing? And, as I will do in the future with subjects like Renaissance art or hang gliding, I plan to explore these subjects by literally diving in. So, in 2011, I will visit a different natural hot spring every month of the year. Iceland and Japan, here I come!

"At the heart of great leadership," says Chip, "is a curious mind, heart, and spirit."

JEFF DACHIS

FOUNDER:

RAZORFISH

THE DACHIS GROUP

INTRODUCING JEFF DACHIS

In the early '90s, Razorfish was the Studio 54 of online agencies, and Jeff Dachis was one of the iconic figures of the East Coast IT world. There's always been a theatrical, rock-star quality to Jeff. But if theater were all there was to Jeff and his companies, Razorfish would not have survived the dot-com downturn of 2001, and it certainly wouldn't have grown to one of the largest digital-services agencies in the world. Jeff created real value for his clients, pioneering innovations like the animated websites that we all take for granted today.

Now, with the Dachis Group, Jeff is doing for social media what he did with the world of the Mosaic Web browser in 1995. In the past, his predictions have been spot-on. Whatever direction the Dachis Group takes in the future, expect the rest of the market to follow.

JEFF'S STORY

Jeff's approach to building companies is summed up in the original Razorfish motto: "Solutions to Hard Problems." Jeff cofounded the digital agency in 1995. The company was an extremely early entry into the world of online advertising, and, unlike other offerings developed at the time, Jeff wasn't attempting to create one of the algorithmic models that would eventually give rise to "pay-for-performance" advertising. Razorfish applied the tools and tactics of traditional advertising to a new medium.

Jeff Dachis: We had a crystal-clear vision of Razorfish from the moment we founded it. It hit me like an epiphany: it was very clear to me where the market was headed, and I knew I had something very powerful in my mind. It took a long time to map that vision into a concrete plan for the business that we built. I did a lot of sketching on whiteboards and paper in order to clearly lay out the core components. I talked to a lot of people to vet those components. Most of the time, I'm misunderstood, because what I'm saying doesn't fit into the framework that people are used to. But I eventually get good feedback, and use that as a starting point to gain traction in the market. That's what happened with Razorfish.

Razorfish gained traction by being one of the first agencies to aggressively exploit the slightest technical advantage to give their clients something unique. Razorfish had its origins when Craig Kanarick introduced Jeff to Netscape's Mosaic Web browser, the first tool that allowed users to interact with the Internet using a graphical interface rather than text commands. This led the partners to the insight that would eventually form the company's second motto: "Everything That Can Be Digital Will Be." Nothing, including the fact that Jeff had to wait tables in the early days to make ends meet, was going to change his mind on that point.

Our perspective on the world was unique at the time. It was extremely tough early on, but we had done the hard work and we had done the research. I don't want to call us the smartest guys in the room, but we were ready to say, "We're right, and everybody else doesn't get it yet."

Jeff's time as a waiter was short-lived. In their first year, Jeff and Craig landed a major client: Time Warner's Pathfinder division. The company was backing a "virtual garden" for the New York Botanical Society and they asked Razorfish to design it. They did and added another feature, an early e-commerce platform that allowed visitors to the site to buy Time-Life gardening books.

THE RAZORFISH STORY

Jeff cofounded Razorfish with Craig Kanarick in 1995. The company's revenues were $300,000 in the first year (a rare feat for early Internet startups) and grew to more than $260 million within five years. When the dot-com bubble burst in 2000 and 2001, Razorfish's revenues fell accordingly, dropping to $50 million. But unlike so many other companies in those days, Razorfish survived. Following a series of acquisitions, it eventually became part of Microsoft, which sold the digital-services company to Publicis Groupe in 2009 for $530 million. That year, Razorfish posted $380 million in revenue.

In its first year, Razorfish's revenue reached $300,000. They grew to $1.2 million the following year, and $3.6 million in 1997. That year, Razorfish made the first of a series of acquisitions that would give it global reach. By 1999, sales reached an astounding $170 million and Jeff had more than 1,000 employees—but still the cost of acquisitions and operating expenses were outpacing growth.

"[W]e were ready to say, 'We're right, and everybody else doesn't get it yet.'"

That same year, Razorfish went public and raised $48 million, but the dot-com bubble was about to burst. As was the case with so many other Internet startups in 2000, Razorfish's stock began to drop. Unlike those other startups, however, Razorfish's growth in the market didn't stop with their decline on NASDAQ.

That was a very difficult time for me, professionally and personally. We were being whipsawed by stuff that was out of our control. The universal lack of health among Internet companies really had nothing to do with us. Still, as those companies went bad, the perception of our company went bad.

In the end, while many of those other companies couldn't survive the downturn, Razorfish did. It's one of the largest digital-services companies in the world today.

In 2003, Razorfish was acquired by SBI Group. A few years later, Jeff would move on to his next venture: the Dachis Group, which he founded in 2008.

THE
JEFF DACHIS
PLAYBOOK

Build Backward from a Future State

The issues I tackle are often wildly complex and years into the future. You have to see where markets are going and envision a solution set that will solve the entire problem. That solution is often far ahead of where the market is today, so the next challenge is to vet what that future state is going to look like and work backward to something that can gain traction in the current marketplace. It's provisional, but it will be a building block toward the complete solution.

Be a Renaissance Man

I've studied many things, from capital markets to classical ballet, and I suck at most of them. But that diversity of experience has given me a knowledge base that includes user experience, design, information architecture, finance, accounting, and the creative expression of ideas. That unique combination of skills has benefited me greatly, especially when it comes to solving problems that aren't always linear. You need to understand the dynamics of nonlinear thinking and craft businesses around that.

Get Laughed At

When you first enter a marketplace, you'll get laughed at and ridiculed and have tomatoes thrown at you. I'm routinely laughed at for the things that I say, because people don't understand my approach to solving problems. It's difficult, but it's the only way to see if your arguments stand up. Over time, you'll continue to be validated by the marketplace.

BUSINESS OPERATIONS

Pursue Multiple Tactics

Leave your company open to pursuing a variety of things. If you're making a platform play, consider multiple partnership opportunities. If you're building a professional services business, don't limit your offerings in the early stages. Don't limit yourself to a single geographic market; go deep into some and narrow into others. There is risk in unlimited optionality, but you can mitigate it by quickly eliminating tactics that prove unsuccessful.

COMPETITION

Beat the Market

To me, success isn't about monetary gain. It's about winning the game because I'm smarter, faster, or better than the competition. We articulate a big vision; the tactics that support that vision may change over time, but the vision has not changed one iota. Entrepreneurial success is measured by playing on a global stage and winning on a global stage. An exit isn't a win. Beating the marketplace is a win.

DEPLOYING CAPITAL

Only Take Risks When You Can Affect the Outcome

It's important to focus on eliminating risks. That doesn't mean that you shouldn't take risks. Taking risks is essential to business, and especially startups. But you should only take risks when you have an ability to affect the outcome.

FOCUSING TIME & ENERGY

Don't Get Lost in Lists

I used to be an obsessive-compulsive list maker. I had enormous lists, and it gave me a great deal of satisfaction to check items off those lists. Eventually, I realized that I'd been using far too much energy prioritizing negligible tasks. The real goal is to identify the handful of value-drivers in your business and spend most of your day focused on those. Everything else is trivial.

LEADERSHIP

Sign Up for a Brutal Experience

The idea that everybody can be an entrepreneur and create a startup is simply false. Building a startup is a ton of work. It's brutal. If you want to do it, sign up for a brutal experience and sign up to be brutal. You need the ability to see the future and manage your way through a crisis. That prospect needs to excite you, to make you jazzed to wake up in the morning. You won't get that feeling just from reading a book. It's you and you alone: your wildness, focus, and capabilities; the expertise you bring to the table will drive your success in the marketplace.

MARKET DEVELOPMENT

New Technology Takes Twenty Years to Go Mainstream

I never thought it would take eighteen years for the digital marketing space to develop. I thought it would happen in two. But when I started, investors who had experience building companies always said that it took twenty years for a new technology to go mainstream. They were right, and I was surprised, but the data supporting their prediction had been there all along.

PRODUCT DEVELOPMENT

Build Solutions, Not Features

A lot of what you see today in the startup world are little feature sets or vitamin pills for small problems that, when the game is played out, will ultimately become small parts of a much bigger solution. The volume of these types of narrow-focus startups in the marketplace is baffling to me. Over time, all of that stuff will be aggregated and consolidated into the solution people are actually looking for. To achieve a real success, build toward that solution instead of a narrow piece of it.

VISION & MISSION

Be Unwavering in Your Purpose

To be good at what you do, you have to believe that you're right. At Razorfish and the Dachis Group, we haven't wavered one iota from the original whiteboard sketch of where this business was going and where it is today. When I speak to new employees, I pull out that sketch and tell them, "This is what we set out to do, and this is what we're doing. They're exactly the same." The tactics that support my thesis might vary along the way. But until my thesis is proven wrong, we're going to assume it's right and run it as hard as we can.

JEFF'S VISION FOR THE FUTURE

As Jeff has said, he only tackles very big problems. Today, he is building the Dachis Group with an eye toward leveraging the rapid growth of online engagement. "The generation that's coming of age today has been acclimated to technology in an unprecedented way. Their degree of connection and engagement is a fundamental change, and it's not yet being reflected in the business world. With the rapid growth of online networks and the power of mobile computing, companies are going to benefit radically from being more connected and engaged. That thesis is driving my development of a number of business cases as I design a market opportunity that is both current and future-ready. I want to create an offering that meets clients where they are, where they're going to be, and where they eventually need to be."

MICHAEL & ELLEN DIAMANT

FOUNDERS:

SKIP HOP

INTRODUCING MICHAEL & ELLEN DIAMANT

When I was running corporate development at an e-business and interactive firm, we came very close to buying T3 Media, Michael Diamant's Internet services firm. When he started iClips, an early video-streaming site, in 1999, I was an early investor. Yahoo! nearly bought the company in 2002, but the deal fell through and iClips failed. But that didn't end up mattering. The following year, Michael and his wife, Ellen, founded Skip Hop, makers of beautiful products for babies and their parents. My wife and I invested immediately, as we will in anything Michael and Ellen ever do. When you find great entrepreneurs, stick with them for life.

Unlike so many entrepreneurs in the digital age, Michael is not a "visionary" who runs roughshod over the details. He's closer to a retail owner: he pays attention to every dollar, every nut and bolt. (He also has the fiduciary responsibility of a traditional small-business owner; when his previous venture failed, Michael made sure that every friend and family member who invested was made whole. That sense of honor informs everything he does.) In an industry saturated with venture capital, it is easy to forget that this is how nearly every company in the world is actually built: dollar by dollar. Michael is very familiar with the venture-capital world, but he has still built Skip Hop by paying attention to every component of the business and optimizing it to the most efficient outcome.

In his wife, Ellen, Michael has found the ideal partner. She is a creator, a modern designer, and craftswoman. Ellen is Skip Hop's special sauce. Everything she invents is a brilliant solution to a real problem, as well as a beautiful object. Michael has said that his role is to make a "bubble" around Ellen and her team, allowing them to focus on creating products. That's true to an extent, but Michael and Ellen don't simply operate in autonomous spheres. They are true partners. When cofounders work in concert and pull in the same direction, they can achieve things at a magnitude beyond what either could do alone. I can't think of a better illustration of that truth than this remarkable husband-and-wife team.

MICHAEL & ELLEN'S STORY

Skip Hop was started at a time when consumers were looking for genuinely new innovations in consumer products, not just redesigned packages for the same old function. Michael and Ellen saw an opportunity not to simply join a market, but to expand a stagnant one, in this case, baby products.

Ellen Diamant: When we started Skip Hop in 2002, design had already become central to our everyday lives. People wanted something special and they weren't settling. Target played a big role in that. Oxo transformed the way people think of kitchen tools. Simplehuman even changed the way people think of trash bins. But baby products were all teddy bears and gingham and pink and blue. Baby was still in the dark ages.

Skip Hop is a consumer brand for babies, parents, and toddlers. Our goal is to create beautiful products that always have an extra touch in form and function. In everything we design, we're trendsetters. We never follow trends.

Michael Diamant: I had two other businesses before Skip Hop. My second company, iClips, actually went under in the 2002 crash. We lost a lot of money for our investors; it was not an easy time. But I'd had a success prior to that with T3 Media, so I've seen both sides of the startup experience. At any rate, I wasn't working immediately after iClips, and I wasn't looking for my next gig yet.

Ellen: At that time, I had been working as an art director for at least ten years. My focus was in graphic design and branding. I'd always loved product design, but I never thought I'd go into it.

Then I had a baby boy, Spencer. When he was a year old or so, I realized that I wanted much better products for him, and one in particular: a simple diaper bag that hung on a stroller. In New York City, a stroller is like your car. For a diaper bag, you want to be able to get to everything quickly, you want something that looks cool, and you want it to be easy to hang on the stroller. That didn't exist. I came up with this concept that I just wanted personally, never thinking that it would be a business. I was happy with my design business.

Ellen came up with the design for the Duo diaper bag, a messenger-style, modern diaper bag that could hang on a stroller or be unclipped to wear as a shoulder bag. This meant it could go anywhere in a city like New York, from the back of a stroller into a restaurant, and still look cool.

THE SKIP HOP STORY

Skip Hop started in 2002 as a mom-and-pop company, in the most literal sense. They began with one product—a diaper bag called the Duo—that was more functional than anything else on the market, and stylish to boot. They've since rolled out innovative, beautiful products one at a time, many of them blockbusters like the Moby bath-spout cover. Now they make baby-oriented décor, toys, tools, and safety items that are distributed in more than forty countries.

Ellen: So I had the idea, but I didn't know how to get it made. My plan was to sew up a few for myself and my friends. But Michael came up to me and said, "If you're going to do this, it's not going to be a hobby. We're going to make it into a business."

Michael: It was about taking a simple need seriously. If you need it, someone else might need it as well. Then again, the market is littered with products that were great ideas for the founders, but nobody wanted them when they hit the marketplace. There's always that risk.

Manufacturing was a new frontier for Michael, but he became determined to figure out the most economical way to achieve quality.

Michael: We had no idea how to actually make the bag. Ellen searched the Internet for people who make backpacks or messenger bags. What we discovered is that a lot of companies that make products that are similar but not competitive will do private-label work. If they have a factory with excess capacity, they want to put that capacity to work. Some of the biggest brands in fashion do private-label work.

Of course, we couldn't afford to make a lot of inventory. We only put a tiny bit of capital into the company: $25,000 or so. There are usually big minimum orders for raw materials like fabric or plastic, but we actually made everything with remnant canvas that was lying around the factories from their existing products.

"It was about taking a simple need seriously."

Amazingly, manufacturers and suppliers were willing to give us credit terms in the beginning. We'd basically say to them, "We'll give you 30 percent up front on our first order to show that we're serious, but after that it's net 30 terms, or net 60." We'd order really quickly, get our products into stores, and use the revenues to fund the next order. It's an amazingly cheap form of capital, and the least risky. To this day, utilizing credit to get ahead is one of our top sources of capital.

Part of the challenge of designing a product, by the way, is bringing it in at a price that people can afford. That can be a big challenge. Often it means deciding what you're *not* going to include. You have to make smart sacrifices to create an affordable product.

Ellen: Some people out there dream of making cashmere baby blankets. Well, how many people will pay for that? Be realistic about what people can actually spend. Sure, we could stay small and sell really high-end products at little boutiques, but we wanted a wide range of consumers.

As the company grew, Michael never stopped seeking ways to make manufacturing more efficient. On that front, he discovered a revolution had taken place behind the scenes.

"We don't want to put all of our resources into one, two, or three retailers. We diversify."

Michael: One of the most fascinating things we've found in this business is the macrochange in manufacturing and consumer products and distribution in the last ten years. Skip Hop may not be a tech business per se, but it's very tech-driven. The way a container moves around the country with your goods, from the factory floor to the retailer's shelves, is as miraculous as the Internet in some respects.

If I were a manufacturer in the twentieth century, we would own our factory, employ herds of factory workers, and have a warehouse. But we're a twenty-first-century manufacturer. We have no factories and no warehouse. We outsource all of those tasks to people who are better at it. This allows us to focus on mission-critical tasks: product design, sales, marketing, and support. We don't have a huge permanent staff, but at any time there are a thousand people doing work for Skip Hop somewhere in the world.

Skip Hop's popularity grew quickly. With that came opportunities to place the brand in big-box stores.

Michael: Over the years, we've gotten interest from some very big retailers who want to carry our brand, which is always tempting because of the huge scale of these companies. We don't want to put all of our resources into one, two, or three retailers. We diversify. Our goal is not to have three big customers. It's to have one thousand customers in thirty different countries. That way, if that one "big" customer goes out of business, we're not going out of business with them.

Ellen: We knew that we didn't want to just stay in bags. We wouldn't be able to build a company as large as we wanted to, so we had to take some risk.

One of the things you'll see if you look at our products is that we are using much less plastic than "cut and sew" materials, which means our business was less risky financially, since plastic products require a much greater capital investment. But we wanted to prove our versatility. The next product we came up with after the Duo, the Splash Bottle Drying Rack, was plastic, and it was the most expensive product we ever tooled.

The Splash was a big success for us. It has a number of different tools: a bottle-drying rack, a brush, and a shelf for nipples, straws, and valves. It won an international design award, but we also think it's cute. ("Cute" doesn't matter in most businesses, but it's a huge factor in baby.) In creating the Splash, we made a statement: we were more than just bags.

Skip Hop's aesthetic began with that core bag: a very simple, clean, modern design. As we move into other areas, we continue to evolve our design philosophy. Toys, for instance, can't be clean-line functional, but they can still be "Skip Hop."

"People are going to judge you by your image in two minutes."

THE
MICHAEL & ELLEN DIAMANT
PLAYBOOK

Select and Bet on Trusted Partners

At Skip Hop, we rely on outside partners to make, ship, and distribute our goods. If you rely on others as much as we do, you have to pick them carefully. When we pick manufacturers, we want to see that brands we respect are being made at their factory.

Then, of course, there's our partnership as founders: we're also a married couple—partners in life. Because we trust each other, this works. Every argument affords an opportunity to find the best solution. We listen to each other, and then try to arrive at the optimal answers for the business. Leave egos or personal issues out of it. If you're always fighting to win, that sets up a bad dynamic. At Skip Hop, we've made our unique partnership work. In fact, we consider our partnership to be a competitive advantage.

Clearly Divide Roles

Partners and executives should split responsibilities very cleanly. If you are working with a talented and trustworthy team, you won't have any doubt that the other part of the business is being handled amazingly well. We're very lucky, because we easily fall into our respective roles here. Ellen is ultimately responsible for the company's products, and while she can make business pitches or review year-end statements, she couldn't do her job as lead creative if she had to deal with the millions of operational challenges that my team and I handle every day. And one of my major strengths as a CEO is that I'm a very good bridge between the creative side and the business side. I can speak business to businesspeople and creative to the creative team. I'm not the creative force, but I understand what creatives need to function well. And I'm lucky enough to be married to the best creative of them all.

Act Big, Even When You Are Small

People are going to judge you by your image in two minutes, so it's important to look established. Even if you're a one-person company, you can look like a fifty-person company. Don't hand-draw your own logo; hire a professional designer. Don't build your own website; invest in one that looks decent. It's common for mom-and-pop companies to use their mothers and sisters and wives for photo shoots, but photography is your number-one online sales tool. A professional brand is a really good investment.

MICHAEL & ELLEN'S BEST ADVICE

BUSINESS OPERATIONS

Outsource Business Operations and Focus on Your Core Mission

Business operations and logistics are extremely complicated, no matter what industry you are in. They can easily overwhelm you and your team. Luckily, there are third-party solutions for nearly every task you need to support your business. Use those and add value by focusing on your core competency.

FAILURE

If You're Not Noticeably Failing, You're Not Innovating

The world is full of people who are afraid to bring a product to market because they are afraid of that initial risk. But failure is a huge part of this business. It often provides the best data you can get. A good percentage of your products will never really take off in the marketplace. That's OK! You can't be successful in product design without occasional failures as well. You are going to need to invent and fail ten times for every success. Invent.

MARKET DEVELOPMENT

Improve on the Marketplace with Every New Product

There are certain "absolutes" for any product to just get into our market. Everything has to meet a certain level of quality. Everything has to be safe. If you don't have that, you won't even get started in the marketplace. But that's not enough. You have to make smarter products, and that means that every product you introduce has to be a demonstrable improvement on what's already in the market—twice as good. Everything needs to have a distinctive and separating function. Don't follow trends; create a culture that sets them.

MARKETING

Don't Assume Customers Want What You Want

You can't assume that people want your product just because you want to sell it to them. You have to do research and you have to listen to the marketplace. Don't rely on a sample size of one.

METRICS

Broadcast Your Goals and Metrics to the Entire Team

Every startup is driven by sales and margins. You have to have monthly and daily revenue goals. And when you're living close to the edge financially (and every startup is), your entire team has to know how your business is doing, 24/7. At Skip Hop, our key metrics are broadcast on an LED sign right in our lobby. Your team should always be kept abreast of the company's financial health, the challenges it is facing, and its major milestones and successes.

PRODUCT DEVELOPMENT

Start with a Target Market and Price, Then Build Backward

A lot of people get into the manufacturing business and think they can start by designing a product and figuring out the target and price later. They calculate the costs, double it wholesale, double it retail, and assume the consumer is going to pay for it—whatever it is. That's not going to work. Part of the challenge is bringing the product in at a realistic price that your customers can afford. You have to start with your buyer and price, and build backward from there.

RAISING CAPITAL

Offer Friends and Family the Opportunity to Grow with You

A lot of people are rightfully scared to ask their friends and family for money. But if you really believe in your idea and think it's a moneymaker, you'd be doing a them a disservice if you didn't offer them first dibs. If you feel uncomfortable offering a great opportunity to your friends and family, it means you don't actually believe in your business.

VISION & MISSION

Search for Innovations in Related Fields

When you enter a marketplace as an entrepreneur, you're doing so in order to introduce an innovative product or service. There's a void, and you want to fill it. You have to look outside of your narrow category for ideas and inspiration. (If you're impressed with what you see in your own space, you're going to have a real challenge introducing improvements.) Be a collector of ideas from outside your industry.

MICHAEL & ELLEN'S VISION FOR THE FUTURE

The Diamants intend to keep growing at a massive rate, without turning over ownership of their company. Michael sets the bar high, insisting on a target of 40 percent growth year over year. Skip Hop is among the most diverse brands in the baby market, and that, coupled with their diversity of retailers, means they can afford to push boundaries to explore new products and markets.

Their partnership in the company is a family affair. As Ellen puts it, "Our eleven-year-old, Spencer, loves that his family has their own business, and he's very integrated into ours. He helps us at trade shows, travels with us to Asia for manufacturing, and participates in all the events. He spots parents on the streets with our products and points them out. He would like to be part of Skip Hop one day, but we want him to understand that he has to follow his own heart and do what he loves."

CHRIS DIXON

FOUNDER:

SITEADVISOR

FOUNDER COLLECTIVE

HUNCH

INTRODUCING CHRIS DIXON

Chris Dixon possesses a pair of skills that are rarely found together in technology entrepreneurs: he's as good at picking companies to invest in as he is at building them from scratch. For Chris, the two activities can't really be separated. As far as he's concerned, you can't be good at building companies if you're not also good at building and protecting your equity. But what makes Chris especially rare, in addition to his aptitude as a technician/technologist, is his understanding of market valuations, equity structures, and the entire venture-capital process, which gives him a powerful strategic advantage in the marketplace.

Chris was a personal investor in such early-stage technology companies as Skype, Foursquare, Kickstarter, and Invite Media. His Founder Collective is as good as it gets. As a seed-stage venture-capital fund built by a collection of successful entrepreneurs, it has a killer record, and nobody else in the marketplace is more pro-entrepreneur.

Too many first-time entrepreneurs undervalue the importance of financing. They're frantically at work building their companies, assuming somebody will take care of them if they succeed. But Chris's playbook tells a different story, one, by the way, that he often generously shares on his wildly popular, eponymous blog, cdixon.org.

CHRIS'S STORY

Chris started out as a computer programmer. But rather than remaining a one-sided tech guy, he was determined to cultivate a new skill, putting his knowledge of technology, business, and even history to work as an investor. He landed at Bessemer Venture Partners, early investors in Skype and Dick's Clothing & Sporting Goods.

Chris Dixon: Initially, I was just a computer programmer, and I got to be pretty good at it. But my ideal was to be very good at two different things, which has exponentially more value. I consider myself to be mediocre at about twenty things, but I'm particularly good at two things: software development and startup financing.

His time at Bessemer gave Chris a comprehensive look at the tech-startup landscape. He discerned significant unmet demand in one particular area: Web security, where he put his long-term goal of becoming a "technical inventor" to use.

While I was at Bessemer, I tracked online security very closely for years. At some point, I was confident there was going to be a very interesting angle there. Eventually, I noticed a historical pattern. Every five years, a new security threat comes along and a couple of midsize companies arise to address it. First there were viruses, then there was spam. When I was researching the industry, a new threat called "phishing" (phony emails or sites that trick users into revealing personal information) had just emerged, but nobody had built a tool to protect users from it.

I mentioned the idea to a college friend, and we quickly built a simple application called FraudEliminator, which did only one thing: indicate whether or not you are on a phishing site. Very quickly, we realized our idea was too narrow. Phishing wasn't the only threat on the Web. What if you were visiting an illegal Canadian pharmacy? Or a site that is infecting your computer with spyware? There needed to be a simple tool that rated every kind of threat on the Web. Using FraudEliminator as a foundation, we decided to build it.

Chris's more comprehensive offer eventually grew into SiteAdvisor, a simple browser notification that flagged potential spam and malware sites with a Caution or Warning tag. The idea seemed so obvious that Chris worried that he wasn't the first person to have this insight.

THE SITEADVISOR STORY

Chris's first independent venture was SiteAdvisor, an Internet-security company—and one of the quickest wins in recent memory. SiteAdvisor simplified online security via a browser plug-in that labeled every site a user visited with a Safe, Caution, or Warning sign. Chris and his team debuted SiteAdvisor at a hacker and technology conference on February 10, 2006. Fifty-four *days* later, the company was acquired by computer security giant McAfee.

Since 2007, he's cofounded two major ventures with fellow *Startup Playbook* contributor Caterina Fake. In addition to Founder Collective, there is Hunch, a personalized search engine known as a recommendation engine, which, Chris and Caterina hope, will create "a taste graph of the entire Web." Hunch was acquired by eBay in late 2011.

If I hadn't actually built FraudEliminator and seen exactly what was out there and what the real problems were, I would not have realized that SiteAdvisor was a good idea. I would just have dismissed it as being too obvious; if it was that obvious, somebody must already be on it, or had decided *not* to build it for good reasons.

That would have been incorrect. I was underestimating the domain expertise I had gained over four years. In addition, security is a highly technical domain, which gave me an advantage over less technically adept Internet entrepreneurs. Developing that advantage was a deliberate strategic decision.

The strategy paid off. Chris secured funding for SiteAdvisor in 2005, debuted the product in 2006, and sold the company that same year to McAfee. At first Chris stayed on, but he was soon drawn back to the startup world, this time both as an investor and as an entrepreneur.

In 2007, Chris cofounded Founder Collective with seven other startup entrepreneurs, including Caterina Fake. Rather than invest in scaling companies, The Founder Collective is entirely focused on seed-stage investments. "There might be more lucrative things we could do with our time, but that's not why we're doing this," Chris has said. "We're doing this to partner with entrepreneurs and help them get through early startup stages—particularly early team building, product development, and financing."

His other venture, also cofounded with Fake, is Hunch, a personalized recommendation engine.

In my first venture, I built a startup that exploited an obvious gap in the marketplace and quickly sold it. But this time, I decided to pursue a labor of love. I consider the work I do at Hunch to be a species of artificial intelligence, which has been an interest of mine for a very long time. My high-school thesis was on a very similar topic (making smart genes out of large data sets). It may not be the optimal economic path for a company, but this was the area where I wanted to focus next.

Today, Chris is a very active member of the New York startup community. He's a frequent speaker at New York–area tech conferences, and often conducts technical interviews with IT innovators there and in the Bay Area. A repository of Chris's thinking is his invaluable personal blog, at cdixon.org, which is a vital resource for budding entrepreneurs. Summing up his efforts, Chris calls them "propaganda for the good guys."

"The best way to predict what's going to happen in a business is to look at the past."

THE CHRIS DIXON PLAYBOOK

Find Your Founder/Market Fit

I explained founder/market fit in one of my most popular blog posts. An extremely useful concept that has grown popular among startup founders is what eminent entrepreneur and investor Marc Andreessen terms "product/market fit," defined as "being in a good market with a product that can satisfy that market." Andreessen argues persuasively that product/market fit is "the only thing that matters for a new startup" and that "the life of any startup can be divided into two parts: before product/market fit and after product/market fit." But this takes time. Founders have to choose a market long before they have any idea whether they will reach product/market fit. In my opinion, the best predictor of success is whether there is what David Lee calls "founder/market fit." Founder/market fit means the founders have a deep understanding of the market they are entering, and are people who "personify their product, business, and ultimately their company."

Be a Historian of Business and Technology

Today, the study of politics is usually referred to as "political science." It's the attempt to create a science of explaining and predicting political systems. In the past, the field was called "political history," and I'm a big believer in the historical model. The best way to predict what's going to happen in a business is to look at the past. In trying to predict how Facebook advertising is going to play out, for example, it makes sense to know the history of Google AdWords. If you're building a plan for creating a new business or a new economic model, learn everything you can about the history of business and the history of technology, especially since the beginnings of the Internet.

Identify and Fill Whitespaces

"Whitespaces" are areas where there is latent demand without supply. Large companies have entire teams of researchers looking out for these areas, but still they often miss them because they have strong biases. While those biases may have helped them become successful initially, they prevent them from seeing large gaps today. Outsiders are often better able to discern those gaps. Startups that fill whitespaces aren't usually world-changing companies, but they often have solid exits. They force incumbents to see a demand they had missed, and those incumbents often respond with an acquisition.

━━━━━━━━━━━━━━━━━━ **CHRIS'S BEST ADVICE** ━━━━━━━━━━━━━━━━━━

CULTURE

Don't Underestimate the Value of Ambient Learning

I no longer believe in the wisdom of having remote product development or remote employees. Especially in the early research-and-development phase, you need a small group of people rapidly cycling through iterations of your idea. That team needs to meet in a single place, overhear each other's conversations, and develop the same set of rhythms. Until you try remote development and fail, you simply can't understand how important ambient learning is.

FAILURE

Don't Overextend the Definition of Failure

I once had a conversation with a young entrepreneur who asked, "What if we end up with a MySpace instead of a Facebook?" It's actually an absurd question: MySpace was a $600 million exit! In 2010, there were 514 venture-backed exits that each averaged more than $75 million. Thanks to movies like *The Social Network*, there's the perception that you're either the next Mark Zuckerberg or you're broke. The view that you're either building the next Facebook or doomed to failure does a great disservice by discouraging entrepreneurs who aspire to moderate success.

FINANCE

Don't Hit Half a Milestone

A fairly high percentage of startups fail because of poor financing. They underestimate the amount of capital they need, don't raise enough money, and hit half a milestone. Each round of funding should do one of two things: get you to your next round or get you to profitability. If you didn't raise enough money to either get a higher valuation in your next round or pass the break-even point, then you should have planned things better. It's a very common mistake.

METRICS

Avoid Vanity Metrics

A lot of businesses focus on vanity metrics: comScore numbers, number of downloads, number of total users. For the most part, those are false, misleading signals. If you're building a software application, for instance, the number of downloads doesn't matter for the most part. You need to know who your active users are. Which subgroups are you reaching, and which are you failing to reach? How can you improve reach in the demographics where you're missing your targets? Unfortunately, there are times when vanity metrics can become a self-fulfilling prophecy. The press sees great numbers and talks you up, and that can lead to its own sort of success. Don't plan for those scenarios. Optimize the metrics that really matter.

RAISING CAPITAL

Raise "Patient" Capital

Founders too often view raising capital as a transaction, when it is actually a very deep relationship. They think of money as money, when there is actually smart money, dumb money, high-integrity money, and low-integrity money. Most important, there is patient money and impatient money. If you raise money from your rich uncle to pursue a dream, he'll probably be very patient and leave you alone. Whereas if you raise money from professional institutional investors, they'll invariably fire you within two years. It is critical to know how patient your capital is.

SALES

If You Aren't Getting Rejected on a Daily Basis, Your Goals Aren't Ambitious Enough

The most useful training I had for running a startup was trying to get my first job. When I was trying to break into the world of VC-backed startups about eight years ago, I applied to hundreds of jobs: low-level VC roles, startups jobs, even to big tech companies. I got rejected from every single one. . . . It helped me develop a really thick skin.

I came to realize that employers weren't really rejecting me as a person or on my potential—they were rejecting a résumé. As it became depersonalized, I became bolder in my tactics. I eventually landed a job at Bessemer (thanks to their willingness to take chances and look beyond résumés), which led to getting my first VC-backed startup funded, and things got better from there.

One of the great things about looking for a job is that your "payoff" is almost always a max function (the best of all attempts), not an average. This is also generally true for raising VC financing, doing biz-dev partnerships, hiring programmers, finding good advisers/mentors, even blogging and marketing. I probably got rejected by someone once a day last week alone. In one case a friend who tried to help called me to console me. He seemed surprised when I told him, "No worries, this is a daily occurrence—we'll just keep trying." If you aren't getting rejected on a daily basis, your goals aren't ambitious enough.

TALENT

Find Partners Who Compensate for Your Weaknesses

Before you can select a partner, you have to understand your weaknesses. I, for instance, am an "INTP" (stands for introversion, intuition, thinking, perception) on the Myers Briggs test. I'm an introvert; I'm bad at making lists and getting things done on time in general. Therefore, it was important for me to find somebody who compensates for those weaknesses, like Hunch's cofounder Tom Pinckney. If we were both Js or both Ps, we wouldn't be as effective.*

WORKING FOR YOURSELF

Don't Overestimate the Risks or Upsides of Entrepreneurship

People overestimate the likelihood that you will go broke as an entrepreneur, but on the other hand, they don't recognize how unlikely it is that you will become a billionaire. Bill Gates is the richest man in the world because he executed everything perfectly. He flipped fifty heads in a row. That almost certainly won't be any other entrepreneur's experience. It's also extremely unlikely that they will fail so completely that they won't be able live reasonably well.

* As it happens, another of Chris's cofounders at Hunch, Caterina Fake, is also an "INTP."

CHRIS'S VISION FOR THE FUTURE

Many founders recognize startups as part of a major macroeconomic trend, but when Chris and I discussed the economic future, he took the most expansive view of all: "Today, very few people believe that they will be safe at a big company as long as they're loyal and do their job well. The notion of lifetime employment is over." Rather than seeing this as a loss, Chris sees the beginnings of a world-changing movement. "The dream of the last century was to own a home. The dream of this century will be to own a company. Working for somebody else is like being a renter for your whole life. In the twenty-first century, we'll all aspire to own a much larger piece of our lives."

MARC ECKŌ

Fashion designer Marc Eckō is like an air-show jet pilot who builds his own planes. But that doesn't fully capture his ride-on-the-edge lifestyle; he's also one part artist, one part rock star, and one part industrial-grade creator.

In a sense, Marc is an extreme embodiment of a quality all entrepreneurs share: the willingness to give up everything for the belief in his vision. But what distinguishes extraordinary entrepreneurs like Marc is their desire to create scaling value. With Eckō Unltd., the urban-wear flagship of his vast fleet of style labels, Marc has built more than a billion dollars of value.

More than anything, Marc owes his success to his unique artistic vision and entrepreneurial drive. He created T-shirts that look disruptively urban and was willing to undertake the hand-to-hand combat required to produce them at scale. Then there was a moment when the rapid scale of his business threatened to undo all of Marc's success. As he tried to take responsibility for each component of every operation, "I started dropping balls all over the place," he admits. Eventually, he realized something that every visionary entrepreneur should learn as quickly as possible: you must have a CEO, but you don't have to be the CEO.

The CEO needs to be directing the "oxygen" that keeps businesses alive: the money flowing into and out of them. If you want to focus your time on creating amazing products, you need a partner who will run the business.

MARC'S STORY

Marc grew up in eastern New Jersey. His father was a pharmacist turned Realtor whose passion was photography.

Marc Eckō: Every weekend when I was a kid, my father would convert our laundry room into a photography lab. From the time I was six through my college years, developing and editing film was a major bonding mechanism for us. We never talked business, because I knew business sucked and it kept him up at night. He taught me every detail of photography. Developing pictures was my first experience applying the rigor of science to art, which is a huge part of everything I've done.

When I began making my own art, I didn't use a camera. I used an airbrush. I was obsessed with graffiti, and the airbrush was the kissing cousin of the aerosol spray can. I figured out how to create precise, photorealistic illustrations. I made hip-hop–inspired T-shirts and started selling them in school.

Marc searched for ways to mass-produce without compromising quality.

The options for screen-printing back in the late '80s and early '90s were limited. If you go back and look at the early skate and surfboard streetwear graphics, everything's very flat and spot colored. I had to settle for doing the first shirt in what's called CMYK (cyan, magenta, yellow, and black), because they could print slightly higher resolution, but they could only print on white.

Marc investigated further and, via hacking, found a mode of production that could get close to the effect he was going for.

The trend in streetwear at the time was black T-shirts with giant, photorealistic images on them. So I started researching the marketplace and figured out where big brands like Nike and Reebok were going. There was a company called Serichrome, which had managed to hack into Photoshop to do eight to ten color separations instead of the four colors of CMYK. But when I called Serichrome, they quoted about $5,000 for five hundred shirts, or $10 a unit.

It was depressing. I had artwork that I knew people would want, but I had no way to produce it. Then one day I went to a small trade show. At a table near mine was a guy named Ken, whose brand was called Eighth

---

THE ECKŌ UNLTD. STORY

Marc has been in the business of selling T-shirts since high school, when he would airbrush shirts for his classmates. He saw the potential of his graffiti-inspired style for a younger generation growing up in awe of hip-hop. Marc was intent on bringing this new style to the mainstream, and through the '90s the Eckō Unltd. line moved from boutiques to major retailers.

Nowadays, the various Eckō brands—having expanded beyond shirts to watches, leather goods, menswear, and even cosmetics—bring in more than $1.6 billion in revenue. Marc's empire also includes Complex Media, a massive lifestyle media outlet and magazine as well as a gaming company, and "Artists & Instigators," a new branded platform dedicated to the entrepreneurial lifestyle.

Day God. He created amazing photo-real prints of giant marijuana buds because his brand's name mused, "On the Eighth Day God Created Marijuana." He told me he'd cracked Serichrome's formula. He said, "Look, you come out to Tahoe, bring me a bag of dope, and buy a computer from me" (that was his day job). So I did, and then he taught me how to hack channels on Photoshop.

For the next trade show, I had ten shirts printed. I remember printing those in Brooklyn, and those guys were like, "How did you do that?"

I created such a point of distinction in the marketplace that I had a two-to-three-year window to exploit. Stussy, Con-Art, Triple 5 Soul; all of them were stuck with spot graphics. I knew they'd catch up eventually, but during that window my business grew very, very quickly.

Marc knew that it was now time to focus on the business end of his operations, with help from the people he trusted most.

I founded Eckō Unltd. in 1993 with my partner Seth Gerszberg and my twin sister, Marci. Without my sister, I don't know if I would have been nearly as successful—you need to have that figure who's gonna tell it to you like it really is.

Marc began looking for ways to expand his business into other industries while retaining his urban aesthetic.

During the first five years, sales were respectable but not without the company's fair share of hiccups. When we finally reached about $300 million in sales, the perception was that we got there overnight. At our high point, we were doing $1.5 billion in retail sales worldwide. It's a fallacy that it happens overnight. It took almost fifteen years.

But Eckō's expansion came with a few missteps, which prompted Marc to define more precisely what made the brand unique.

With that kind of capital on hand, I got seduced into taking my eye off the ball and straying from my core mission, which was monetizing and merchandizing my art. I thought that I could just go out there and start making snowboard jackets, or working on denim, and it would work because I'd already cracked the code. I was wrong.

When I started out, I was obviously very young and emotionally kind of unhinged. My partner Seth and I would yell at each other like brothers

> *"You need to have that figure who's gonna tell it to you like it really is."*

and Marci would come in and break it up. Part of me was excited to get past that and exercise the rigor of being mature. But as I've gotten older, I'm realizing that it's as important to exercise being naïve.

For fifteen years, I micromanaged every aspect of my business. In the latter part of those fifteen years, I started to bring in really good management because I was overwhelmed by the sheer magnitude of not getting to stuff and was dropping balls all over the place.

Marc knew he was a style pioneer. Through trial and error, he learned what sectors that style could break into, and which ones he couldn't.

I had a big emotional hunch that I could parlay my platform into something else. That big departure came with founding *Complex*, a lifestyle magazine for young men, in 2007. Today Complex Media and all of our websites pull in 500 million unique IPs. It's crazy to think that just ten years ago I launched it by putting hangtags on my T-shirts.

THE
MARC ECKŌ
PLAYBOOK

Manage Your Inner Artist

When doing creative work, it's important not to get trapped by your emotions. I've learned that by managing creative young people; I see them get too emotional about their positions. With age, I've learned how to nurse that feeling, but also when to turn it off in my brain. It's a mechanism that you have to exercise: performing an honest inspection and determining when the emotion is driving good work, and when it might lead to unintended consequences.

There's No Shortcut to Perfection

When you put pencil to paper as an artist, you get immediate, gratifying feedback just seeing the image. But there's a longer process involved in honing and perfecting that work, and there's no way to speed it up. As a kid, I remember geeking out with my father in the darkroom: measuring everything to exacting standards, getting the water temperature right, adjusting the red light, then finally seeing the image burn into the paper. There was a kind of magic or alchemy in following that process. In the same way, you can't expect instant gratification in the business of selling art.

Don't Let Yourself off the Hook

To run a business, you have to be a kind of masochist. You have to be willing to compete against yourself and call you on yourself. That's especially rare in my industry. I know a lot of fashion designers who build a Great Wall of China around themselves, not allowing any bad input to touch them. They're up in an ivory tower and they become deluded. I'm not that guy; I'm more of a populist.

FAILURE

You Can't Cheat the Learning Curve

You have to get lost in the woods of your own doing and discover a way out. You have to find the right path over the creek, under the rock—whatever mechanism is good for your body's size and your stride and your cadence and your tolerance for wet or cold or humid weather. That kind of learning comes from having a tolerance for failure, and extracting lessons from your failures. Life is a composite of lots of failures, but hopefully, you net the end of the day with more wins than losses.

FOCUSING TIME & ENERGY

Every New Business Direction Has a Price

The fact that you've gone through all the pain to build one business doesn't mean the next ones will be pain-free. Getting involved in a new enterprise without testing the waters first is a drain on your time and money, and can even take a toll on your established businesses.

LEADERSHIP

Let Evolution Happen

You have to create an ecosystem of governance that doesn't depend entirely on you. The organization has to be an organism that's able to learn and grow organically. If you micromanage everything, that won't happen. It can only work if you bring in a really, really good management team and let them share in the learning curve.

MARKETING

Exploit Every Technical Advantage

Technical advantages can give you a window of time to distinguish yourself, but inevitably that window's going to close. The market will eventually catch up. The important thing is to use those windows as opportunities to create an edge and keep your competitors chasing you.

PRODUCT DEVELOPMENT

Decode Problems Yourself

Every time I've gotten lazy and relied on somebody else to decode problems for me, I've run into more problems. You have to apply yourself and find the mechanisms that drive your business with your own hands. Later on, you can teach managers the formulas you discover; but if it's your company, you need to be the one to blaze the trails.

RAISING CAPITAL

Leverage Every Asset

I didn't do the private-equity thing; Eckō Unltd. was always self-funded. We used our inventory to finance the business. It's actually a best practice in the apparel industry called factoring: sell a portion of your receivables at a discount and use that capital to finance future business. As the business grows, so does the value of your trademark and your brand. Eventually, this gives you leverage to negotiate good terms with banks and to scale very fast.

TALENT

Allow Senior Managers to Participate in Your Company's Success

When *Complex* launched in 2007, it was under the leadership of Rich Antoniello, who is CEO. In the early years of the business, I made him suffer when it came to giving him upsides. I was an equity hoarder. Eventually I saw that I was alienating him and gave him a piece of the magazine's success. You have to share; you can't do all the learning by yourself.

WORKING FOR YOURSELF

Don't Let Academic Models Take the Place of Lived Experience

Entrepreneurs often think that there is a formula for running a business: measure this, check that box, and you're done. But it never looks like that on the ground. It's messy, but it has to happen organically; that's heuristics. Academic types are really scared of that; they want to believe it's just Xs and Os. But you can't always learn everything in school. Sometimes your philosophy develops from your interaction with the world.

MARC'S VISION FOR THE FUTURE

There can be no doubt that Marc will continue to expand both his empire and his profile as a public provocateur. No summary of Marc's story would be complete without mention of one of the great public stunts of our time. At auction, Marc paid $752,467 for the baseball that signaled Barry Bonds' record-breaking, 756th career home run. He then started a website that allowed the public to vote on whether to launch the ball into space, donate it to the Baseball Hall of Fame, or brand it with an asterisk and then give it to the Hall of Fame—the last a nod to the controversy over Bonds' alleged use of performance-enhancing drugs to achieve his record. Bonds publicly stated that the whole vote was stupid, and in response Marc offered to make him a custom shirt that read "Marc Eckō paid $752,467 for my ball, and all I got was this 'stupid' T-shirt." The voters decided that Marc should hand the ball over to the Hall of Fame . . . with an asterisk.

In addition to pushing the envelope in public life, Marc is involved with charities focused on improving education and providing mentoring programs for children in need.

KEVIN EFRUSY

FOUNDER:
IRONPLANET
CORIO

GENERAL PARTNER:
ACCEL

INTRODUCING KEVIN EFRUSY

When I spoke with Marc Cenedella of TheLadders, he told me the old joke about sculpting an elephant. "How do you sculpt an elephant?" someone asks. The sculptor replies, "You start with a block of marble and chisel away everything that isn't an elephant." Kevin Efrusy is that chisel. As an investor and a board member, he fearlessly hammers away, removing everything extraneous in big, dramatic chunks until only the essential idea remains.

While Kevin is best known today as a partner at the Silicon Valley venture-capital firm Accel, where he sourced the firm's investment in Facebook, he began his career as the cofounder of two successful startups: Corio, an enterprise software pioneer, went public and was acquired by IBM for $182 million in 2005. IronPlanet.com, a heavy-equipment marketplace, has annual gross merchandise sales of approximately $600 million. By any standard, Kevin is an extraordinary investor and mentor.

KEVIN'S STORY

In 2003, Kevin joined Accel Partners, a major Silicon Valley venture-capital firm. Accel focuses on early investments in visionary entrepreneurs, and Kevin quickly defined himself at Accel as a tenacious pursuer of those visionaries. In 2005, for instance, he spent several months pursuing Mark Zuckerberg—a meeting that eventually led to Accel's heavy investment in Facebook, where Jim Breyer has represented Accel on the board. After that investment, Kevin continued to focus on consumer Internet software investments for Accel. He now serves on the boards of Groupon, BranchOut, MindLab, Medio Systems, and Couchbase.

Accel Partners focuses on finding great entrepeneurs before anyone else, and Kevin knows what to look for.

Kevin Efrusy: Look at Larry Page at Google or the recent social-media company founders. It would be easy to ask these guys, "Aren't you done? Didn't you prove everything you needed to prove? Isn't your company valuable enough?" Their answers would clearly be, "No. We've done just a fraction of what we want to do." And they're talking in terms of five, ten, fifteen years. Just the other day, Larry said that Google was doing about 5 percent of what Google would eventually achieve.

It's that constant pushing forward that makes these guys great. Most of us would have left that job several billion dollars ago. What more would there be to prove? How much more money would we need? But it's not about that. It's about being completely energized and fulfilling a vision.

While I've been involved in both sides of entrepreneurship, I certainly don't claim that I was ever near the order of magnitude of the guys in the pantheon of entrepreneurship. But, those who can't do—teach!

While Kevin takes pride in the achievements of the teams at Corio and IronPlanet, he sees his greatest achievements as a board member. In that role, Kevin places an unusually high value on CEOs who fight for their vision, even when that vision clashes with the need to keep a business stable and collect quarterly profits.

The founders of the recent crop of social-media and social-commerce companies had to make many bets that ran contrary to the conventional wisdom—to the point of getting pilloried in the media, by partners, and by outraged user bases that initially reacted to the changes with fear. Look at Steve Jobs' battles with the music and wireless carrier industries. If he

---

THE IRONPLANET STORY

Kevin helped found IronPlanet.com in 1999 as a place for the purchase and sale of used, heavy equipment such as asphalt pavers, combine harvesters, and trucks.

THE CORIO STORY

Corio was a platform for a full suite of enterprise business software, which was sold to clients for a monthly fee. Kevin cofounded Corio in 1998 and brought it public in 2000. In 2005, IBM acquired Corio at a 40 percent premium over the stock price. Today, it is part of IBM Global Services.

would have compromised his vision to accommodate the music labels or big cellular companies, it's unlikely the iPod and iPhone would have achieved the same levels of success. I'm told Larry Page and Sergey Brin had to fight very hard to preserve the clean, simple utility of the Google homepage and prevent the clutter that had oozed into the other portals of the day. The controversies around the social-media and -commerce companies (privacy, spurned M&A suitors, etc.) are well known. But in every case, the ultimate decision was made with passion for the user experience and ultimate mission in mind. Only special entrepreneurs can resist these pressures.

Of course, taking these massive risks doesn't always lead to immediate success. We've seen that very clearly with Reed Hastings of Netflix. He won the DVD business and destroyed Blockbuster. But very early on, he saw the seeds of his own destruction in video-on-demand. He knew that if Netflix wasn't the one to innovate on that, someone else would, and he'd lose. So he's pushed extremely hard over the past year to reorient the company in that direction. He's stubbed his toe pretty hard in the process, and a lot of people have asked why he would take the company in a completely new direction when the DVD business is profitable. But he thought Netflix would fail if it remained complacent. And he was right.

The major disruption that Kevin sees in the market today is more widespread. It isn't simply a matter of creating new ways for companies to interact with consumers, but of transforming consumers into producers in significant, if modest ways.

Startups enable a whole new class of small entrepreneurial businesses to use new tools and thrive in ways they couldn't have in the past. Rather than saying that everyone in America is going to start a company like eBay, I point to the way that eBay has enabled thousands of people to make their livings online. Groupon is beginning to do the same thing for small businesses, and Etsy for handicrafts. And since almost the beginning, Google has allowed small businesses to grow by reaching new customers online.

I think we'll see a lot more of that. There won't necessarily be more technology companies. But new tools will allow many more people to create proprietary companies. If you're good at using these tools, it's easier to start a small business than ever.

"It's about being completely energized and fulfilling a vision."

THE
KEVIN EFRUSY
PLAYBOOK

Don't Optimize a Melting Ice Cube

Entrepreneurs often fail because they aren't willing to risk everything on a radical transformation. They aren't willing to make the harsh changes that moving in a new direction usually requires. Instead, they insist that they're just "one big deal away" from saving their company. They are refusing to address the problem. They're not being bold. Making this kind of transformation is hard. But if you're not willing to make it, you're going to get stuck optimizing a melting ice cube. It's funny because the dynamic is what often strangles big companies, so it's tragic to see startups suffer the same fate.

Stay on the Bleeding Edge

Companies shouldn't become too big and lumbering early in their lifecycles. You have to stay hungry and bet companies on things that you believe are critical to move them forward. Most companies don't do that: they simply optimize a particular advantage.

Don't Miss Major Disruptions

When a major disruption is coming, don't miss it. We can't allow companies to be happy dominating the world they're currently residing in. They have to move on to the next one. No matter how well they might be doing, if they miss a major disruption, they'll suffer. Being the board member who loudly insists that fundamental new capabilities need to be built can make you extremely unpopular, but it's an absolutely crucial role.

CULTURE

Hire Unsexy Optimizers

Accepting the fact that people are going to be loyal to an idea or a mission rather than loyal to you is extremely difficult. But if you don't accept it, you'll never hire the unsexy optimizers that you need to manage a company effectively. You don't want to hire so many of them that you'll stop reinventing your business and finding new areas to generate revenues, but you need people who are going to stand up to you and do what needs to be done to execute on specific tasks.

FOCUSING TIME & ENERGY

Don't Clutter Your Time

You make your best decisions, sign your best deals, and find your best investors when your time isn't cluttered with a bunch of random stuff. When you're conviction driven and proactive, you'll set the bar much higher and do better work. Fewer cocktail parties and press events and more unstructured time to think.

HIRING

Interviews Are Worthless; References Are Everything

Forget the interview. The interview is worthless. I don't care how smart someone seems or how many spreadsheets they show you or how much they wowed you with their intellect in an hour. The only thing that matters—the only real predictor of the future—is a potential hire's references. Most often, references don't say bad things, but they also don't say good things that aren't true. Silence can be very telling. It gives you hints, and your job is to probe those hints. Make sure to find references other than those supplied by the candidate.

LEADERSHIP

Professional CEOs Can't Replace Startup Founders

Companies that lose are often the ones that bring in new CEOs. Professional CEOs tend to be very good at optimizing. They're great managers. They can take your advantages, exploit them, hire great teams, and build all the systems and processes you need to achieve profitability. But optimizing isn't the same thing as advancing. When companies bring in professional CEOs, they often become very static. And in those cases, the founder needs to return and instill the momentum for moving forward. You saw that at Dell. You saw that at Yahoo. And you certainly saw that at Apple. Jeff Weiner of LinkedIn is probably the exception to this rule, but perhaps Jeff is an exceptional person.

MARKET DEVELOPMENT

Create New Markets

Successful companies either create markets or disrupt markets. They don't live in between. If you create a market and quickly establish yourself as the leader within it, that always works out well. But the same thing can happen when you disrupt a market and transform it into something else. In that role, you're essentially creating a new market, even if it seems to be occurring within the confines of an old one.

PRODUCT DEVELOPMENT

Don't Compete Against Big Checks

The most difficult situation to deal with is one in which an entrepreneur has a really great product—better than anything you've ever seen—and they find themselves up against an infinite checkbook. We once pledged $20 million toward a product, but then Steve Ballmer at Microsoft swooped in with $100 million in the same area—not for product development, but simply to subsidize a necessary partner. It is difficult to compete in situations like that.

SALES

Create Self-Serve Tools

If you've created a new market or reinvented an existing one, you'll find yourself with an open field and a clear value proposition. In those situations, you won't need a sales team. The best software companies, Dropbox for instance, don't have salespeople. They have self-serve products that are clearly valuable.

TALENT

Don't Clone Yourself

There are strategists, and there are executors. It's very rare to find someone who can do both. Most often, the CEO takes the strategy role and the COO executes. Problems arise when CEOs clone themselves with their first hires instead of finding someone who compensates for their weaknesses. Your COO doesn't need to be someone you want to spend time with or hang out with at parties. Most often, they're boring, calm, measured . . . but highly skilled. And that's exactly what they need to be.

KEVIN'S VISION FOR THE FUTURE

When speaking about the role of venture capitalists and boards, Kevin always stresses the importance of noticing every major disruption. Recently, he has noted a shift in terms of how quickly businesses expand their global reach. "Companies are going global much, much faster than they ever did. Worldwide revenues are starting to appropriately reflect the world balance of trade: the United States is big, but it only represents a fraction of the global market. In fact, markets are beginning to emerge that are far bigger than the United States.

"Others have noticed these trends, but they haven't applied these lessons to a systematic approach to scaling companies worldwide. We're still in the old model: wait four years, hire a GM of Europe, hire a GM of Asia Pac, hire a GM of Latin America, and just wait for it to happen. That is no longer necessary. The entrepreneurs in these new markets are now so sophisticated that they can be full partners with American startups. American startups need to become partners with local entrepreneurs.

"The new model will be to find entrepreneurial teams in emerging markets and cut them loose. Get a great team, give them a playbook, and tell them to go ahead."

As a venture partner at one of the country's major investment firms, Kevin is uniquely situated to transform this vision into a reality.

CATERINA FAKE

FOUNDER:

FLICKR

HUNCH

FINDERY

CHAIRMAN:

ETSY

INTRODUCING CATERINA FAKE

Get underneath Caterina Fake's happy, laissez-faire vibe, and you'll find she's carrying a weapon—her ideas. She is the cofounder of the now-legendary Flickr, a photo-sharing site with more than 50 million users that was sold to Yahoo! in 2005. She is a partner at Founder Collective, an influential fund that invests in startups. One of her investments is Etsy, the online marketplace for handmade and vintage goods, where she also serves as chairman of the board. And, in 2008, she cofounded the recommendation engine Hunch, which is like a customized version of an online search engine.

Caterina is a headstrong optimist, yet she's always looking around the corner at what could go wrong. She is not a wishful thinker. She's fully aware of all the problems that can arise when you build a company, but she doesn't shy away from taking risks. When she's committed to an idea, she commits full stop.

It would be impossible for Caterina to be anything but a founder. Her goal isn't simply to solve a problem, but to create a framework to solve all the problems facing a startup. The "how" and "why" are just as important to her as the "what" of a particular product.

If there is one talent in particular that differentiates Caterina, it's her acumen for usability. While the rest of the marketplace builds features, she builds experiences, recognizing that functionality is only one component of an effective product. It also has to be beautiful, exciting, and impossible to live without. Knowing how to accomplish that is her specialty.

CATERINA'S STORY

Caterina offered this reflection by the English philosopher L.P. Jacks as an epigraph to her story:

A master in the art of living draws no sharp distinction between his work and his play; his labor and his leisure; his mind and his body; his education and his recreation. He hardly knows which is which. He simply pursues his vision of excellence through whatever he is doing, and leaves others to determine whether he is working or playing. To himself, he always appears to be doing both.
—*L.P. Jacks,* Education through Recreation

Caterina Fake: This is, I think, a very important distinction between entrepreneurs and nonentrepreneurs. For the latter, there is a very strong distinction between work and leisure. For us entrepreneurs, there can't be.

There are certain things that define a working person and a playing person. When I have lunch with my lawyer, he wears a suit. When I go to the doctor, he wears a lab coat. While I don't wear my yoga gear to work, I think that our industry has in many ways eliminated the accoutrements of working. This is what you'd be doing even if nobody paid you to do it.

In 2002, Caterina cofounded Ludicorp, a game company whose pilot game was Game Neverending, *a multiplayer, online game. The company ran out of money and the game failed, but what emerged in 2004 was one of the most influential Web startups of the decade. Flickr went through many stages: a chat room, a real-time photo-sharing site, a site for exchanging images found online, and, finally, a tool for uploading and tagging digital photos. More than that, it was one of the first sites to feature user-generated content.*

A lot of people think that companies start with an idea. Many of them do, but Flickr did not start with an idea.

We assembled a group of supersmart, incredibly talented developers to build *Game Neverending,* and the game failed. But it was from that team that Flickr emerged. I've seen it happen so many times that the accidental side project becomes the main product, like Twitter or Flickr. The way Flickr came about was very organic. It's like putting a band together—it's an art. Flickr emerged out of an extended failure. We ran out of money at the company. We were broke. We were failing. We were about to go out of business. When you're in a company death-spiral like that, there's a tendency to panic. You've raised the flag and said, "Follow me!" You've convinced a team

---

THE FLICKR STORY

Caterina Fake cofounded Flickr, the revolutionary image-hosting online community, which today has more than 50 million registered users. Flickr emerged out of tools originally created under the auspices of a Canadian company called Ludicorp, also cofounded by Fake. Just one year after its launch in 2004, Flickr was acquired by Yahoo!.

THE HUNCH STORY

In 2009, Fake and Chris Dixon (along with a team of eleven MIT graduates) cofounded Hunch, a website dedicated to building a "taste graph" of the entire Web, using "decision trees" to offer recommendations to users based on their own affinities and interests. Both Jimmy Wales, founder of Wikipedia, and Gideon Yu, former CFO of Facebook, have joined the Hunch board of directors, and in 2011 the company was acquired by eBay.

of people to give up their highly paid, big paycheck jobs, and you're about to walk them off the edge of a cliff. It's just no good.

I realized that I was in a state of such intense anxiety that I was being counterproductive. That sort of anxiety was going to spread out into the organization, and you need to protect your employees from it. So I actually left for an entire month. I went to Europe. I went to museums and I bicycled around quaint villages. I completely cleared my mind. And when I returned from that trip, Flickr had started its upward ascent.

One of the lessons I came back with is that you need a high tolerance for failure as an entrepreneur. You have to define failure differently. You have to define it as the failure to try. They say that kids who are told they are smart do very badly in the long run: they don't want to fail because they wouldn't be considered smart anymore. Entrepreneurs can't do that. You have to keep trying and failing and then you have to try and fail again. Even having an entire company fail—entrepreneurs think of this differently. It's not career death, it's just a chapter in your book. You just go and start a new company.

It was the team, not the ideas, that made Flickr successful.

Because we had assembled such a remarkable team, we were able to go at the problem of online community in a complete different way and change gears from a gaming to a photo-sharing site. After the death spiral of *Game Neverending*, it was extraordinary to watch Flickr's upward ascent. It's what I imagine the early days of the space program were like: you spend years and years trying to put all of these pieces together and then suddenly you have liftoff. It's an amazing feeling, like flying.

When Yahoo! purchased the company in 2005, Caterina notched a major success. What was next? She decided to focus on investing in exciting new ideas and mentoring up-and-coming entrepreneurs with Founder Collective, a venture-capital fund she participates in with other successful entrepreneurs.

Recently, I had a video chat with an entrepreneur we're working with at Founder Collective. He's a young guy who just dropped out of Columbia in order to build a photo site, one of my special areas. He spent a month at my house in San Francisco. I showed him all of my favorite places, and we stayed up late at night eating tacos and discussing the ins and outs of community management. A reporter asked me if this was common, and I told her, "You know what? It kind of is."

The relationship I have with the entrepreneurs we work with is just like the relationship that I have with my coworkers and colleagues. These are my friends. They camp out at my house and know my daughter. "Playing with the chairman's toddlers" isn't part of the job description, but it's just seamless. That's part of the reason that I'm an entrepreneur.

After a couple of years incubating the ideas of other entrepreneurs, Caterina knew it was time to start another project of her own. Hunch is a leader in the new field of "social search." If Google revolutionized the search engine's ability to provide a thorough survey of online information and organize it by popularity, Hunch's goal is to revolutionize search's ability to be perfectly relevant.

THE CATERINA FAKE PLAYBOOK

Make Something People Want to Use Every Day

Flickr is a social network. A lot of our focus went into building something that you had to go to every day and that you would invite your friends to join. We were building a community. There was no other way that it would work. But once you figure out that recipe, you just have to apply it over and over and over again.

Working on the Right Problem Is More Important than Working Hard

My work and my life are seamlessly integrated, but that's not the same as working twenty-four hours a day. There's an ethos among entrepreneurs that working 24/7 is the road to success. Staying late at the office, working for the sake of working—there's a sort of heroism around it. "Gosh, you know I never sleep. I was at the office until midnight last night." I don't believe in it. As I wrote on my blog in 2009, "Working Hard is Overrated." If you're working on the wrong problem, it doesn't matter how hard you work at it. There are two things

I go back to again and again: having the right people and working on the right problem. Work heroics can be counterproductive; working on the right problem is so much more important than putting in hour after hour on the wrong problem.

A Side Project Often Becomes the Main Event

Very often, accidental side projects become the main product. Flickr is a great example. Twitter's a fantastic example. They were not the main thing that the team had been working on, but they suddenly came to define the company. Once you have a great team, you can switch direction. (The common word these days is "pivot.") You can throw out the thing you thought you came together to work on and build the new thing, the new idea that everybody falls in love with.

CULTURE

Drop the Accoutrements of Work

In other industries, there are certain things that define a "working person" and a "playing person." I think the ideal is to have a fairly seamless existence in who you are all day long.

FAILURE

Have a High Tolerance for Failure

Failure is part of discovering the problem you need to be working on. If, as an entrepreneur, you are afraid to fail or to admit the failure of your efforts, then you completely lose any chance at being able to adapt and succeed at finding the problem that needs solving.

FIRING

Accept the Need for Judicious Firing

I had a colleague at Yahoo! who had a fantastic team. I asked him how he did it. He said, "Judicious firing is often part of the program around here." I have been in the unfortunate position of firing people who have been passed around: people who've moved from group to group, but people will not fire them. Employees like that can be poisonous to an organization.

HIRING

Value Teams over Ideas

A lot of people think that companies start with an idea. Many of them do, but the vast majority do not. If you assemble a group of super-smart, incredibly talented people, amazing successes can grow out of the ashes of some of your initial failures.

LEADERSHIP

Never Allow Your Anxiety to Infect Your Company

As the leader of a team or company, you will always have to deal with anxieties. You cannot let those anxieties spread out past you, the decision maker who can deal with them. You need to protect your employees from them, even if you cannot deal with them immediately.

MARKETING

Build Marketing into Your Product

A well-built product markets itself. Many popular books are great examples. You get to the end of the book and there are listings for book club discussions, websites, and places where you can donate. All sorts of actions that you could take after reading the book—marketing built into the product design itself. And at the point at which your enthusiasm is at its peak—you've just turned the last page.

TALENT

Balance the Ps and Js on Your Team

My Hunch cofounder Chris Dixon and I often talk about Ps and Js. The Myers-Briggs personality test breaks people up into four sets of pairs: Introversion vs. Extroversion. Sensing vs. Intuition. Thinking vs. Feeling. Judgment vs. Perception. The one I use when hiring is Perception (P) vs. Judgment (J). The Ps are the visionary types; the Js are execution oriented. If you have a lot of Ps, you'll have a lot of great ideas, something awesome that people will love; but you never get it done. It doesn't ship. Nothing happens. If you have too many Js on your team, you're executing like mad, things are getting built, and you're shipping like crazy—but you're building something that nobody wants. If you have a good balance of Ps and Js in your company, you're more likely to stay on track. Those people complement each other.

CATERINA'S VISION FOR THE FUTURE

Hunch is a recommendation engine based on the collective knowledge of its community members. "Which digital camera should I buy?" "Where should I move when I retire?" "What British crime or mystery series should I watch next?" Hunch has answers for every one of these questions and thousands of others. Every time a user answers a question, Hunch uses that bit of data to make its next suggestion.

Unlike other recommendation engines, Hunch asks users questions about every topic imaginable. "At a social gathering, do you interact with strangers or stick to people you already know?" "Do you prefer your sandwiches to be cut vertically or diagonally?" "Do you like to dance?" Every one of these questions helps this new kind of search engine make better recommendations. It also compiles a set of data that tracks the tastes of every entity available online, and finds connections between those tastes.

After eBay purchased Hunch in late 2011, Caterina, always looking for new ways to innovate, quickly moved on to her latest venture: Findery, a service that allows users to "find and leave" geo-tagged notes all over the world.

MITCH FREE

FOUNDER:

MFG.COM

INTRODUCING MITCH FREE

To Mitch Free, entrepreneurship is just another trade. He began his career as a machinist, and he strongly believes that no amount of market research or academic dithering is going to outweigh a perfected sense of craft wisdom. His philosophy boils down to, "Build it and see." Although this sounds simple, it can be far riskier than writing a business plan, getting financing, and then building a company.

When Mitch launched MFG.com, he didn't try to game the system; he simply built and tweaked, blocked and tackled. He didn't seek venture capital. His approach didn't put him on the fast track to success, but it did produce a much better outcome than anybody could have imagined at the time.

The "niche" that MFG.com serves is one of the largest in the world: the manufacturing industry. Within that sector, MFG's online marketplace has the unimaginable dominance of an eBay. It's hard to imagine competitors making significant inroads into their business. That said, I expect that Mitch will continue to compete, very rigorously, against himself.

MITCH'S STORY

Mitch began his career as a machinist and a mechanical engineer (he didn't go to college). After time spent producing metal stamping dies and plastic injection molds, he moved to reverse engineering and producing aircraft parts at Northwest Airlines in the early '90s. While there, he earned two patents for complex devices that he invented: "a method for treating jet engine components with high-pressure water" and "a method and apparatus for noncontact inspection of engine blades."

An early adopter of CAD/CAM (computer-aided design/computer-aided manufacturing), Mitch has always looked for ways that software technology could improve manufacturing. His first company, 3DATUM, produced CNC software applications to automate machine tools. While there, he recognized a major need in the marketplace. "My design customers were asking me if I knew someone who could manufacture what they had designed, and my manufacturing customers were asking me if I could introduce them to potential customers who needed something manufactured." After hearing a radio commercial for LendingTree.com, Mitch decided to build an online manufacturing marketplace.

Mitch Free: I knew there were a lot of people trying to create new types of marketplaces when I started MFG.com, but I didn't spend any time studying or obsessing about them. My early employees would all try to follow those competitors, and it was my job to tell them to stop. "Let's cut our own road," I said, because if you spend your time studying what others are doing, you tend to fall into the pack. We wound up doing some things very differently, and I think that was the key to our success. Had we been too obsessed with analyzing our competitors, we would have probably just fallen into their draft.

MFG.com was founded in 1999, at time when funding was widely available to most serious Internet entrepreneurs. But Mitch was committed to building his company from scratch.

I bootstrapped the company for five, six years. There were times when I thought that I was the dumb one in the room for doing this. Here I am struggling, and everybody else is raising $50 million with a bunch of big investors. But had I raised money, I wasn't exactly sure how I would deploy it. I wasn't sure that I could really grow the company much faster. And I always valued equity very, very much. I felt that there was no reason to take capital and lose equity unless I had a clear need for that capital. So the

THE MFG.COM STORY

Mitch Free founded MFG.com in 2000 in order to bring together the two constituencies he'd worked with at his first company: designers and manufacturers. Designers of custom goods can place requests for quotes on MFG.com along with detailed technical specifications, and the system automatically matches them to manufacturers with the capabilities required. It is the first marketplace of its kind, bringing a unique degree of efficiency and transparency to one of the world's largest sectors. Today, MFG.com has over 200,000 members trading in more than fifty currencies.

approach we took was to sell a subscription to our service; buy a stapler. Sell another one; buy a chair. We grew the business organically.

In its first eight years, MFG.com experienced exponential growth, on the order of 40 to 60 percent a year. Then, the global recession of 2008 slowed down manufacturing, as it did nearly every other sector. The company's growth leveled off.

> ## *"Failure is extremely important."*

It's interesting to manage a culture when the euphoria of huge growth goes away. The people with you in the early years thrive on a high-growth environment. When that levels off, they become bored. They want to go find that next high-growth opportunity. In the case of MFG.com, the recession caused some transition in the company. I told certain people, "Maybe it's time for you to go start your own business." I needed people who would come in with a fresh perspective and see us as an exciting opportunity.

Mitch's job changed along with the reality around him. Rather than maintaining his craftsman's focus on product development, he shifted to the role of evangelist-CEO.

I've become more and more of a communicator. I spend time freshening up our marketing, or communicating directly with customers. At one point, I flew three customers in to walk around the office and tell us their stories—of the impact MFG.com was having on their businesses and how much value we were creating for them. That kind of feedback helped allay some internal fears and reinforced the picture of growth.

Despite the downturn in the world economy, MFG.com has continued to grow. But Mitch's impatience with the company's rate of growth is another indication of how high he sets the bar.

I've had to point to other companies in this recession in order to show that we weren't the only ones going through slow times. If everybody else was still growing 40 to 60 percent a year and we weren't, then we'd have a problem. But they're not growing at all, and we are. We slowed down to about 12 percent growth in 2009; in 2010 it was about 15, but it's still decent growth in this market. Comparatively, though, it looked like we'd hit a wall.

Whatever adjustments he's had to make, Mitch has continued to lead MFG.com with considerable success. And despite the current financial environment, Mitch still isn't afraid to take necessary risks.

Failure is extremely important. If you don't fail, then you're probably not trying enough new things. You're not pushing the edge far enough. "If you're not pushing the edge, you're taking up too much space." That mantra pervades my company. I don't want people standing in the middle, I want them to get out there on that edge and push. Failure is how you learn; it's how you iterate. Obviously, you can't bankrupt your company with failure, but you've got to have small failures.

THE
MITCH FREE
PLAYBOOK

Let Ideas Find You

In my experience, you don't find ideas. They find you. Whether it's a result of how you grew up, your education, or your job experience, you're uniquely prepared to do something. Entrepreneurs recognize the moment when that preparation intersects with opportunity. If the intersection happens too early, the infrastructure or the marketplace won't be ready for you. If it happens too late, you'll have missed the opportunity. This is what it means to have "the right idea at the right time." If you go out seeking ideas to start a company, on the other hand, you're much less likely to be successful.

Build Quickly and Test the Market Reaction

If you're going to do something disruptive, there is no way to analyze it on the basis of historical data. The only way to analyze it is by building something relatively simplistic quickly. Then you can test the market reaction. Do people like it? Do they use it? It's impossible to say, "If we build this new thing, people will use it in this way." You have to build a proof of concept. When it's in the marketplace, let people try it, listen intently for their reaction, and iterate based on that feedback.

Bootstrap Your Company

Bootstrap your business for as long as you can. Now, not everything can be bootstrapped; some businesses are too capital-intensive. But if you can prove that customers are willing to pay money for your offer *before* you raise money, you'll get a much higher valuation. On the other hand, if you take the easy road and accept a lot of money up front, you'll suffer a tremendous amount of dilution. A lot of entrepreneurs wind up owning something like 5 percent of their businesses. A great salary on Day One often means significantly less upside later on down the road.

BUSINESS OPERATIONS

Recognize the Life Cycles in Your Team

People have life cycles within companies. From zero to $5 million, you need a sales manager who's entrepreneurial, scrappy, hands-on. But from $5 million to $25 million, you need a real manager who can inspire, and also enforce rules and consistency. Then, from $25 million to $100 million, you need somebody who is much more analytical. And so on. The sales manager who gets you to $5 million is probably not the one who is going to get you to $25 million. Not everyone will transition as your business scales.

CULTURE

Always Reinforce Your Core Values

Every action a CEO or founder takes ripples through an organization. Every decision you make impacts your organization's culture. But the bigger an organization gets, the more important it is for you to explicitly communicate with your team. Deliver the message about why the company is doing what it's doing, how it's delivering more value to customers, and why your team should be proud to work there. Sometimes, delivering that same mantra over and over can seem boring. It can be like a rock band that gets up on stage every night and plays the same songs. But they do it with energy and enthusiasm, and that's what you have to do.

DEPLOYING CAPITAL

Be Respectful with Your Investors' Money

If you invest $100,000 of your own money in something and it goes belly up, at least you've only lost your own money. But when Jeff Bezos or Fidelity invests in MFG.com—that's *Jeff's* money I'm putting at risk. That's money that belongs to Fidelity's investors. Those people are counting on me, and it's a very heavy weight to bear.

FIRING

Share the Blame When Letting People Go

When you have to terminate somebody, it takes a heavy toll. It obviously takes a toll on the person being let go, on their family, but it also takes a toll on the company itself. When I have to fire somebody, I always make sure people realize that if it wasn't a fit, if there was a failure, then it was a failure on both of our parts. It's never, "Screw you; you didn't work out," but "I'm sorry that we didn't assess the fit properly."

HIRING

Let People Reveal Themselves During Interviews

I don't ask profound questions during interviews. I like to talk with people about things that aren't necessarily work related in order to get a feel for them and what they value. If you let people talk, they will reveal a lot. I ask people to stop giving me their sales pitch. "Tell me what you look like with your makeup off." I make it clear that if they work with me, I'm going to find out anyway. How people respond to that question is quite telling about whether or not they're authentic.

LEADERSHIP

Appreciate the Impact of Your Position

I'm a very detail-oriented entrepreneur, especially when it comes to the product, the level of service, and how we interact with our customers. But once you have a layer of management, the CEO is really on a different plane than most of the employees. In the early days, if I saw something that wasn't right I could just walk over and say, "What the fuck, man? You used the wrong color in the logo!" And they'd just go, "Oh, fuck you, I'll fix it!" But if I were to say that to someone now, they'd start crying and go home. That divide builds as your organization grows. In the beginning, you can be brutally honest with people. But in a larger organization, your words have to be much more metered and measured.

MARKET DEVELOPMENT

Don't Try to Prejudice the Marketplace with Money

Throwing money at the adoption curve won't make a dent. There is an unintended brilliance to the market: it will only adopt your offer if that offer adds value. People will always try to prejudice the marketplace with money, but that will never make a significant, long-term difference.

METRICS

Optimize EBITDA Margins

In the early days, you're taking the market by brute force, and your focus will always be on top-line growth. But as the company grows, the focus should shift to EBITDA margins (a measure of a company's operational profitability). Rather than simply trying to build revenues, you should be focused on operational excellence and stripping costs out of the operational structure, and get some cruising efficiency. Rather than asking where revenue growth is, ask, "Are we growing the bottom line by 30 to 40 percent?"

MITCH'S VISION FOR THE FUTURE

Mitch believes manufacturing, broadly defined, is the world's largest industry. Given the state of the global economy, any recovery will depend on a resurrection of that sector. Aware of this fact, President Obama appointed a manufacturing czar in 2009. The following year, Mitch published his thoughts on the position, in an article entitled "If I Were the Manufacturing Czar." In addition to calling for tax reform and TARP funding for the manufacturing sector, Mitch proposed the bold idea of "Special Economic Zones":

"Special Economic Zones (SEZs) like Free Trade Zones have been established in China, India, and even in Iran. By designating SEZs with reduced tax burdens, relaxed or (in some cases) altogether eliminated regulatory requirements, and streamlining bureaucracy and administrative compliance, we can begin to attract real investment and encourage growth outside of that attained merely through a falling dollar. I would also investigate the possibility of helping states develop regional SEZs to distribute technologies or create industrial clusters. This could also have the ancillary effect of delivering high-paying jobs to regions in distress."

Mitch has already remade the manufacturing marketplace. What's left for him now is to remake the economics of the entire industry.

LISA GANSKY

FOUNDER:
OFOTO

INTRODUCING LISA GANSKY

Lisa Gansky is a true entrepreneurial pioneer. GNN (Global Network Navigator), where Lisa became CEO in 1995, is often credited as being the first commercial website. Ofoto was an established photo-sharing site long before digital cameras became ubiquitous. When Lisa discusses the business of IT startups, she speaks with the authority of somebody who has participated from the beginning.

In recent years, technology has advanced to a point that allows Lisa to combine her two great passions: entrepreneurship and environmentalism. In everything Lisa does, there is a clear commitment to sustainability. Dos Margaritas, the charitable organization she founded in 1999, is directly involved in fostering environmentalism and development in South America. But Lisa's commitment to sustainability is even deeper and subtler. Her embrace of "the mesh," where sustainable efficiencies match up exactly with economic ones and excess capacity is eliminated, is the ultimate bid for a sustainable economic system.

As information technology encroaches upon the physical world, online efficiencies can finally start to become tangible realities. When she's unpacking this insight, Lisa sounds professorial, both in the breadth of her knowledge and the confidence of her opinions. But, at heart, she remains a startup junkie who's always looking for a new, disruptive business to found and lead. The next great "mesh" company may very well be that venture.

LISA'S STORY

With Tim O'Reilly and Dale Dougherty, Lisa founded GNN, Global Network Navigator, in 1993. This early portal service was among the first websites to offer clickable ads, which brought it to the attention of the reigning Internet giant of the time: America Online. AOL acquired GNN in 1995, and Lisa became the CEO.

Lisa Gansky: When we started GNN, the Web was still a very new thing and we were already redefining it. We saw it as an opportunity to connect ideas and people all over the world on the kind of level playing field that wasn't available before.

At the time, we were extremely excited, but we weren't necessarily thinking about how much money we would make. It was about creating an incubator for new ideas and new business models. Our goal was to frame what was possible on the Web. The really exciting websites of the moment were, like, feeds of video cameras outside the physics lab at MIT that could tell you whether or not there was Coke in the Coke machine. It was an incredible time for invention.

The GNN team was excited about the AOL sale, but they were also concerned about maintaining their company's integrity. Those concerns turned out to be prescient.

We had mixed feelings about the sale to AOL, but we thought they'd give us a bigger platform. But after being inside there for about a day, it was clear that the acquisition was just a defensive play on their part. AOL was a walled garden: people paid a monthly fee for limited access to the site and the Internet. I thought that needed to change fundamentally, and I was naïve enough to believe that I could effect that change myself. I didn't understand anything about the pressures of being in a highly volatile, valuable, publicly traded company.

GNN was sidelined after AOL changed their model, and I see now that they made the right business decision for them. From a branding perspective, they needed to remain "AOL." There was no room for "GNN." What I learned from the AOL experience is that, after an acquisition, you lose control completely.

THE OFOTO STORY

Ofoto launched their site on December 13, 1999, in a marketplace that was *immediately* competitive—Shutterfly was brought live on the same day. The initial offer was simple: users could store and share JPEGs they uploaded to the site, or they could order standard prints. Gansky and her team released new features over the following two years, until they became a wholly owned subsidiary of Eastman Kodak in 2001 and renamed Kodak EasyShare Gallery. Eastman Kodak has since filed for bankrupcy, and sold the Kodak Gallery to Shutterfly as part of the dissolution.

Lisa regained control in 1999 when she founded Ofoto, pioneering online photo-sharing. The company raised $60 million in its first round of funding and was immediately successful. A major component of their success was a commitment to meeting customer demands.

At Ofoto, our major business starts after Halloween and goes through New Year's. During that window, we made sure our customers got everything they asked for. If you ordered a photo book as a Christmas gift and didn't get it until two days after Christmas, you'd probably get mad, refuse to pay us, and tell everybody that we stink. So we bent over backward during this period, and the investment in doing that was absolutely worth it.

Lisa recognized that other investments might prove less valuable, and carefully avoided the distractions that increased cash flow might have led to.

A few months after we got our Series A, we had a bunch of money and people were constantly coming at us with their ideas du jour. "You should do Ofoto Pro." "You should do Ofoto Lite." It was crazy. I wanted to make it clear that we wouldn't be going down all those paths, so I had T-shirts printed up that said "O-Focus." If you're focusing on the wrong thing, then you should change focus; don't try to do thirty things when you only have the capacity for two.

In 2001, Eastman Kodak purchased Ofoto. This time, Lisa was ready to manage a realistic acquisition.

The ability that you have to control your company postacquisition depends entirely on your ability to maintain your brand and identity. When the Kodak deal came along, my deal was essentially that I would stay at the company for as long as it remained Ofoto. But the second they changed it to *Kodak* something, I'd be out. They tried to alleviate my concerns. They said, "As far as we're concerned, Ofoto acquired Kodak; the lifeboat has become the cruise ship. We need to go where you guys are." I knew the reality was different. As soon as film tanked, they would have to touch the brand.

She was right. As digital cameras became more popular, Kodak's film business began shrinking to zero. The result? The cruise ship remained the cruise ship, and the lifeboat was rebranded. In 2005, Ofoto became the Kodak EasyShare Gallery and Lisa stepped down as CEO.

Today, Lisa is an adviser or investor in numerous startups, including Loose-cubes, TaskRabbit, RelayRides, Pi.pe, Scoot Networks, Squidoo, and GreenBiz.

THE
LISA GANSKY
PLAYBOOK

Just Enough Friction

I know what I'm good at, and I know what I really suck at. The importance of teams and cultures is that they allow you to find people who can go extremely deep in areas where you're personally weak. The reality is that you're hiring people with different and sometimes incompatible personalities, but that's OK. You want enough friction to generate sparks, but no so many that the whole thing burns down.

Immerse Yourself in Ideas PreLaunch

At my first company, I got completely sucked into the specifics of my job before I could get a clear picture of our launch plan. In subsequent projects, I've always set aside ninety days of "soak time," which allows us to become completely immersed in everything we need to know about the business. During that time, we articulate the problem and how we can make it irresistibly fun to solve. How are we going to make a major difference in the marketplace? In the end, we either kill the idea or we go for it.

Define, Refine, Scale

The three components of business are "Define," "Refine," and "Scale." In the Define and Refine stages, you're rapidly designing products, testing them, and improving them. This should be highly iterative and relatively inexpensive. The expensive part is going from Refine to Scale. If you look at companies' B, C, and D funding rounds, those are scaling rounds. Though a lot of businesses fail in the early stages, the real risks are associated with scaling because a failure is much more costly at that late stage.

BOARDS

Build Boards That Break Things

I'm a big fan of breaking things; a lot of interesting cocktails come together in that way. You need people outside your organization who aren't spending all their time telling you how great you are. (If you need that, have some applause go off when you open your office door and get it out of your system.) Your board should engage and disrupt your company; it shouldn't simply affirm it.

CULTURE

Form a "Molecule" with Your First Ten Hires

When you start a company, it's tempting to hire a team of people who have worked together before and finish each other's sentences. It's important to introduce different voices and approaches, though you don't want to end up with a team that looks like a mutant Mr. Potato Head. Your first ten hires should form a molecule. The team will be composed of different elements, but it will cohere.

FOCUSING TIME & ENERGY

Be Willing to Push the Off Button

In startups, people often refuse to turn things off because they get personal. The attitude is "This is *my* project" when it should be "This is *a* project." You need to be willing to turn things off when they're no longer effective. If you hire a great person to work on a project and that project fails, keep the person and end the project. If you need to ramp up your operations for a specific project or season, turn it off when that need goes away. Too many startups keep their sprinklers running in February.

HIRING

Avoid False Positives

The most expensive hiring mistake is a false positive. False negatives are a bummer, but if you pass on a hire only to realize two months later that it was a mistake, at least it's not a very expensive mistake. On the other hand, if you hire someone who is wrong for the role or who just doesn't fit into your company, it could be a huge deal to fix.

MARKET DEVELOPMENT

Create New Categories, Not New Businesses

What gets me excited is looking for ways to create new categories, as opposed to just building a particular business. Instead of just adding a new piece to the environment, new categories reframe the entire ecosystem. Think about the moment when the existing ideas or businesses or products in your category came to be and fundamentally shook things up. That's where the opportunities to effect real change are.

PRODUCT DEVELOPMENT

Paranoia Isn't Always a Bad Thing

Paranoia is a sensory-nervous sensation that can alert you to the possibility that you missed something. Founders are used to putting out fires in their companies, so it's a relief when you can come in to work three days in a row and not have to call the fire department. That's a good thing, because it demonstrates stability. But at the same time, while you're feeling comfortable, something could be changing in the marketplace that will make you completely irrelevant.

TALENT

Meet Your Immediate Needs

Young entrepreneurs often want to hire a core group of people who will stay together forever. But the reality is that, in the first days of your business, you aren't in a position to attract the financial officer or the operations person you'll need in a year or two. You have to realistically ask, "What's essential for *right now*?" The answer to that question is going to be different one or two or five years out. People who join the team early in a company's life can't take it personally when there needs to be a change.

VISION & MISSION

Look Ahead, but Be Realistic

When Ofoto merged with Kodak, they were very complimentary and insisted they would adapt their business to ours. I accepted their assurances, but saw plainly that they'd take over the Ofoto brand as the market continued to go in the inevitable direction of digital photography. Being realistic allowed me to make a secure, graceful exit from the CEO role when the time came and to be prepared for my next step.

LISA'S VISION FOR THE FUTURE

In this book, we've spoken to a number of entrepreneurs about their visions for the future. At least one theme keeps coming up: the future lies in "the mesh." Unlike traditional companies that sell goods and services outright, mesh companies sell access and convenience on an as-needed basis. Nobody has thought more deeply about this topic than Lisa:

"The historical strategy for businesses has been to build out their own infrastructure, their own platform, their own team, and their own customer base. This is both time-consuming and expensive, especially in the early stages. The mesh is a way for us to leverage things that we already have in order to get a lot of scale and utility out of existing assets and tools. It's much less expensive to design interactions with the help of partners than it is to build things from scratch, and it allows early-stage businesses to iterate much more rapidly."

In 2010, Lisa published *The Mesh: Why the Future of Business Is Sharing*, which lays out her beliefs on this topic in much greater detail. Additionally, she launched the global Mesh Community directory at www.meshing.it.

TOM GARDNER

FOUNDER:

THE MOTLEY FOOL

INTRODUCING TOM GARDNER

Tom and his brother Dave didn't just found a company; they launched an entire movement. It began in 1993 when they created a monthly newsletter with the goal of sharing the investment lessons their father had taught them. *The Motley Fool* was aimed at people like them: amateurs with a passion for investment.

With the Motley Fool Channel on AOL, Tom and Dave expanded their reach and set themselves an ambitious goal: to get one million fools on the road to financial freedom. From the beginning, the Fool was both irreverent and insightful. (If he hadn't cofounded the Motley Fool, Tom Gardner would have undoubtedly made it as a standup comic.) As the brothers and their audience grew more knowledgeable and sophisticated, so did the Fool's advice and analysis. In 2008, Tom and Dave's efforts culminated in the launch of Motley Fool Asset Management (MFAM), their own mutual fund.

Throughout their journey, the brothers have remained inherent rebels. They know everything there is to know about Wall Street, but they're not insiders. In an insulated, self-serving, "black-box" sector, the Gardners are incorruptible and altruistic. These days, it's hard to imagine a mutual fund being a trustworthy source of financial advice, but that's exactly what the Motley Fool provides.

TOM'S STORY

Tom Gardner: My father taught my brother, David, and me to invest, but neither of us pursued business or finance at first. We both became English majors. Eventually, we combined our passions and launched *The Motley Fool* as a monthly newsletter in 1993. We didn't have a business plan; all we had was investment advice sent to friends and family. Frankly, I was surprised that anyone subscribed. Who were we but two relatively recent college graduates? But we did have subscribers: thirty-seven of them! The original newsletter was sixteen pages long and cost $48.00 a year.

Without a business plan or even the knowledge of how to incorporate, it was their passion that drove them to explore how to conduct a business. Tom is the first to admit that mastering the role of CEO took longer than he thought.

I thought I'd mastered things earlier than I actually had. If anyone thinks they've achieved mastery, they'll probably discover five years later how little they actually knew when they decided to call themselves a true master.

I like the point Malcolm Gladwell makes in *Outliers*, where he says that it takes 10,000 hours—5 or 6 hours a day for ten years—to achieve mastery in a field. For us, that milestone passed in 2003, but in some ways we were just moving from competence to mastery at that time. It probably took us 15,000 hours instead of 10,000 hours. We're probably slow.

In August 1994, The Motley Fool took a significant leap. The newsletter's circulation was stagnant, so Tom and Dave started broadcasting their advice on a new Internet service called America Online.

Our original model was built around AOL's per-hour fee structure. Users paid $4.00 an hour to use AOL, and we basically got 40¢ for every hour spent on our site. We built our whole business around that model, and we became incredibly profitable. We had a very small employee base and tons of people coming to our site. We went right to the top.

Business was booming, but as an executive Tom found that success brought new questions. Among them: what would he do with his company's profits?

Our first six or seven years, we were all over the place. We talked about starting a Motley Fool Café. We even talked about buying a minor league baseball team! All these things can actually work for an investment organization. It can work, but you've got to be deliberate about why you're making

---

THE MOTLEY FOOL STORY

The Motley Fool started as a monthly newsletter in 1993. The next year, the Fool accepted an offer to join AOL as a content provider, rapidly becoming the most popular area of AOL's finance section. In 1995, *The Economist* wrote, "Part of The Fool's attraction is that it stands out as an ethical oasis in an area that is fast becoming a home to charlatans running penny-stock schemes to woo the gullible."

These days, the Motley Fool provides a plethora of financial advisement and services. Their mutual funds, launched during the economic turmoil of the late 2000s with an emphasis on small and midsized American holdings, have exceeded expectations. The Independence Fund (FOOLX), which holds a minimum of 50 percent American companies, has a one-year trailing return of nearly 16 percent.

each acquisition. Does this fit with your purpose? Will it help you meet your outcome? But in the beginning, our only question was, "Would this be cool or would this not be cool?" Today we have our entire investment strategy written out on a single page. We call it the Road Map. And we can state our purpose in a single line: "To help the world invest. Better."

Tom's next challenge arose when the Internet entered the next phase.

> *"Every entrepreneur needs to ask why they are being paid."*

In 2001, AOL changed their business model to a flat-rate monthly fee. Suddenly, the usage payments we were getting went to zero. We were screwed. We had hundreds of thousands of people coming through our site each month, but only one customer: AOL. If you have one customer and that customer changes directions, you're in trouble.

Stage Two was advertising, and we had a lucky strike. About a half dozen discount brokers were paying us quite a bit of money to advertise on The Fool, that business went away when the brokerage market dropped. We had eight customers carrying our business, but all in one industry, and they all cut their ad budget by 80 percent. It was one thing when the bad news came from AOL. But when the bad news came from our advertisers, I thought, "Fool me once, shame on you. Fool me twice, shame on me."

Tom had to act fast to reclarify the company's function in the marketplace.

In 2002, we realized that the greatest thing we could do is create a membership business. Today, we serve thousands of people directly: they pay us and renew at the end of each year. Once we learned how to diversify our customer base, it brought tremendous stability. After a bumpy seventeen years, we've learned why our customers stick with us. Every entrepreneur needs to ask why they are being paid. But when we talked to customers and asked them what they needed, they said, "I want great investment returns." They wanted to learn, but what they really want is great returns.

Their next opportunity arose out of an uncommon place: Major League Baseball.

It all started when Barry Zito, a left-handed pitcher, signed a seven-year, $126 million contract with the San Francisco Giants. I found out about the deal when Zito's father called The Fool: "I read your newsletters. I believe in you guys. My son just signed a $126 million contract and I want you guys to manage that money."

We were flattered, but our first response was, "We can only give you a newsletter." But then our customer-service team made the same point. When people call to cancel, we had listened. Again and again, the reason was, "I don't have the time to manage my own investments." Or related factors, like "I don't have the temperament for this." There was a huge opportunity there—many people who don't want to be making stock-by-stock decisions. We finally woke up to that in 2008 and built our own mutual fund.

THE
TOM GARDNER
PLAYBOOK

Define the Perfect Outcome

There's more than one way to succeed, but you have to nail down what outcome you are seeking. Do you want to be the fastest-growing software company in your first five years—like Netscape—and then sell to America Online? That would be very profitable. Netscape is completely irrelevant today, but was it a success or a failure?

Someone else might say, "Get the concept. Raise some capital. Kick butt. Cash out. That's my game plan." That's fine as long as it's clear and deliberate. Know yourself. Are you out after you go public? Or is this something you want to do for the rest of your life?

If you don't know your outcome right away, that's OK. I've definitely talked to a lot of entrepreneurs who had breaks with their partners and founders because they hadn't nailed down their ideal outcome, and there was a huge disagreement late in the game. You don't want to end up in that position.

Diversify Your Long-Term "Customer" Base

A key for any entrepreneur is to ask, "What are my sources of cash? Who are my real, paying customers?" You may have millions of visitors to your site, but if it's a free site, those aren't your paying customers. Your advertisers are. It's important to recognize your actual revenue streams and diversify them. No matter how successful you seem, you can end up in trouble if all of your money comes from the same place. A diverse customer base can bring stability to your business.

Be Transparent with Your Entire Community

Kip Tindell, the CEO and founder of Container Store, came to speak at the Motley Fool. He told us that their communication policy is to internally share every important piece of information with every employee at every point of time. That's their standard, and it's one that more entrepreneurs should strive for.

TOM'S BEST ADVICE

BUSINESS OPERATIONS

Review Your Purpose Statement Every Year

I believe an organization should review its purpose statement once a year. The primary aim is to reaffirm it, but in an active way. I believe the great organizations see their purpose statements changed once every five to ten years. No company and no individual should be put in position to stop learning and growing. And one of the most educational journeys to be on is the journey toward your purpose.

CULTURE

Create an Environment That People Would Make Sacrifices to Join

One of our core values at the Motley Fool is "Be Fun—Revel in Your Work." The list is long of the people I admire who have taken pay cuts to take on jobs that they flat-out love. If you get this right in your career, you'll be on a path to mastery and to prosperity . . . without working another day in your life.

CUSTOMER DEVELOPMENT

Iterate Constantly

The Internet is the greatest test-and-learn platform in human history. The companies that know this are acquiring customers less expensively and more continually.

DEPLOYING CAPITAL

Deploy Capital Like an Investor

The best deployers of capital are those who lead business and who invest. This is one of Warren Buffett's key principles. Superior capital deployment is a primary responsibility of the CEO and their leadership team, and in my experience, trained investors are best at this.

FINANCE

Find a CFO Who Will Watch Every Dollar

The most important hire that an entrepreneur can make is the CFO—someone who counts every dollar, challenges every assumption, raises capital with sound long-term contracts, and pushes the company through survival mode.

HIRING

Don't Try to Solve Every Problem with a Hire

I learned an important lesson from Marti Morfitt, the former CEO of CNS (the company that makes the Breathe-Right strips you see athletes wearing on the bridge of their noses). There is almost always a better option than taking on another full-time employee. The key word is *almost*. Growing businesses definitely need to hire, but the very best of them do so very carefully, with a strong focus on finding people who share their core values.

Every entrepreneur—every businessperson—will tell you to "hire great people." That's fine, but how do you define that? My brother Dave came up with a clear guideline: "Hire people who are smarter than you are."

HUMAN RESOURCES

Do Away with "Sick Days" and "Vacation Time"

We have a performance culture at the Motley Fool. We want you to be a high performer and we're going to push you. But if you need to be out every morning for the next three weeks because there's something going on with one of your children at school, you're out. Do it. Make your time. It's not just that I trust you. It's that I want you to be fired up. So, at the Fool, there's no vacation policy, no sick day policy. But we do review you every ninety days. We're checking in.

METRICS

Never Slacken Your Goals

The more you measure and the higher the standards you create, the better the odds that you'll succeed. But once you stop counting your score and start kicking the golf ball out from behind the tree, your organization will begin its decline.

TALENT

Build Systems That Foster Talent

You can hire real talent, but if you don't have systems in place to develop that talent every month of the year, and every year for the rest of their career, you're going to leak away infinitely more talent than you'll ever hire.

VISION & MISSION

Value Operations as Highly as Vision

In my experience, the very, very best operators are the ones who leave their dog out of the fight on strategy. They simply want a defined vision toward which they can plan and execute, and recognize that providing that vision is someone else's job. The best organizations see the brilliant strategist and the brilliant operating leader as equally important.

TOM'S VISION FOR THE FUTURE

With the launch of their asset-management platform, the Fool stepped into the center of the investment world, but Tom remembers that they started on the outside. They still offer their original product: great, inexpensive advice for do-it-yourself investors. Now they also offer to manage millions for everyone, from Barry Zito to your next-door neighbor.

One of the remarkable things about the Motley Fool's new efforts in money management is that Tom has retained the company's dedication to transparency. He has a challenge to issue to other financial people: "Why, with the simple tools that are available on the Internet, can't two customers of any broker, planner, advisor, financial fund manager, anyone, speak to each other? Because if they did, they'd get a lot of second opinions and people would realize who the bad brokers are out there. So in our case, our customers are always able to talk to every other customer at the Motley Fool about anything."

Given their reputation for ethical behavior and good advice, Tom refers to their mutual funds as "the next logical step." It's not hard, however, to see the Fool's ascendency during a time of public disgust with the rest of the investment world as something bigger: the arrival of a new kind of financier.

FOUNDER:

BLURB

INTRODUCING EILEEN GITTINS

Eileen Gittins is a self-described technology geek who studied English and journalism at UC Berkeley and ended up falling in love with photography for its ability to tell stories. After gigs at Eastman Kodak (she got her first job there by pestering them until they caved) and the launch of two successful startups (Salsa and Personify), she wanted to pay tribute to some of the "Bay Area Renaissance people" she had worked with in her various ventures by photographing them. But when she then tried to assemble those portraits into a format that gave them depth—a book—she was shocked to discover that with all the great digital and other types of innovations out there, you still couldn't create your own high-quality book without spending tens of thousands of dollars. As an entrepreneur, she knew she'd found a problem to solve that married her love of photography, technology, and books.

In 2005, she started Blurb, a do-it-yourself, book-creation platform that special-izes in high-quality, four-color books in a variety of formats. Blurb has not only changed the conversation about book publishing, but has also helped millions of people around the world tell the stories that inspire them. In 2012, the company will do an excess of $85 million in revenues.

EILEEN'S STORY

Eileen Gittins was already well established as an entrepreneur and an executive before founding Blurb in 2005. After holding a variety of positions at Eastman Kodak and launching a startup that didn't work, Eileen followed up by helping to found Salsa, where she was VP and general manager.

Salsa was a part of Wall Data Inc., an early (pre-Web) software company. In her time there, Gittins built a department with more than one hundred employees and helped launch seventeen new products. One of those products allowed computer users without significant technical expertise to build their own databases. Giving control to end customers was a key component in Eileen's vision.

Eileen Gittins: The Internet was poised to explode, and I wanted in. The Internet was shaping up to be where consumer experience and technology were converging—on steroids. It was 1996, and I was still working out of Seattle. But if Seattle was the church of where the Internet was happening, Silicon Valley was the Vatican. I knew I had to move there.

It was in Silicon Valley that Eileen started really connecting with the larger tech and venture-capital communities, and where she built her next two companies, Personify and Verb. But these were "bubble plays"; the companies weren't immediately profitable, so second-round funding was hard to come by.

Because there just wasn't enough funding available at that time, most of the startups that weren't instantly returning profits were forced to either close their doors or sell. It wasn't a time for resting on laurels or hanging out in your villa in France—it was a whirlwind time, like a boot camp for several years running, after which I spent some time not in startup mode, consulting.

One of Eileen's consulting clients at the time was an investment bank, which made her yearn again for something more creative. She began taking pictures of some of the entrepreneurs she had worked with over the years, and one by one, they began to share their stories with her.

During this process, for the first time, I got to know them as people and not just as colleagues. I wanted to somehow share that content with all the members of that group, to sort of honor that community. At first I thought I would create a website, then I thought, "This is supposed to be a gift to them," and decided to make a book. I realized a book is the best vehicle on the planet through which to create and share something with lasting

THE BLURB STORY

Back in 2005, Eileen Gittins was surprised to realize that though Adobe and desktop publishing had been around for years, there was a complete lack of resources when it came to easy, fun, high-quality, do-it-yourself book creation. As a systems person, Eileen thought, "How do you build book-designing software for people who aren't book designers, and how could printers profitably produce a book in a quantity of one?"

After identifying the challenge and the business model, she had to convince investors that even though the world was going digital, creating a print-on-demand book platform was viable. Her passion and track record enabled her to get her first round of investment. The Blurb website launched in 2006. Since then, they have expanded their services to offer a wide range of print formats, to launch a variety of apps and other storytelling devices, and to provide an e-book offering. In 2010, *Inc.* magazine named Blurb "The Fastest-Growing Media Company."

relevance and meaning. The problem with the Web is that "lasting" and "meaning" are not words associated with a typical Web experience.

That decision is what led Eileen down the path of establishing Blurb. She discovered that it would be impossible to do what she wanted to do—create fifty beautiful, glossy, high-quality hardcover copies of the commemorative book she envisioned—without spending less than $15,000 and printing far more copies than she actually needed. Thus, the idea for Blurb was born.

I wanted four-color and a good-sized book, but I soon realized that not only would I have to spend a lot of money I didn't have, but I would also have to become an expert in printing and book design. So I gave up. But the idea just wouldn't go away. I thought, "This is crazy. Why does it have to be so hard?" I'd bet on the future of desktop meets e-commerce on the back-end. I knew about digital printing and was printing out photos at home via Photoshop. Come on! There had to be an integration opportunity there. Finally, I got irritated enough that someone wasn't out there fixing the problem for me that I decided, "I'll be the one to fix it."

Given her past experience with startups, Eileen's next step was to carefully analyze the market opportunity, focusing on three central questions. The first was, "Is the opportunity big enough?"

My next question was, "Could we make money on a print run of one book?" We were looking to disrupt the publishing industry, where typically publishers are venture capitalists for authors: investing a lot up front, taking on a lot of risk, and hoping that they hit one or two out of the park. We needed to find a model that allowed us to profit on books that sold a single copy. The last question was, "Will I go to jail? What happens the first time somebody claims copyright or plagiarism on a book we released?" We would need to do everything we could to minimize our liability.

Minimizing costs and liabilities weren't the only issues Eileen and her team faced. They also needed to minimize the amount of time it would take people who weren't book designers to make a beautiful book. They solved this problem by creating BookSmart, a simple, free, online tool for laying out and designing books. Blurb's final hurdle was to engage a printing industry optimized for much larger print runs.

We wanted to be good at the online experience of making, sharing, and selling books, but we didn't want to be our own printers. We needed to get people in print manufacturing excited about this business. It should have been easy; we would be providing them with the cleanest file they'd ever seen. Print on demand isn't seasonal, so printers can keep their capacity running full-time. And because we'd be a technology company, we could write to APIs and deliver the files in any format they wanted.

It turns out there are two kinds of printers in the world: those who are in the printing business and those in the systems business, meaning word processing and fulfillment. We needed the latter. But the obstacle was that their usual business involved shipping two orders a day, each of which would go out on palettes. We'd be in the business of shipping 5,000 orders a day, each of them going out separately in a FedEx envelope. In the very beginning, we worked with one player who had some nascent technology, and a second we brought in. Thereafter, we had enough volume to attract more players.

All that rigorous technical, financial, and market analysis was always in service of a single goal Eileen never lost sight of.

THE
EILEEN GITTINS
PLAYBOOK

Be a Storyteller

She jokes that her title should be "chief storyteller." It's through telling stories—about the business, the founding, the customers—that people take on the spirit of the company. Blurb holds its own town halls every month, where Eileen uses the occasion to tell stories about what she's hearing out in the marketplace. Stories drive clarity and team alignment, and they get people motivated. Leadership is, in part, the art of storytelling—it's a discipline, from your pitch to the story of the company; from personal stories to specific "sparkplug stories" that can be used to to motivate your team.

Make Sure You Aren't Seeing Your Idea Through Rose-Colored Glasses

Your bias will get you started, but it can also kill you. You need to practice tough love early—is this an idea for the next five to seven years of your life? Every entrepreneur needs to be in love with their idea, but you also have to be willing to listen to others telling you your idea is crap—that's how your idea gets honed into a lasting opportunity. That's the dichotomy: you're simultaneously paring down your mission and reaching a point where you can't not do it, in the process putting yourself out there nakedly for all the world to see—just as an artist would.

Think in Threes

What are the three questions you need to answer about your idea in order to validate it as a business, rather than just as a fun, cool thing you want to do? Coming up with these questions is as difficult as coming up with the answers, but limiting yourself to three is a forcing function. Stay focused on the three things that really matter.

Unpack the Entire Business

There is one question that every founder needs to ask. What is the size of the opportunity and can you reach it with your resources? The market needs to be fairly large, growing, and within your reach.

EILEEN'S BEST ADVICE

BOARDS

Cultivate Outsider Perspectives

One way to keep yourself honest is by cultivating people who are willing to say, "This isn't working." They're the ones who are really going to advance your business. In fact, as painful as it is, every founder needs to have a board of directors. They're going to present a more dispassionate, colder point of view—an outsider's point of view. When you have a boss, they force you to think about the metrics of your business rather than getting buried in all the other stuff. That's really important.

BUSINESS OPERATIONS

Fit Current Frameworks, Even When You Seek to Change Them

With Blurb, we entered an industry that had an extremely institutional production process. The manufacturers that we needed for our product just didn't deal with low-volume, high-frequency orders; they dealt with the polar opposite. Even though the high barrier to print-publication was exactly what Blurb is meant to demolish, that didn't mean I could refuse to play ball with the printers who controlled my access to the manufacturing. Our solution was to take the reins by tailoring software for their process. If we couldn't provide printers that easy transition, Blurb would not have been possible.

CULTURE

Enable Global Reach with Global Production

You have to decide whether you're going to be a domestic business or a global business. It's very expensive to ship products from the United States to other parts of the world. You might as well dip them in diesel before sending them out, because it's just a really big carbon footprint. If you want a global business, you have to be committed to worldwide locations.

FIRING

Ineffective Team Members Cause More Harm Than Terminations

Whenever I've waited too long to fire someone, my excuse has always been that it would harm morale. "If we lose this person, the team's gonna be destroyed." The obvious truth is that the rest of the team already knows when somebody needs to go. In fact, they'll think you're an idiot if you don't make a move. As CEOs, we're often insulated from this obvious truth.

LEADERSHIP

Don't Write Your Manifesto; Live It

As you start hiring people who are not part of your inner circle, you need to communicate what really matters in your company. Who do you want to be? What's your manifesto? Your manifesto shouldn't be a mission statement that you write and put up on the wall; it should be consistently stated through all your actions.

PRODUCT DEVELOPMENT

Ensure Success by Building Successful Partners

If we had to build everything from scratch each time we brought a new product to market, it would be a huge operation. Product development would become so costly that it would stagnate completely. Having worldwide supply-chain partners gives us much more flexibility. We make it a priority to help them succeed, but we do so in an advisory role. We don't invest directly in their businesses.

TALENT

Grant Your Employees Autonomy, Mastery, and Purpose

In his book *Drive*, behavioral scientist Daniel Pink writes that three elements really motivate people: autonomy, mastery, and purpose. It's easy to see that in a company like ours. Engineers absolutely want a role in defining how they build; they want autonomy. Then, they have to demo their work to the whole company; that provides mastery. Finally, it's very important that a startup culture be motivated by Purpose with a capital *P*.

VISION & MISSION

Maintain a Core Purpose

Building a startup is just hard; it's an emotional roller coaster from day to day. Ask somebody at a startup how they're doing, and they're likely to respond, "Ask me ten minutes from now." If you don't have a key mission that explains why you're all here, you'll suffer major attrition. The center will not hold.

EILEEN'S VISION FOR THE FUTURE

Books have always been a solo experience (both creating and consuming) while at the same time being fundamentally social (ergo book groups, book readings). Much like movies, we experience books as individuals, but then can't wait to begin talking about what we've read with friends.

Strangely, the actual physical form of the book has likely impeded the book's inherent power as provocateur. When too much time elapses between the reading and the opportunity to discuss . . . well, we all know what happens. Life moves on and an engaging discussion that should have sparked, doesn't.

How many times have you read something and thought, "Really?" or "That's just beautiful." What if you were reading a digital book and could have that conversation right there and then—without leaving the book? Or what if you could subscribe to a book—where the subscription was a curated conversation among a community with shared interests, and moderated by the author herself?

That's what Blurb is building: a platform to enable authors to create inherently social books and readers to participate in the conversation, or not. The future will be the campfire again—where the telling and the collective response are experienced live and in concert.

SETH GOLDMAN

FOUNDER:
HONEST TEA

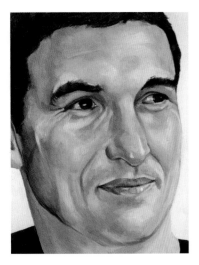

INTRODUCING SETH GOLDMAN

Seth Goldman is a marathon runner, both literally and in his approach to building companies. When he started Honest Tea in 1998, he set out to build a beverage company that would change the definition of what a beverage should be. The standards he set for the company are immovable: fair trade, low sugar and caloric content, a commitment to organic ingredients. But within that formula, there was also room to be creative about the way he built the business.

Seth is clearly brilliant. He has degrees from Harvard and Yale, and hails from a family in which both parents were professors with a history of commitment to education and activism. He's also a patient and powerful listener, willing to test new ideas so long as they don't violate his core mission.

There are many different types of personalities that can build companies. Seth is a clear example of one type in particular: the thoughtful, caring parent. He devotes constant attention to his work, his employees, his customers—and his own family—and he expends infinite patience in nurturing their growth. In a little over ten years, Seth has built a company with more than $70 million in sales. He has made such an impact on his industry that Honest Tea is now a part of Coca-Cola, the company that once exemplified the attitude about beverages that Seth set out to change. And yet, when we spoke, Seth mentioned the fact that a former intern now runs Honest Tea's West Coast division is one of his proudest achievements. It's a clear indication of his priorities and his character.

SETH'S STORY

Like a lot of entrepreneurs, Seth got his start with a lemonade stand and has since remained committed to working in and transforming the beverage industry.

Seth Goldman: My commitment to change formed early. My parents were professors, so our dinner conversations weren't typically about sports or anything trivial. From an early age we were taught to think globally, with the expectation that we would do something we believed in. After I earned my MBA from the Yale School of Management, I knew that a traditional finance job wouldn't be enough.

Seth needed to determine what manner of company he would found. Sustainable businesses need to sustain themselves through profit, so he had to find something that would make a positive impact on the world while remaining a cost-effective, marketable product.

Since high school, I've been a runner, and I would get frustrated when I reached for a drink after a run. There were always new drinks available, but there was nothing that was 20 or 30 calories a serving that I could get excited about. Years later, when I was going for a run in New York after an investment presentation, I realized that this idea of a less-sweet drink was still an opportunity. It was something I had no expertise in, but I'd been aware of the *absence* of this kind of product since high school.

At that point, two fortuitous events pushed me to keep going with my idea. First, an investment my father had made in my name seventeen years earlier matured and I got a $50,000 check. At the same time, a former professor from Yale, Barry Nalebuff, came back from a fact-finding trip in India, where he was studying the tea industry for a case study. He learned that nearly all American brands used cheap and inferior tea leaves. He even had a name for the alternative: Honest Tea.

I took the train to Barry's house and we sat around his kitchen table and talked it out for pretty much the whole day. We didn't really spend much time on details and minor business differences. The real question was, "What is your life plan and how does founding this fit into it?" Barry never became involved in the day-to-day operations of the business, but he has been critical to our success. Neither of us had any experience in the beverage industry before we started Honest Tea, but he knows the right questions to ask.

THE HONEST TEA STORY

Honest Tea got its start in 1998, when Whole Foods took on an order of 15,000 bottles of the tea that he'd brewed in his kitchen. The company grew steadily over the next few years, and as it became profitable, Honest Tea decided to distinguish itself further from the rest of the beverage market. In 2001, more than half of their offered products became organic. In 2002, when legislation was enacted that brought the USDA Organic seal into being, Honest Tea was ahead of the game in qualifying for the certification.

By the end of the decade, Honest Tea had become known as one of the world's top green companies, with annual sales of more than $70 million. In 2008, Coca-Cola purchased a 40 percent stake in the company. Two years later, the *Washington Post* named Honest Tea one of the top five companies of 2010.

Seth had the right idea, the right partner, and some capital. The next step was to find demand by looking in the right place.

In February 1998, we produced the world's first organic, bottled tea—in my kitchen. We put a sample in a thermos and took it to Whole Foods. They asked for 15,000 bottles, which were on the shelves by June.

As the business expanded, Seth never deviated from the principles on which the company was founded.

As we started to grow, people were pushing us to spend and move more aggressively. But the marathon runner in me reacted against that. The beverage industry is very capital intensive; in order to make it work, you have to deal in tenths of a penny and understand every little component. In the years since we've started Honest Tea, we've seen a lot of other bottled teas boom and bust along the way. The contrast between us was really clear at the trade shows. They'd put on this splashy display, staying in fancy hotels and spending all sorts of money. We had a simple booth and shared rooms at the Best Western. What I always told people then was that we'd be back next year, and those other brands would come and go. That's always proven to be the case.

When we started, nobody else offered low-sugar, low-calorie tea. But now, the rest of the beverage industry is moving toward us. Eventually, even Coca-Cola took the bet that this is where consumers were headed and bought a minority stake in Honest Tea.

Seth had a product he could believe in and revenues that allowed him to avoid the expensive traps that new entrants have to deal with in order to attract consumers. But, make no mistake, he does promote his brand with flare.

We don't spend our money on advertising the way other companies do. We're always looking for alternative ways to connect with people, so we engage in guerrilla marketing campaigns that are unique in our sector. We've leveraged our retail relationships to introduce widespread product sampling—we even released a rap video ("Rethink What You Drink" features Seth himself on vocals). In particular, we got a lot of attention with our Honest Students campaign last year. We went out to a number of different cities and put up these free-standing booths that offered bottles for a dollar each, on the honor system. We wanted to see how honest people were. It was a fun and interactive way for people to get introduced to our brand.

That's not to say that we haven't made mistakes. Looking back, our really bad decisions often involved moving away from our core task: to create and market great-tasting drinks. For example, we owned a bottling plant for six years. It was a disaster. It took up a lot of time. We got entangled with some shady partners, some legal issues arose from it—it was a bad investment in many ways. All told, we probably lost a million dollars. It could have taken us under. Less dramatically, we went into tea bags. It didn't take us under, but it certainly didn't help us because there wasn't a margin in it and there wasn't growth in it; worst of all there was no meaningful differentiation between our product and the rest of the marketplace.

It wasn't always easy and profitable for Honest Tea to stick to its guns. But fighting the temptation to bow to traditional advice has worked in the long run.

Early on, we had distributors who told us that our product wasn't going to have any appeal in the marketplace because it wasn't sweet enough. But we refused to add the level of sugar they wanted. We were confident that the world didn't need another sweet tea. In the long term, that allowed us to create something we believed in.

THE
SETH GOLDMAN
PLAYBOOK

Be an Activist

The challenge, as I see it, is not, "How do you sell products?" It's, "How do you communicate your beliefs to people and make them into believers?" You want everybody who interacts with your brand to be excited about it. That could mean getting distributors to give you more shelf space, or getting your employees to believe in the opportunities you offer. It also means making your customers feel invested in your cause. To me, that's been a much more powerful driver than the financial incentive.

Develop and Grow Talent

It is crucial to develop your own talent. To do that, you have to offer more to your employees than great compensation. You have to make it clear to them that as the company grows, they can grow along with it. People who start as interns need to believe that they'll one day have the opportunity to run entire divisions. It's a great way to organically develop your internal leadership, and it's also very satisfying. You shouldn't only produce great products. Produce great people.

Don't Stray from Your Core Mission

Often, our really bad decisions can be traced back to moving away from our core task. Sticking to values will help you survive. When you stick to what you do best, you are much more likely to differentiate yourself in the marketplace. Nonessential endeavors will only distract you. Run on belief, and that will help you overcome a lot of other challenges.

BUSINESS OPERATIONS

Structure Financing Alongside Investors with Warrants Next to Stock

Instead of providing penny stock to our founders, we provided warrants. This allowed us to invest alongside our investors on the same terms and gain more control of the company as we grew.

CUSTOMER DEVELOPMENT

Develop a Long-Term Relationship with Your Customers

One interesting aspect of our growth has been the great response we've received to our Honest Kids line. It's really fueled a lot of our sales today. More important, it helps assure future sales. Honest Kids is for children who are still drinking from juice pouches. But those kids are going to be Honest Tea and Honest Ade drinkers in the decades ahead.

DEPLOYING CAPITAL

Be Aware of Every Cost

In order to make a business work, you have to understand every component and deal in tenths of a penny. For us, that means understanding the cost of every label and every bottle cap. Whatever your industry, you have to break down the business to its very smallest components and then build it up again.

LEADERSHIP

Model the Behavior You Expect of Your Employees

We want our employees to have a healthy balance between work and life, so we always tell people to take holidays and make time for their families. But if the other executives and I are working late every night, it's hard to be credible. So I try hard to leave the office by 5:30 p.m. every day. I coach my son's baseball team. If there's something meaningful happening with my family, I'm almost always able to structure work around that. Obviously, I'm committed to the work and I'm not afraid to work late into the night if I have to. But life is happening while you work. I want to make sure I have real time together with my family, and I want the same for our employees.

MARKETING

Engage in Guerrilla Marketing

It's not only about having a unique message, but presenting it in a unique way. You should always look for alternative ways to connect with people. Guerrilla marketing campaigns can be very effective, and they allow you to discover fun and interactive ways to introduce people to your brand.

PRODUCT DEVELOPMENT

Balance Your Values Against Market Realities

When we started offering a 17-calorie drink, the average tea was 100 calories per serving and we were just too far from where consumers were. We upped it to 30 calories, but we didn't have to keep it there for long. During the low-carb craze that started right after we came to market, people started reading labels on beverages for almost the first time. Two of the biggest segments to lose share at that time were beer and orange juice. But our low-calorie, low-sugar alternative was exactly what people were looking for.

TALENT

Empower Your Employees

You want employees to care about the long-term performance of the company, so you should give them as much control over their part in the business as you can, including giving them ownership of their P&L. Stock options are a very direct way of making them feel invested in the future of the company, and a good way to retain them. But, more important, hire people who are passionate about your core mission and make it clear that they can have a direct impact on moving it forward. There's a real satisfaction to building something you believe in; employees should share in that satisfaction.

WORKING FOR YOURSELF

Use Partners as Sounding Boards

When you start a company, you're basically jumping off a cliff. You don't have any sense of where you're going to land, what to do when you land—or what you should be doing in midair. It's very, very scary. But it's much easier when you have somebody to commiserate with who knows what you're going through, and who you know will always be on your side.

SETH'S VISION FOR THE FUTURE

Seth is looking forward to the growth of the organic foods sector, and to continuing his company's role as a leader in it. "The whole organic foods industry is maybe 3 percent of the total U.S. food industry, but then you look at some categories like yogurt, where it's closer to 10 percent. And so I believe that within five years, 10 percent of all food and beverage will be organic," he says.

Seth's commitment is particularly remarkable, given the tactical considerations that first led him to use organic ingredients. "At first, we did it for purely business reasons; our largest target customer was Whole Foods. But as we've learned more about it, we've decided that it's the right thing for our environment and the right thing for our health. If any chemicals are sprayed on tea leaves, those chemicals stay on the leaves until hot water is poured on them, then they get washed into the drink. And it isn't just consumers who suffer. We started to learn about the impact of those toxins on the ecosystem."

Seth is a believer. "Many people say that as you get older you get a little more conservative. But when it comes to what our business can be doing with respect to the environment, and our employee standards, I've become much more progressive."

JOE GREEN

FOUNDER:
CAUSES

INTRODUCING JOE GREEN

It's a little hard to believe that Joe Green was born in the 1980s. He's a character straight out of midcentury radical politics: the laid-back community organizer. It's easy to imagine him wandering the streets of Daley's Chicago with a clipboard and a box of leaflets, advocating for better housing conditions on the South Side. Many of the entrepreneurs I've spoken with have referred to classic works on company building like Chip Conley's *Peak*, Steve Blank's *The Four Steps to the Epiphany*, or Jim Collins's *Good to Great*. With complete sincerity, Joe told me to read Saul Alinsky's *Rules for Radicals*.

In another decade, Joe might have invented picket lines or wildcat strikes. But with his college roommate, Mark Zuckerberg, he has found a way to redefine activism for our time. His organization, Causes, leverages social networks to globalize activism, as a newer venture, NationBuilder.

Joe's path is an important reminder of the wide variety of directions that the same purpose can take. He began in traditional politics, managing phone banks for John Kerry's presidential campaign. The same impulse prompted him to build a website (Essembly.com) and, finally, a category-defining Facebook app. His motivation has remained consistent and pure. In the future, it is certain to open many new paths.

JOE'S STORY

Causes is one of the most innovative charitable organizations of the past decade, but it grew out of Joe's commitment to traditional grassroots organizing and the amazing human connections it gives rise to.

Joe Green: When I was working on John Kerry's campaign in 2004, I helped organize phone banks in Arizona, which was an important swing state in that election. The volunteers' commitment was extraordinary. One woman could only use one arm, so it was very difficult for her to pick up the phone, dial numbers, hang it up, and so forth. Another volunteer was a Vietnamese woman who both didn't speak a lot of English and had a speech impediment. So we teamed them up: the Vietnamese woman would dial and the other lady would talk on the phone. At most companies, unfortunately, that would make no sense, because you inherently want to do as much as you can with the fewest number of people. But at a volunteer organization it's awesome; you're getting stuff done and now these people are inspiring everybody else. Even if someone is sitting in a corner doing nothing, if they're happy and adding energy to the room, it's a net positive.

Despite his enthusiasm for old-school phone banks and door-to-door campaigning, Joe was one of the first people in the world to realize that grassroots organizing was about to be revolutionized. It started when he discovered a site called Friendster and talked with his Harvard roommate about it.

If you had asked me in college if I was going to work for a for-profit, much less start one, I would've thought you were crazy. But grassroots organizing is all about working through people's networks. Then when Friendster came along, I realized I could actually see what people's networks looked like. I tried to convince Zuck [Facebook founder Mark Zuckerberg] to start a political social network. Instead, he started a college one. I didn't join Facebook because I was still passionate about politics, so I went to work for the Kerry campaign.

But this networking idea kept nagging at me. When I got back to Harvard from the campaign, I started this site called Essembly. I had no idea what I was doing. I got together some buddies from high school to code the thing in my friend's borrowed guest house in New Jersey. Our angel investor was an oil and gas guy from Pennsylvania who Mark introduced me to.

THE CAUSES STORY

Causes expands on the idea behind Joe's first venture, Essembly.com, a nonpartisan social network with a focus on politics. Like Essembly, Causes is agnostic. Users can create or join any number of social causes—charitable, religious, political, or otherwise. Originally planned as a website, Causes was launched as a Facebook app. Today, it is one of the largest apps on the site: more than 100 million Facebook users have contributed $40 million to nearly half a million causes.

Essembly evolved when, in 2006, Joe met Napster founder and former Facebook president Sean Parker.

We spent the summer of 2006 wandering around Los Angeles, hanging out at various Coffee Beans and thinking pretty broadly about how we could organize opinion on the Internet. That was how we ended up with Causes. One of the core ideas was that people have a desire to be altruistic, but getting them from motivation to action is pretty hard. We realized that relying on people's relationships with other people is the key to activating them.

> *"[P]eople have a desire to be altruistic, but getting them from motivation to action is pretty hard."*

Causes was originally conceived as a website, but before launching in 2007, a curious "movement" on his old roommate's network caused him to reconsider.

Before we started the company, Sean and I had been observing the viral characteristics of various causes. One of the first things that happened after Facebook launched the news feed was that a lot of protest groups sprang up to try getting rid of it. The funny thing was that the only reason these protests grew was *because* of the news feed.

Another type of group we noticed growing a lot were the ones that said they would send a dollar to Darfur or some other charity for every thousand people who joined their group. There was no evidence that this was actually true, but those groups grew very fast. That reminded me of one of the all-time classic chain-emails: "Every time you forward this email, Bill Gates will donate a penny to charity." That obviously couldn't be true, but this was back in the era when people thought Bill Gates was omniscient.

Joe and his team decided to make Causes a Facebook app. It was a fortuitous choice. Within weeks of launching, they had a million members. Soon thereafter, they hit upon a model for scaling at an even faster pace and generating revenue.

In late 2008, the Facebook sales team called us about a cause-marketing deal they were working on with Ben & Jerry's. This was around the time of Obama's inauguration, and they had a new flavor called "Yes Pecan."

As part of launching the flavor, they wanted to make a donation to Common Cause, a nonprofit that focuses on campaign finance reform. We launched a campaign announcing that Ben & Jerry's would donate a dollar to the organization every time somebody joined the cause. It worked so well that in a couple of hours, the $50,000 they had budgeted was gone.

We thought, "Well, this is very interesting!"

It took time to develop, but Joe was close to finding the model—philanthropic matching for Cause membership—that would be the primary driver of revenues and charity dollars at Causes.

THE
JOE GREEN
PLAYBOOK

Compare Fleshed-Out Ideas

The first stage of any startup is to talk through some really high-level ideas, and then at some point you start to take one of those ideas and drill down. Draw some sketches. Do some market research. Mock up a few wireframes. The mistake a lot of people make is once you get to that level of specificity, it's tempting to stay there. But it's important to go back up and do the whole process twenty more times. It's much more labor intensive and tiring to compare theoretical ideas than it is to compare fleshed-out ones, but it's crucial. Then you can get a better picture of how they translate into things that you can look at, see, and feel.

Lead Your Customers

Teaching people how to organize is very hard. In any grassroots movement, you need to motivate action by creating relationships. Connect with people on a personal level, not just at the level of issues or ideas. Those connections will lead them to hold meetings, invite their friends—and help you expand your network. It's not the same thing as building a consumer product and waiting for customers to respond. It's more like an enterprise task: you have to lead your customers toward the actions you want them to take.

Let Tactics Drive Strategy

Everyone gets dealt a certain number of lucky opportunities. The number of opportunities and their magnitude will vary depending on your situation, but the key thing is to capitalize on them as they present themselves. Sometimes, you have a plan for how things are going to go, but then have side projects that may suddenly work incredibly well. You may decide not to completely shift directions as a result, but you have to be open to the possibility. Rather than sticking at all costs to your original vision or framework, you need to be willing to adapt.

CULTURE

Build Power Through Relationships

The best employees and volunteers aren't necessarily the ones who are most gung-ho, but the ones who are mostly tightly wound into the social fabric of your organization. Political campaigns have to ask volunteers to wake up at six in the morning and go knock on strangers' doors. When the alarm clock goes off, it's easy to remind yourself that the candidate doesn't really know whether or not you're showing up. But the buddy who's picking you up does know. There is power in those relationships. That's a core part of any successful organization's culture.

FOCUSING TIME & ENERGY

Pursue a Clear Goal, but Be Willing to Pivot

Building a company is like climbing a mountain. You have to decide which peak to climb and work your way toward it. As with climbing a mountain, it's hard to see anything ahead of you. Are you about to fall off a cliff, or are you just going over a small bump? If you trust your gut and feel like you're going to fall, you have to be willing to invest all the effort in going back down and starting toward a new peak. It sounds like a contradiction, but it's an important reality about company building. You have to balance a commitment to your primary goal with a willingness to pivot quickly when necessary.

HIRING

Exercise Leverage Through Recruitment

One of the hardest things about being a founder is avoiding the temptation to micromanage. The product is your baby; you're the one who knows everything about it. Eventually, you need to focus on the high-leverage things you can do to grow your company, so the first and *highest*-leverage thing you can do is recruiting. It's much easier to step back and empower your team to get things done when you have devoted a significant amount of time to hiring really great people.

HUMAN RESOURCES

Compensate Early Employees with Equity

In the early days of your company, you have to make a trade-off between compensating people with cash and compensating them with equity. Ideally, you should tend more toward equity. Of course, there's only so far that you can push that, because your employees need to pay their bills. But when your compensation skews heavily toward equity, your team's incentives are more fully aligned with your organization's goals. They won't be there just to pick up a paycheck; what they have is only worth something if the company succeeds.

MARKETING

Target Customers Who Signal Their Interest

When we first launched Causes on Facebook, we overestimated how easy it would be to get random people to organize. There's a lot of hand-holding involved. At every stage you have to say, "Now do this. Now do this. Now do this." Over time, we've realized that many of the best organizers on the platform are existing nonprofits or people who work for them. We've ended up devoting much more time and energy to targeting that demographic and helping them be successful.

METRICS

Don't Micro-Optimize Yourself into Oblivion

With the proliferation of tracking tools and A/B testing, there is an extraordinary amount of data available to startup founders. Yet if you overreact to immediate feedback, you'll micro-optimize yourself into oblivion. You can't be *completely* oblivious to feedback, but you also have to be willing to trust your gut. Constantly adapting to every minor variation in your metrics will prevent you from ever making big bets. Visionaries are forced to set goals and strategy without perfect information.

PRODUCT DEVELOPMENT

Expand the Product Conversation

Creating products by committee doesn't work. On the other hand, people on your team get really inspired by being part of the product conversation. You have to strike a balance between getting things done and giving a wide variety of people their say. Every employee wants to feel that they've made an impact on your product, and more important, they'll often provide good ideas.

TALENT

Recruit and Organize Yourself out of a Job

Fundamentally, building an organization is about recruiting yourself into obsolescence. In a grassroots campaign, initially you might have one phone bank and you're running it yourself. Then you'll recruit some vounteers to man that phone bank, then you'll recruit someone to run the phone bank. The only way that you can scale in any type of organization is by organizing yourself out of a job.

VISION & MISSION

Align Revenue and Impact

When we started Causes, we tried to build a business that was focused on both revenue and impact. That double bottom line doesn't work unless those two things are fully aligned. If you focus half your time driving revenues and half your time making an impact, you won't do either well. You have to find a business model that accomplishes both goals at once.

JOE'S VISION FOR THE FUTURE

In recent months, Joe has found the business model that "aligns revenue and impact," as he puts it. By leveraging the Causes platform, corporations can highlight their philanthropic efforts while building their Facebook fan base and strengthening their brand equity. Joe knew that this was the perfect model to grow his business virally when "we realized that the marketing people were willing to both pay for the matching grant and pay us!" Rather than simply targeting the charitable arms of their corporate partners, Causes can work directly with marketing teams. "We thought that we were going to repurpose additional charity dollars, but we ended up creating new charity dollars out of the marketing budget," said Joe. "In a completely unexpected way, focusing on revenue actually advanced our mission." Causes is a new, unique form of advertising that *drives* further user engagement rather than detracting from it.

SCOTT HARRISON

FOUNDER:
CHARITY: WATER

INTRODUCING SCOTT HARRISON

At first, Scott Harrison's story might seem familiar. He was raised in a conservative Christian family and, as a teenager, rebelled against his upbringing. He abandoned his faith, family, and home city of Philadelphia to become rich and famous in New York City. He joined a band and grew his hair long. With a partner, he went into the lucrative business of nightclub promotion, which he did for almost ten years. He'd gotten the success he'd wanted, but it wasn't enough. Scott came to a painful realization: "I'd become a scumbag. I was selling trash for a living." He left New York for a hospital ship in Liberia, West Africa, to serve God and the poor.

What makes Scott unique is that this epiphany led him to take transformational action. Even more important, it's a transformation he's sustained.

I first met Scott in 2008. He'd founded charity: water two years earlier, and he was still white-hot in his commitment to bringing fresh, clean water to everybody in the world who doesn't have it (a staggering one billion people). The organization was growing at a remarkable pace, and Scott wasn't flagging a bit.

The clearest evidence of Scott's continuing passion for his work is the way that he speaks about it. He never says, "I'm going to do this for ten years before moving on to the next project." What he says is, "I will do this and nothing else. This is my true purpose. This energy will animate my entire life." There is never any talk of "exits."

Many entrepreneurs fade soon after they get started, especially if they launch their endeavors from powerful, personal experiences. When that initial enthusiasm meets the overwhelming complexity of building a business, most lose direction. Not Scott. His transformational experience wasn't an isolated spark; his faith ignited an energy that persists.

For Scott not to do this work would be to violate a spiritual covenant. He's made a commitment to God and to himself to see this work through.

SCOTT'S STORY

Scott Harrison: I came to charity work in a very nontraditional way: through nightlife.

I was brought up in very conservative Christian family in Philadelphia. Tragedy struck my family when I was four; my mom was knocked out by a carbon monoxide leak in our house and became an invalid. After that, I took on a lot of responsibilities. I was basically playing mother of the house.

At eighteen, I rebelled and moved to New York City. Eventually, I learned that there is a job called "nightclub promoter," where you get paid a lot of money to drink for free. That sounded like a great way to get back at everybody. I spent the next ten years building a pretty successful promotion business. My life looked great on the outside: everybody wanted to be the promoter surrounded by beautiful girls. I was going to work at 11 p.m. and coming back at noon the next day—and I only worked two nights a week. My business grew and grew, but it was all pretty empty.

After a full decade of that decadent lifestyle, I was on a three-week vacation in Uruguay with all the right people and it just sort of hit me: I had become emotionally and spiritually bankrupt.

I decided to re-explore faith as an adult, not just what was force-fed to me as a child. Leaving everything behind, I set out for West Africa. It was a pretty radical life change from life in a nice New York apartment, with a great dog and a model girlfriend to two roommates in a 150-square-foot cabin in war-torn Liberia. And with all of that, I actually had to pay about $500 a month to be on the ship. I was $30,000 in personal debt and running up credit cards to volunteer!

That was the beginning. I was there for two years. I'd never seen poverty before. I probably wept fifty times during that two years, seeing people at the end of their ropes, living in a country with no hope. I left New York as an a-hole and came back with a newer heart. At the end of that experience, I was thirty years old and I knew that I was going to do this for my whole life. There was no going back into nightlife.

**THE
CHARITY: WATER
STORY**

Charity: water's mission is simple but herculean: to provide safe, clean drinking water to the estimated one in eight people in the world who don't have it. And in the process, they want to reinvent charity.

In their first four years, Scott and company raised more than $63 million from more than 300,000 donors. Every dollar of that is traceable, so donors can see exactly what their money is spent on—100 percent of public donations go directly to the people they are trying to help.

Charity: water also documents—with photos, video, and even a GPS system—the struggles they are helping to ease with the construction of solutions like wells, spring protectors, filters, and rainwater-harvesting systems.

In 2009, charity: water reached a benchmark of funding enough projects to serve bringing clean water to one million people.

There was one problem in particular that I was really interested in: a billion people in the world don't have clean water, something so basic. A billion customers who needed to be served. It's a very straightforward problem, and I founded charity: water to solve it. But after my experience in Africa, I thought that the nonprofit model needed to be different, and I had a couple of big ideas about what a reinvented charity might look like. First off, charities are awful at branding. To build charity: water, we needed to create an epic brand, so I was more interested in watching what Nike and Apple were doing than any other not-for-profits out there.

The first person I hired was someone with experience working on water projects. The second was our designer, Viktoria. She came out of a job working for Time Warner and L'Oreal. Making beautiful things, but ones that didn't have redemptive meaning. She helped me build the brand. (By the way, that designer I hired four years ago is now my wife.)

When I started, I learned about Paul Tudor Jones who had started the Robin Hood Foundation. He said, "My buddies and I will fund the staffing operations of Robin Hood so 100 percent of the public's money will go directly to projects." I thought that was so powerful and loved that clean separation. So I said, "Great, let me borrow that model." The only problem is that I didn't know any billionaire philanthropists; I had a negative bank account. But I believed that I would find a way to make that work.

Second, I wanted to show people where their money was going. We wanted to get to their hearts. We want them to understand the impact they are making. I got an idea at Best Buy: why not show online where every water project is, using handheld GPS units? They were $99, we could easily train all of our field partners to use one, along with an HD camera. We've made 200 videos in the last four years. We crank these videos out in-house and it doesn't cost us anything. That way, every donor knows where the projects are and that they were completed.

Explaining the big, imposing statistic at the center of our water problem wasn't going to net the response we want. We needed to tell the personal stories of people affected by the issue. In our second month, we built a giant outdoor exhibition in New York City, taking dirty water from the Hudson River and the East River and putting it into tanks to show people what it would look like if they had to drink from a river. It's disgusting, yet it's the reality for hundreds of millions of people.

I launched charity: water at a nightclub because that's the only way I really knew how to do a fundraiser. Promoters always have big birthday parties, so I invited everybody I knew to come out for my thirty-first. And I charged them $20 at the door. We raised about $15,000, which we used to build and rehabilitate wells in Uganda a couple of months later.

I wanted to scale the promoter birthday experience, but it didn't scale. So I got this idea to give up my birthday and mail out invitations for everybody to stay home and just donate money. When I turned thirty-two, I asked everyone for $32. We wound up raising about $52,000 online. Then, I thought, "I'm not the only guy born in September!" I got another ninety people in our small network to give up their birthdays and we raised $150,000. And we did it all by hand-coding little HTML pages with PayPal buttons.

We'd done ten times better than our opening night exactly one year later. A year after that, we said, "Let's just get more birthdays." We got about 900 people to give up their birthdays and raised a million dollars. That idea now has literally spread around the world.

THE
SCOTT HARRISON
PLAYBOOK

Emote Passion and Purpose

Everything that you do—every dollar you raise, every message you broadcast, every product that you release—must express your passions and your purpose. When an investor gives you money, are they doing it to further the core mission of your organization? When you make a statement in the press or release an advertisement, does it communicate your core values? When you put a new product out, is it a clear expression of the passion that went into building it? Clearly define your purpose, and communicate it to all of your partners—both in your organization and outside of it.

Have an Audacious and Clearly Stated Goal

"There are one billion people in the world without clean water. Our goal at charity: water is to help all of them." If you can't state your goal with that degree of power and clarity, you won't be able to create enduring, meaningful relationships with your partners, your investors,

or your customers. Making money or consuming a great new product is secondary to a larger commitment. You started your business in order to make a positive impact on the world. Tell people what that vision is and how you're going to achieve it with them.

Build an Epic Brand

Every great business is trying to solve an extraordinary problem, but you can't do that without building an epic brand. I left the world of nightclub promotion when I founded charity: water, but I didn't forget the lessons that I learned there. There doesn't need to be any conflict between purpose and presentation. You have to express your passion, and you have to do so in the most visual and striking way possible. This means investing in design and making your brand *immediately* recognizable in every detail: from your font and your color scheme to the production value of your videos. A clear message might help you win an argument, but an epic brand will help you win hearts.

BUSINESS OPERATIONS

Show Your Partners and Customers the Impact Their Money Is Making

A well-built product markets itself, so you shouldn't hide it. Show people where their money is going. Make them understand the impact they're making. When you're creating real value, that's easy. Similarly, show your investors and customers the *concrete* impact of their dollars. You'll earn their hearts, and that will translate into a greater commitment.

CUSTOMER DEVELOPMENT

Tell Concrete and Impactful Stories That Express Your Purpose

If I'm telling you about water and statistics, that there are a billion people who don't have water and all the diseases caused by impure water . . . it's just information that most people already know, and it's not very interesting. Connection is about storytelling, not just citing facts. We hunt for stories to bring this issue alive. We need to show people, not tell them.

DEPLOYING CAPITAL

Run Lean

Nonprofits don't need a lot. They need talent and conviction, which are free as long as you are diligent in hiring the right people. One designer can handle the entire brand, and your people can learn to solve their own small IT problems. At a nonprofit, everyone understands that the money spent on shallow conveniences of other businesses goes to other, better places.

FAILURE

Tell the Messy Truth

Not every one of your endeavors is going to be successful. But when your investors and your customers care about what you do, you don't have to hide the downturns. Invite your partners to join you for the whole experience. Let them experience the heartbreaks with you. It will make the victory celebrations all the more meaningful.

MARKETING

Try Everything

Not every marketing initiative is going to work, so you have to be willing to try everything. As long as you stay true to your core mission and values, you have nothing to lose.

PUBLIC RELATIONS

Use Technology to Enable Transparency

Years ago, producing high-quality videos and leveraging GPS technology was prohibitively expensive. Today, it's cheap and simple to employ. We knew that we needed to show people the results of our project, and shooting videos to post online was the no-brainer way to do so. With communication as it is today, you can bring your customers and partners into your factory floors and boardrooms. Make your customers feel a real investment not only in your end product, but in the entire process that went into producing it.

RAISING CAPITAL

Appreciate the Power of Networks

When you have a large enough network, every sale and every small bit of fundraising can contribute to significant windfalls. At charity: water, we get no money from governments and very little foundation money. But we've got an extraordinary number of people around the world involved, and that has allowed us to grow at a rapid pace. With an average donation size of about $200, we've raised more than $40 million in five years. Expand your network widely enough, and you can make economies of scale work for your business as well.

SALES

Be a Tenacious Salesman

You have to constantly be pitching, pitching, pitching. Telling your story. Saying, "Here's my vision. Here's what I want to do with my organization." Almost everyone says no, but you can't allow that to frustrate you. Eventually, someone will say, "Here's $25,000." And then you pitch again.

SCOTT'S VISION FOR THE FUTURE

Scott initially envisioned moving on to other charity efforts once his work on water was done, but he realized that he has already arrived at his ultimate mission. "I originally thought that the 'charity' colon was going to mean lots of initiatives," he explains, "First came charity: water. But then maybe it would be charity: education. And then maybe we'd move on to charity: health. But I learned that half of the world's schools didn't even have clean water. And that there were clinics throughout the world that also didn't have clean water. After that it might be charity: AIDS—but there are places where AIDS medication is literally administered with river water.

"So for now, we've decided to keep our focus on water. Without clean water, what have you got? It's water; there's nothing else. It's not water at 75 percent or water at 80 percent. It's water all the way."

SCOTT HEIFERMAN

FOUNDER:

I-TRAFFIC

FOTOLOG

MEETUP

INTRODUCING SCOTT HEIFERMAN

Scott Heiferman is an extraordinary and irreverent leader. Still shy of forty, he's already built three companies. That can't happen without a willingness to lead a team on every step toward the realization of your vision. Yet Scott was also passionately committed to a hyperdemocratic decision-making process, which he balanced with good leadership to build a great facilitator of democracy: Meetup.

Meetup began with a modest goal: Use the Internet to get people off the Internet. Scott wanted a more human touch after a decade in online advertising, but he couldn't shake the Web altogether. He thought the site would help fanboys organize club meetings, but it became the backbone of presidential campaigns. Scott was tapping a much larger and more complex marketplace than he'd originally envisioned.

From Day One, Scott wanted Meetup's values to inform how the company ran: transparently, collaboratively. But as he's the first to admit, that turned out to be an immature theory: "People want leadership, and you have to be willing to provide it."

I've known Scott for many years, and I was surprised at first to see how enthusiastically he took up that call. My first impressions were of a kind idealist with a deliberate naïveté about the world. I was only partially right. Scott is smart as hell, kind, and he is passionate about his ideals. But he's not the slightest bit naïve, though he may intend you to think so. He is an open and intentional listener, and this can obscure the steel rebar of belief that keeps him standing upright. Every decision is communicated with a smile, but it's communicated unambiguously: "I will do this; I will not do that."

In a sense, Scott has come full-circle to a true understanding of the democratic process. The end goal of that process isn't endless deliberation; it is the discovery of principled, committed leaders. That's precisely what Scott has become.

SCOTT'S STORY

Before going to work at a Manhattan McDonald's, Scott spent four years building a pioneering online advertising company, i-traffic.

Scott Heiferman: When I started it back in 1995, I was a dumb twenty-two-year-old kid who'd just quit a job at Sony to run a business out of my apartment. I didn't know all that much about the Internet and I didn't know much about advertising. All I saw was "Hey, there are TV commercials, and there's the Internet . . . There's the chocolate and there's the peanut butter, links and traffic are the currency of the Internet. I'm going to make an Internet ad agency."

Pretty quickly, I realized that I had no idea what I was doing. Part of it was lack of experience, but it was also the fact that we were doing something new. That's what makes it interesting. Online advertising was new, and I'd stumbled upon it at the right time. Amazingly, it worked. A huge part of the reason was the team we'd put together. Rather than hiring people like me, I hired people who complemented me as well as each other. Within a few years, i-traffic was a 100-person agency. Larger firms took notice.

When i-traffic's client accounts became highly valuable, the big players in the advertising world decided they wanted in on the action and Scott decided he hated the ad business, he chose an unconventional next step.

Right at the peak of the tech boom in 1999, Agency.com bought the company. I was twenty-seven and I was miserable because I didn't know what I wanted to do or how to contribute. After years of being surrounded by corporate wonks, I needed to get back in touch with customers and really understand business.

Getting a job at McDonald's was pretty straightforward. I filled out their application with my contact info, my availability, and my most recent school and work experience. I wrote that I was still employed part-time at i-traffic. The manager asked me about that in the interview. "It's an Internet thing." That was enough; he asked for my waist size and got me a uniform.

Crain's New York Business, an online magazine, eventually caught wind of the story. I posed for a picture after work one day and they put it on top of a story about "Dethroned CEOs." People started thinking that I was doing this as a publicity stunt. But it really wasn't some sort of circus shtick. I was lost, and I needed something radically different.

THE MEETUP STORY

Meetup was founded in 2002 to bring together groups of people with common interests. Scott's idea was that it would be used by hobbyists and enthusiasts, so it was a surprise when Howard Dean's 2004 presidential campaign began touting the website as their most important organizing fund-raising tool. In a *Wired* article on the phenomenon, Dean stated: "We fell into this by accident. The community seized the initiative through Meetup. They built our organization for us before we had an organization." Meetup had allowed for a genuinely grassroots political movement to gain force.

In 2006, eBay purchased a minority share in Meetup.com, with founder Pierre Omidyar explaining, "My belief that business can be a tool for social good is validated by eBay and Meetup's ability to connect people over shared interests through a for-profit model."

Meetup is now a global phenomenon with more than 11 million members.

I punched in five days a week, burned my arm on the fry basket, and went home smelling like McNuggets. I made a little over $30 each day, and quickly learned a huge amount about management and leadership. As a manager myself, I never took much time to thank people. I figured that good people got enough satisfaction from doing their jobs well and getting paid. Being an underappreciated employee taught me how wrong that was.

"Meetup began with a modest goal: Use the Internet to get people off the Internet."

The most important lessons I learned were about how to interact with the people. At i-traffic, I spent a lot of time with bankers and lawyers and accountants, but I didn't interact with any customers. At McDonald's, I encountered hundreds of customers every day. At the time, their tagline was, "We love to see you smile." But I went from job application to an interview to a couple of hours of training to working the front counter, and they never told me to smile. Here I was, the face of McDonald's on Fourth and Broadway, and there was this huge dissonance between the marketing tagline and the training of the employee.

After the cloistered experience of working at i-traffic, Scott knew that his next company would have to be about human interaction.

Bob Dylan's grandmother said to him, "Be kind, because everyone you meet is fighting a tough battle." I wanted to discover what problems there were in the world, what problems people had in their lives, and build businesses to solve them.

I'd spent a year thinking about this, until events a few blocks from where I worked gave me a renewed sense of urgency. After the attacks on September 11, I came up with thirty ideas for new companies and narrowed them down to two. The first was Fotolog, a photo-sharing site. The second was Meetup.

The site was designed to help people organize in-person meetings about any topic. I figured that it would help like-minded people—hobbyists and enthusiasts, fans and followers—get together. It became much bigger. As I wrote in the *New York Times* in 2009, I had no idea that Meetup would help people form "new types of PTAs, chambers of commerce, or health support groups." And I certainly didn't expect it to become a political platform. But people first noticed us when Howard Dean's campaign team made Meetup a crucial part of their 2004 presidential run.

In recent years, I've had some pretty radical ideas about extreme flatness and extreme democracy in organizations. That's what Meetup was all about: helping people interact and create ideas together. While I still believe that ideas can come from anywhere, I've learned that people need good direction. They need leadership, and you have to be ready to provide it.

THE
SCOTT HEIFERMAN
PLAYBOOK

Let Your Curiosity Grow into an Obsession

If you're going the route of doing this crazy thing and starting a company, that's got to be the product of some obsessive-compulsiveness around the idea. It's like falling in love. It's joy. But you want to think through everything. I seek product ideas that make me say, "I'm gonna drop everything and just sketch and plan and plot and think it through."

Become Obsessed with Useful Things

Artists can become obsessed with paintings they want to create, musicians with songs they want to write, and that's wonderful. But if you're an entrepreneur, you'd better have your obsession tuned to things that are of use to people. This is not about do-gooderism, it's about making stuff that people need and like. You can tinker with ideas that are technologically interesting, or artistically interesting, but that's not enough. I don't need a cup with mustache. I need something useful.

"Paint Paradise"

Bill Bradley was on our board, and he criticized me for being all over the place. He said to me, "Listen, you've got to paint paradise." What he meant by that was that I needed to get a clear vision of what the world would look like if we were successful and repeat that ad nauseam. Even if you are trying to build a small business, imagine what it would be like in your town if the amazing restaurant you want to start were successful. How would that be; what would it feel like, smell like? Achieving that mission is what it's all about.

SCOTT'S BEST ADVICE

BOARDS

Ignore Your Board; Embrace Your Customer

Learn to ignore the board and to get your employees to ignore the board. If you always say, "We need to do this to make the board happy," you are sending the signal that your organization is about pleasing your board. It's not. The purpose of every business is to please its customers. Do that, and your board will be happy anyway.

CULTURE

Treat Company Culture as a Means to an End

It is important to create a positive company culture, but not simply to make your employees happy. You do it because it's going to produce the best product and serve the most people. I love Tony Hsieh at Zappos, but I disagree with his theory that as long as there's a great culture, everything else will fall into place. I think that culture is only a means to an end, and your end is to serve the people.

CUSTOMER DEVELOPMENT

Manifest Your Core Values with Every Customer Interaction

There can't be any disconnect between your company's message and what you do. If your customers see that rift, they will call into question everything about your operation. And if there is such a disconnect, they won't be wrong when they walk away.

LEADERSHIP

Don't Be Too "Flat"

You want an organization in which everyone knows they can provide ideas, at any time, that will be considered on their own merit. You need to accomplish goals every day. To accomplish goals, someone needs to decide what the objectives are and close the discussion.

RAISING CAPITAL

Don't Raise Capital for Validation

Too often, entrepreneurs are looking for validation as much as they're looking for capital. When you're putting yourself out there and sticking your neck out for an idea, a lot of people are telling you you're an idiot. And yet, someone is going to write a check and invest in you. That's so validating. But you have to ask yourself: what do I really need capital for? Funding is not the best way to be patted on the head and made to feel good. You want to build a great product or a great service that the people really need and love, and everything else is a means to that end.

VISION & MISSION

Don't Read This Book; Live and Learn!

Don't spend too much time reading books like this one. Many great companies were built before there was a canon of startup materials. You need to balance an expertise about startups with an expertise about whatever it is that you're doing. If you want to create a great business about X then it's about X it's not about "business."

WORKING FOR YOURSELF

Don't Go It Alone

People often don't realize the importance of having partnerships, a sort of "band of brothers or sisters" across the different parts of the company. It's not just a matter of hiring a COO. If you can have a CFO as a cofounder, that frees other people to focus on *their* areas of expertise. Doing anything well is hard, cultivate relationships where there's trust and true partnership.

SCOTT'S VISION FOR THE FUTURE

Scott's vision is to keep Meetup growing and evolving so that it becomes even more of a go-to platform for community than it already is. He's already taken bold steps to distance Meetup from other social networks, and succeeded. In May 2005, he made the decision to begin charging for the Meetup service. "When it came time to generate revenue, we started charging a nominal fee to meeting organizers. Immediately, people started predicting our demise. The fact is, when we went from free to fee, we lost 95 percent of our activity. But we knew that what we were doing was a quality filter as much as it was a revenue model, and we knew that good Meetups would continue. They have. In July 2009, we had our first profitable month. We've maintained those profits ever since."

Now, there's ten times the activity on the site than when it was free, and Meetup is able to stay in the black while Scott and his team further perfect the business and the function of the website. Quality and quantity came with patience. Not all the social networking companies of the current boom will last, but Meetup.com has solidified its ability to bring people together in the real world. It's not just a network, it's also a tool, and that's worth paying for.

REID HOFFMAN

FOUNDER:

LINKEDIN

INTRODUCING REID HOFFMAN

Reid Hoffman founded LinkedIn on the basis of a profound insight: Even for individuals with a career at only one company, we live in a world where everybody is becoming a professional free agent. Rather than companies making decisions for our careers, each individual is the CEO of their own career. Professionals decide how to invest in their own skills and advancement; they decide which risks to take in order to create bold opportunities. Employers will select the talents that are best correlated to their needs. Industries are transforming in such ways that we will no longer be making decade-long career decisions. Every professional will have a network to navigate the changes in their industry. This shift of the professional universe has been going on for some time; and Reid recognized that the growth of the Internet made a new platform of Linkedin possible.

Reid is capable of assimilating a jetstream of data before making decisions. Is your idea really any good? Does your team have the ability to execute on it? Are the capital markets ready to fund it? Will the marketplace be ready to receive it? Have you identified key strategic levers—which he calls "Archimedean Levers"—that will drive the idea? This is the kaleidoscope of considerations that he keeps in mind when deciding whether to execute (or, in his capacity as venture capitalist, whether to invest).

When Reid does execute, his goal is to put the pieces together and arrive "a little bit too early." There's an important contrarian twist in that last clause. Reid doesn't want to be "on time," which would mean that everybody in the market-place could see the value of his idea. He wants to stake a claim before others catch up. With the most successful IPO in recent history, LinkedIn's success has proven his insights are exactly right.

REID'S STORY

Reid doesn't follow the entrepreneurial strategy of keeping his ideas to himself. When he started work on LinkedIn in late 2002, for example, he sought feedback from as many people as he could. Their response was nearly unanimous: "You're crazy."

Reid Hoffman: When I started LinkedIn, a wide variety of my friends said, "You're out of your mind. It'll never work." Their main criticism was that it was impossible to start a network product from scratch. "What's the value to the first member? Zero. What's the value to the second member? Zero. What's the value to the third member? Zero." You've got to get a large number of members before you begin to get any value whatsoever for anyone. "How is this ever gonna work?" is a perfectly logical question. But usually, really good ideas come down to saying, "There are reasons why this hasn't worked before, but I have a solution." You always want that contrarian check—for example why it wouldn't work before but could work now.

If users were going to join LinkedIn in the early days, they would have to do so with a spirit of adventure, a sense of participating in the creation of something new.

Part of how we solved the critical-mass challenge—and why LinkedIn exists today—is that we analyzed the question, "What do people most look for when they show up to a networking site?" One thing we knew they'd ask is, "Who is else is here?" We needed to give users the power to affect the answer. So we included an address book, which was at the time really just an email uploader, but it tells you who else is there. We predicted that a higher percentage of people would start uploading address books thereby and then send out invitations. That worked well enough that it changed the growth curve.

But even with LinkedIn's significant growth, Reid had to face the objection that he wasn't generating sufficient revenues.

All throughout the process, I had board members and the investing community asking, "Where is the revenue?" And I had to tell them "I don't care about the revenue right now. That's not the battle I'm fighting!" I needed to solve the growth challenge first. That's how I came up with the Web 2.0 mantra of "growth, engagement, then revenue." We were forced to work in

---

THE LINKEDIN STORY

LinkedIn was founded in 2003, just as social networks like Friendster were beginning to rise to prominence. The public's new familiarity with online networking was a crucial factor in LinkedIn's success. But, as Reid points out, LinkedIn was careful to position itself as a "professional" network rather than a "social" one. By 2011, it had more than 120 million registered users and was rated the 13th most-visited site on the Web by the Web-information company Alexa. LinkedIn went public in January 2011, with shares more than doubling in value in the first day of trading: at $94.25 a share, LinkedIn the company was valued at $9 billion.

that order in the beginning, but it turns out to be a pretty good template for thinking about a number of consumer Internet sites.

Having made the decision to focus on growth and engagement before making a push to generate revenues, Reid was faced with another challenge: proving that his market was a valuable one.

Most people are wrong about what's going to be great; that's why you have to have a hypothesis, and you have to get it to the market and test it as soon as possible. By the way, for years, the question of whether LinkedIn was part of an important category was unclear to most people. Did professional networking really matter to most people? This was one of the reasons I raised money from David Sze at Greylock Partners in our Series B. I knew it was, and I knew I needed to add great product talent to my board instead of just getting cash at the highest possible value. At that moment we were at the head of the "professional networking" pack, but it was not yet generally clear whether this pack was valuable at all.

When looking to invest in a company as a partner at Greylock, Reid also puts a premium on testing hypotheses.

Part of the way I analyze startups is by asking, "Which hypotheses need to be true such that this becomes a really valuable business?" Those are the hypotheses that I'm betting on. Another important consideration is how many hypotheses you have. If you only have one, you're probably not analyzing your challenge and strategy well enough; there are likely other key hypotheses that you haven't figured out. But if the list of key strategic points is too long, then maybe you should be thinking about doing something else. The goal is to have a handful of well-defined hypotheses and to put a very high priority on resolving them as early as possible.

Reid started LinkedIn to test the hypothesis I mentioned at the head of this chapter: that we are all professional free agents. He dominated his marketplace, and LinkedIn's IPO answered the other big unknown—this marketplace was indeed an exceptionally valuable one.

We have a proven market, a proven set of customers, and a working set of growth and customer-acquisition techniques. Because we're profitable, we can invest money back into the system, and the value to our members compounds with the growth of their networks.

LinkedIn's success was not inevitable. There was no guarantee that Reid and his team would create the user base required for a valuable networking tool. Every perceptive analyst would be aware of those dangers. A successful entrepreneur has to be optimistic enough to look past them.

Entrepreneurs have to be irrationally bullish about what they're doing because there are so many ways that their business can die. So how do you know when you should stick to your vision and when you should change? The key is to use your network intelligently. Identify really smart, really helpful people who know their stuff and collaborate with them. If you find that several of them are saying, "You have a problem; you should listen carefully," you might want to listen. If you don't have a good, clear solution to the problem that you really believe; if the only thing you can say is, "All of these people are dumb; I'm the only one who gets it"—well, that's very dangerous.

THE
REID HOFFMAN
PLAYBOOK

Execute on Your Biggest Idea

When you found a startup, you're metaphorically jumping off a cliff and assembling a plane on the way down. If you're going to jump off a cliff, you might as well try to assemble a great airplane. Building up a small idea is as much work as building up a big one in the first phases, so you absolutely want to execute on the biggest possible idea that you can. The big ideas have many benefits. In terms of outcomes, you have a possible huge result, you have a much higher likelihood of an intermediate result, and you have the potential of a small result—e.g., a strategic purchase. Furthermore, you can recruit a much better network to help with a big idea—employees, investors, advisors.

Build Companies with Real Competitive Differentiation

Often, entrepreneurs produce ideas that make only minor improvements on an existing product or service. "No, but *my* thing is built in Java, *their* thing is built in PHP," they might explain, or, "Our interface has Java Script." But if your idea is a little better or a little faster, that doesn't mean anything. The only competitive differentiations that matter are ten-times-greater differentiations. If your idea doesn't offer that, you should be really paranoid that it's not a good one. Otherwise, it won't drive adoption—by customers most especially—or investors or employees.

Be Early to Market

The right time to execute on an idea is when it's not obvious, which means that it should be contrarian. When everybody to whom you mention your idea says, "Oh, that's obvious!" that is a real sign of danger. If it's a no-brainer, why isn't everybody doing it? Better yet, why haven't they done it already and become successful? Of course, you'll (rarely) have a lightning strike that other people didn't have. (By the way, if that's the case, run really fast!) But it's much more likely that others have already had this idea and started moving on it. This relates to the strategy in market timing. The best timing is to be somewhat early. You'll have a harder time raising money, but you'll also have a lot less competition. This allows you to build up your product and develop momentum that makes it much harder for any competitor to catch you later.

CULTURE

Be Aware of Your Organization's Politics

One of the most central items in a company's culture is holding each other accountable to its principles, and that stems from the people who have power. Executives and founders often say, "There are no politics in my organization." That's idiotic. By definition, politics is what happens around people who have power. If you're sitting in a powerful seat and you don't see the politics, you're not seeing what is actually going on around you.

FAILURE

Fail Fast and Pivot

It's paradoxical, but you want to identify the things that can kill you and engage them sooner. This is part of the metric behind "fail fast." Of course, you're not actually trying to fail; you want to succeed. But failing fast is much better than failing slowly, since it enables you quickly to pivot, iterate, and redeploy capital. The one key mistake is that people tend to work first on the problems that they have the most confidence they can solve. In a good startup strategy you actually want to face death soonest because then you fail fast or get on a great path to success fast. Identify the hardest problems and try to solve those as soon as you can.

FOCUSING TIME & ENERGY

Triage Problems

Early in a startup, you won't have enough people to delegate the fires to. One of the mistakes that smart people frequently make is to integrate priorities, i.e., focus on Priority One and Priority Two, while also having an eye on Priorities Three, Four, and Five. That's absolutely the wrong way to do it. The key thing is to not be distracted by the fact that there may be other fatal fires you need to get to. Solve the the biggest problems first, then evaluate the rest.

HIRING

Perform Lightweight Reference Checks

The interview process takes twelve to fifteen hours of your team's time. You need to ask people about their best learning experience, because if they can't actually give you one then it sounds like they think they know it already. Decide whether the person has integrity, collaboration, and truthfulness; whether the chemistry is right; and whether their performance will be at a high enough level. This process is expensive for your team, so you should vet people in advance. A technique I use is to email the references and say, "Rate this person one to ten." No one's going to reply a "five" or a "three" by email; that means they hate the candidate. "Call me" is usally the response for a sub-seven rating. At the same time, nobody is going to reply with a "ten." What you're really looking for is a bunch of "eights" and "nines." This is an exceptionally quick referencing system when you're trying to triage a list.

LEADERSHIP

Make Provisional Decisions, Then Fill in the Gaps

When confronted with a problem, always make an immediate decision, but make it clear that it's a *provisional* decision. The next task is determining what you need to know to make a final decision. In other words, what are the things that might cause you to change your mind? Once you know that, you can analyze those things in detail. But you should always make an initial decision within a very fast time frame.

MARKETING

Take the Risk of Clearly Defining Your Product

The only way to really scale is by taking bets that might reduce your opportunity. This is especially true of your branding and marketing. People have the tendency to say, "I want to define my product as the best in the marketplace." You have to eschew that kind of vagueness viciously. Of course, when you say, "This is who I am," some customers will respond, "Nope. Not interested." But if you don't make those sorts of bold statements, you can never really learn whether people want what you're offering.

METRICS

Don't Let Data Replace Judgment

People say that you should make only data-driven decisions. But for important decisions, data isn't the final answer. The data might suggest continued growth based on past performance, but you shouldn't ignore your judgment about the current reality. That's a judgment call. A lot of businesses fail because managers overrely on data.

PRODUCT DEVELOPMENT

If You're Not Embarrassed by Your First Release, You Waited Too Long

One common piece of advice entrepreneurs get, and one of the worst, is your product has to be perfect before you launch. In technology, this is a holdover from when customers bought a piece of software at a store and installed it on their machines. If they didn't like it, they'd pull it off their machines and you'd be dead. That's not true with the Internet. There are lots of ways to get back to your customers. Products no longer have to be "perfect" right away.

TALENT

Treat Recruitment as a Critical, Long-Term Strategy

One of the challenges of running a startup is solving critical, short-term problems without neglecting long-term ones. Recruiting is a long-term problem; it's almost never the answer to the problem of the month. Clearly, you need to have the right talent on board, but it's not likely to solve the key problems your business is facing *right now*. Yet the longer you wait to do the long-term things, the more likely it is that you're going to die from something that requires a longer time frame to be solved.

REID'S VISION FOR THE FUTURE

"Growth first, then engagement, then revenues" became a defining feature of Web 2.0. However, when Reid participated in a "fireside chat" at the Web 2.0 Expo in 2011, he wasn't interested in digging into the paradigm he'd done so much to define. He wanted to talk about Web 3.0.

According to Reid, Web 1.0 was defined as "go search and get data"—with limited interactivity. Web 2.0 provided real interactivity: "real identities" and "real relationships." Crucially, these online relationships generate "massive amounts of data," which will form the basis of Web 3.0. While online personal data has already generated a great deal of commentary, that discussion has almost exclusively revolved around privacy concerns. Reid is aware of the dangers, but he's focused on the opportunities.

Expanding on his ideas at 2011's SxSWi conference, Reid proposed two rules that would help companies navigate the dangers of massive amounts of personal data. First, "Never ambush users" and make them feel that you are violating their trust. Second, understand that "Not all data are created equal." (Some, like credit-card numbers, should be treated like passwords.) Within those parameters, Reid is optimistic about what entrepreneurs and inventors can do. We can't just predict the future, he insists. We have to invent it.

JEFFREY HOLLENDER

FOUNDER:

SEVENTH GENERATION
AMERICAN SUSTAINABLE
BUSINESS COUNCIL

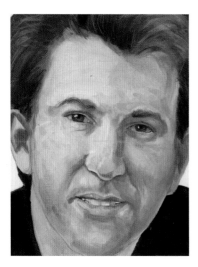

INTRODUCING JEFFREY HOLLENDER

Jeffrey Hollender is the steward of a bold mission: global sustainability. To say he has high standards would be a radical understatement.

In 1988, the company that would become Seventh Generation purchased Renew America, a mail-order provider of environmentally friendly products. The name echoes a phrase in the Constitution of the Iroquois Nations: "In every deliberation, we must consider the impact of our decisions on the next seven generations." Given the path that Jeffrey's career would eventually follow, the remainder of that sentence seems remarkably prescient: "even if it requires having skin as thick as the bark of a pine." Jeffrey has thick skin, and he's needed it.

For the more than two decades that Jeffrey ran Seventh Generation, it was repeatedly recognized for its commitment to sustainability, most recently in the 2011 Green Brands Survey by Cohn & Wolfe where consumers ranked the company as the number-one "green" brand in America. But when Jeffrey's professional relationship with Seventh Generation ended, he was unequivocal in his views. Speaking to an audience at the 2011 Sustainable Brand Conference, he bluntly stated, "Seventh Generation was never a sustainable brand, not even close."

Nothing less than a pure commitment to the mission of sustainability is palatable to Jeffrey. As Seventh Generation grew, it attracted leaders and managers who were committed to the performance of the business, but significantly less committed to the mission than Jeffrey was. As he sees it, they regarded Seventh Generation's mission as a valuable market distinction, while for him it was the essential core of everything the business did and would ever do. Jeffrey pursued his ideal relentlessly, but it wasn't enough. In October 2010, the board of Seventh Generation dismissed him from the company he had built.

Jeffrey's is a cautionary tale—one that he never hesitates to bluntly recount. But there can be no question about one thing: whatever he pursues next, Jeffrey will put his mission above all else.

JEFFREY'S STORY

Jeffrey began his career with an audiobooks business that he sold to Time Warner in the 1980s, then stayed at the company as president of Warner Audio Publishing until 1987, after which he cofounded Seventh Generation. Even before dedicating his career to environmentalism and sustainability, Jeffrey was passionately committed to both causes. In 1985, he published How to Make the World a Better Place: 116 Ways You Can Make a Difference. *Within a few years, he would be running a business committed to doing exactly that. As Jeffrey explains, he would have to go far beyond what was required of his industry in order to live up to the title of his book.*

Jeffrey Hollender: Every year at Seventh Generation, I had an opportunity to see whether I was living up to my standards for transparency. When I wrote the Corporate Responsibility Report, if my lawyer didn't almost have a heart attack reading it, then I knew I was failing to be transparent enough. Your lawyer should always worry about the legal risks associated with the level of transparency you're pursuing. If you never have to worry about that, then you're probably not being nearly transparent enough.

In particular, there is a very tangible and specific way to face that challenge in the consumer-products business: the ingredient list. There are two exemptions around ingredients. One is for ingredients that are below 1 percent of the total volume of a product, based on the notion that if there's less than 1 percent it probably doesn't matter. This is a totally flawed concept. Most of the things that are highly toxic and carcinogenic are dangerous in very, very low percentages.

The second exemption is for by-products. Often, two chemicals react with each other to create a third chemical. Technically, that third chemical is not an ingredient because the manufacturer didn't put it in the product. Nevertheless, it's there, and it can have an impact on you as a consumer. As a result, we decided that Seventh Generation would go beyond the disclosure requirements for ingredients and disclose by-products.

The only lens that makes sense when thinking about these things is the perspective of the consumer who's experiencing your products. It doesn't matter if something is present in very small amounts or if you didn't technically put it in there, it's still part of the consumer's experience and should

---

THE SEVENTH GENERATION STORY

Seventh Generation began life as Renew America, a mail-order catalog of environmental products. The following year, the twentieth anniversary of Earth Day brought Seventh Generation to national prominence, and revenues increased from $100,000 to $7 million. Seventh Generation sold its catalog operation in 1995 in order to focus exclusively on its wholesale consumer-products business, which included cleaning and paper products and, eventually, diapers.

Seventh Generation achieved profitability in 2002. By 2010, the company was generating more than $150 million in annual revenues.

be disclosed. Unfortunately, that kind of thinking is totally contrary to the current practice of the consumer-products industry. In many cases, the way the rules are defined not only allows but encourages deceptive practices.

Chief executive officer wasn't the only position that Jeffrey held at Seventh Generation. He also had another position that was much more congenial to his character: chief inspired protagonist. As the company scaled, the requirements of the two positions often conflicted.

Being the chief inspired protagonist was a reflection of who I am, and who I am didn't always fulfill all the responsibilities of being CEO. One of the places where I was weak, for example, is in process. I'm not all that interested in process, but process is critical to a success. That wouldn't have been a fatal problem if I'd had a management team that could compensate for my weaknesses in this and certain other areas. But I didn't adequately empower the senior managers around me by giving them high levels of responsibility, so they often weren't able to complement me as the leader of the company. I didn't really have a COO who could have taken the lead on process. I think that having stronger people whose primary focus was finance and process would have allowed me to build a stronger business and continue to focus on what I do best.

Eventually, the conflict between Jeffrey's two positions and his two sets of responsibilities proved untenable. In 2009, he stepped down as CEO and became executive chairperson. Chuck Maniscalco was brought in from PepsiCo to run the company, but he left a year later. In October of that same year, the Seventh Generation board dismissed Jeffrey from his position. At the June 2011 Sustainable Business Conference, Jeffrey offered a blunt assessment of the reasons for his termination.

After twenty-three years, I was fired from Seventh Generation and never allowed to set foot back in the company. I was fired because my view of the role Seventh Generation should play in society fell out of step with the board's view of that role.

Jeffrey offered four reasons why he thinks he failed.

1) I didn't institutionalize values in the corporate structure.

2) I took too much money from investors who weren't aligned with my values.

3) I failed to give enough equity in the company to the employees who would have protected what we'd built.

4) I failed to create a truly sustainable brand.

The last point came as a shock to many in the audience. Seventh Generation was often lauded as a pioneering sustainable brand. But for Jeffrey, it just wasn't good enough.

Seventh Generation was never a sustainable brand, not even close. I struggle to find any truly sustainable brand, though I continue to look. The problem is that we've confused "less bad" with "good." The fact that we make chlorine-free paper towels with 100 percent postconsumer waste doesn't make them a good product. They're just less bad.

THE
JEFFREY HOLLENDER
PLAYBOOK

Transparency Should Hurt

Radical transparency and authenticity should dominate your brand and culture. There may be certain things that need to be kept confidential, but I'm of the radical end of the spectrum. If it's not a little bit painful, and a little bit scary and difficult, you're probably not being transparent enough.

Don't Neglect Corporate Governance

I did not give enough attention to corporate governance issues at Seventh Generation. Building interpersonal relationships is important, but your core values need to be ingrained, officially, into the structures and bylaws of your organization. That makes it much more difficult for those values to be violated. Your management team can change very rapidly, but your bylaws are more permanent.

Don't Build an Egotistical Brand

Businesses often create a persona where they endlessly talk about all of the things that are wonderful about themselves and their products. When you're in a relationship with a human being, you don't want an egomaniac who'll only tell you good things about himself. You want to know the whole person—the good, the bad, and the ugly. I want to know how they handle their faults and flaws and weaknesses. I want them to be willing to have a dialogue about those flaws and weaknesses. It's no different with businesses. If you're willing to reveal your flaws, it will lead to relationships that are much deeper and longer lasting.

CULTURE

Build People

My instinct was always to direct everybody toward the company's mission, then not worry about their personal development along the way. My drive toward the mission was so high that I assumed everybody else would get sucked into it. I undervalued and underinvested in developing my employees as people. I may have built the company, but I didn't build my employees enough in getting there.

HIRING

Avoid the "Perfect Hire"

The biggest mistake you can make is to hire the "perfect" person for a position. Often, they turn out to be utterly wrong. The best people don't fit into predefined boxes. Rather than checking boxes off a list of qualifications, you need to find committed team players. I've found that the best way of identifying those people is by asking them to tell me what they're most proud of. Beware of people who say, "I . . . I . . . I." You need people who say "We . . . We . . . We." When you find those people, the process of making them successful begins *after* they join your organization.

HUMAN RESOURCES

Invest Heavily in Internal Training

At Seventh Generation, we were addicted to hiring people from other consumer-product companies and failed to invest adequately in training and promoting people internally. These were people who really understood our culture, understood our values, and demonstrated their commitment and passion to our mission, but we neglected them in order to pursue outside talent who often were not a good fit. It's one of the hazards of growing quickly.

LEADERSHIP

Find a Role Where You Can Be Passionate and Capable

One of the challenges of starting a business is that you often need to do many things that you don't want to do and that you're not good at. If you put yourself in the position of doing those things too often and too long, you'll end up creating some real problems. To avoid that, commit to designing a role for yourself from the beginning where you are both passionate and capable. From Day One, don't take on tasks in areas in which you are unlikely to be successful.

PUBLIC RELATIONS

Disclose Everything You Would Want to Know Yourself

Being transparent is about going beyond the rules of the game. Rather than asking what you *have* to disclose, ask what someone would *want* to know before buying your product. What you are *required* to tell your customers is irrelevant. It's really about what they would want to know if they knew to ask.

RAISING CAPITAL

Vet Investors like Potential Employees

Before taking money, interview three CEOs who have been recipients of money from that same person. Find out what it's really like to have them as a board member and an investor. Vet your investors the way an HR department vets potential employees. This is a much more significant decision. Think about the whole person outside of the context of how big a check they can write.

TALENT

Beware of Irrelevant Experience

The bigger you get, the more induced you are to hire experienced people. It's easy to lose sight of the fact that those experienced people have often learned extremely bad habits. They've learned that the ends justify the means, or that it doesn't matter what you produce so long as you produce. In our marketing department, for instance, we did things very differently. Success in another marketing department wasn't going to translate into success at our company.

WORKING FOR YOURSELF

Meditate

My daily meditation is the most productive time of my day. The clarity I achieve in those moments is better than anything I do, bar none. Reflection is powerful. You need to find peace and grow.

JEFFREY'S VISION FOR THE FUTURE

Jeffrey announced his next venture at the 2011 Social Capital Markets conference. CommonWise is "a new business that leverages large-scale local, regional, and national cooperative purchasing to lower the costs for all types of social enterprises and cooperative businesses, enabling them to more cost-effectively compete with traditional business." He found inspiration for the model in an Ohio worker's co-op called the Evergreen Cooperatives. As he told the audience at the conference:

"Evergreen is pioneering innovative models of job creation, wealth building, and sustainability. Evergreen's employee-owned, for-profit companies are based locally and hire locally. Their goal is to create meaningful green jobs and keep precious financial resources within our community. I see this as core to building truly sustainable communities. CommonWise aspires to evolve the concept of Evergreen. We want to build and scale a model that exists and is representative of the system solution we feel is needed. This time, we won't be the exception to the rule; we'll change the rules. We'll displace the bad by bringing in the good."

BEN HOROWITZ

FOUNDER:

OPSWARE

INTRODUCING BEN HOROWITZ

Ben Horowitz cofounded Loudcloud with Netscape's Marc Andreessen and two other partners in 1999. It was one of the first software as a service (SaaS) companies in the world, and it developed products around "the cloud" before the cloud was a reality. At first, Ben and his partners experienced tremendous growth. But after the dot-com crash in 2001, they lost nearly everything overnight. What followed was one of the greatest corporate turnarounds of all time.

Rather than trying to salvage a dying business, Ben made the bold decisions to sell Loudcloud's hosting business and build out their internal technology framework into an enterprise-software solution. He gave away the car, but kept the fuel and built a new car around it.

Not only that, but Ben achieved this turnaround at a publicly traded company. He wasn't in a position to simply make an announcement to his team, convince his board, and move forward. He persuaded his shareholders to abandon the company's original model and create something very different, with a brand new set of risks. To make the change as clear as possible, he also renamed the company Opsware. Less than ten years later, the company was acquired for more than a billion dollars.

As radical as Ben's decision making can be at times, it's never inscrutable. It has the perfect clarity of high-level software development: his mind is his operating system, and his thinking is composed of libraries in every area of business and product creation. Read his blog and review his insights, and you'll encounter well-written code.

Today, Ben has shifted his priorities from creating companies himself to fostering those of others. Yet again, he is pursuing this goal with his longtime partner Marc Andreessen. Both have been angel investors for years, and they launched their fund, Andreessen Horowitz, in 2009. They're the new kingmakers in Silicon Valley.

BEN'S STORY

Ben joined Netscape in 1995 as a product manager. He was quickly promoted to vice president and general manager, a position that lasted until Marc Andreessen sold Netscape to AOL in 1998. After a year working as VP of AOL's e-commerce division, Ben knew it was time for him and Marc to start something new from scratch.

Ben Horowitz: John Reed, the former CEO of Citigroup, once told me that the only reason to start a company is because you have an irrational desire to do so. Given the level of stress and torture you put yourself through, it's not worth the money. Don't do it for status—a better car or a bigger house in your neighborhood. Only do it because you have an irrational desire to build something.

Ben was ready to take on that challenge, founding Loudcloud in 1999.

A big part of your output as a leader of the organization is setting direction and making decisions. To be effective at that, you need superior knowledge, and there's a lot of work involved in acquiring that. You need to understand your entire company and its workings. What is the real capacity of the company? Where is it working? Where is it broken? Where is their miscommunication? Who is great? Who is working below their capacity? Systematically collect all of that information. If you don't have all the answers by the time real questions start to come your way, you're going to slow down the company.

Loudcloud's early clients included Ford, Nike, News Corp, and the U.S. Army. The company went public in 2001. Quickly thereafter, however, the business climate soured.

One of the most horrible things about being a CEO is that when your company is facing its biggest risks, there aren't a lot of people to talk to about it. People in the company need you to set the vision and lead effectively, and you can't talk to people outside the company because you don't want to muddy the waters. It's torturous to have these thoughts and not be able to get them on the table. If you keep them in your head, they will drive you insane. You need to find someone you trust completely, someone who has something interesting to say back to you.

THE OPSWARE STORY

Ben started the company that eventually became Opsware in 1999 with Tim Howes and Marc Andreessen, the cofounder of Netscape. Their company, Loudcloud, offered software infrastructure and hosting to major organizations, including Ford Motor Company and the United States Army. After Loudcloud was stymied by the dot-com bust in 2001, the founders sold its managed-services portion to Electronic Data Systems for $63.5 million and realigned the company's focus to automated server-management solutions. In 2002, Loudcloud became Opsware.

Opsware evolved its offer through a combination of acquisitions and internal development. In 2007, one of Opsware's largest clients, Hewlett-Packard, purchased the company for $1.6 billion in cash.

The same year that Loudcloud went public, the dot-com bubble burst and investors couldn't wait to jump ship from another sinking online-technology company. Clients were leaving as well.

It was horrible. When we came out of the gates, we were the darlings of Silicon Valley and we were on the covers of magazines. We had a great business, for which there was a great market. Then the market went away and there was nothing I could do to bring it back. Not everybody realized that. We had about forty competitors in our space and they all went bankrupt. Before that happened, they were all saying the same thing. "We're going to cut back. We're going to burn less cash. We're going to improve the business." But the businesses weren't the essential problem. The problem was the market. You could cut back and improve all you want, but it was just a question of biding time.

> "You can't succeed by making something just a little better."

Horowitz and Andreessen decided to focus on their skill as technologists, not day-to-day support providers. They were in the business of creating powerful automated solutions. Opsware was founded to perfect a technology that was only used as support in the Loudcloud business model. It was not a minor risk, but the partners were confident that they knew what the market would demand on the other side of the turmoil.

We recognized that there wasn't going to be enough of a market to sustain all of these companies, least of all our own. The hardest thing about this time was that we had sold every employee on the fact that this was a giant market, and we had gone public on the same understanding. In everything we had previously said we made the same claim, and then I came to the belief that it was no longer true. Looking back, I can see how everybody else talked themselves out of admitting that.

Ben's intellectual honesty led to a turnaround that was as successful as it was drastic: HP acquired Opsware in 2007 for $1.6 billion. After another major technology success in addition to Netscape, Horowitz and Andreessen decided to focus on angel investing and guiding the other companies to push the IT envelope even further.

THE
BEN HOROWITZ
PLAYBOOK

Build a Great Product

In our businesses, the product drives the company. With something like chocolate milk, people really can't tell the difference between products, so your success will depend more on factors like marketing and distribution. That's not true of technology companies. The first thing you have to determine is what you're going to improve for your customers—which behavior you want them to change. Next, you have to figure out how you're going to build a product that fulfills that. The product is the main thing.

Avoid Incrementalism

You can't succeed by making something just a little better. For a technology company, it can't even be twice or three times as good. People are fundamentally lazy, and they're not going to adopt something unless it's at least ten times better than what they already have. The incumbents are happy to make lots of money offering customers something they're familiar with. To win, you have to build a breakthrough major enough to cannibalize that business.

Create a Monopoly

As Peter Thiel told me, you always want to build a monopoly because that's where you'll get outsize returns. If you think about that in terms of the current marketplace, it can be very confusing. The guy with the Indian restaurant on the corner will talk about all the ways that his offer is unique and better: "We've got better spices. We've got better hours. We've got tablecloths that are special-ordered from this great place." But Larry Page will never come out and say that Google is a monopoly. Instead, you'll hear him say things like, "We've got real competition from Bing, and now Twitter is out to get us." The truth is that they have a unique platform that they can leverage in numerous ways, but they need to stay worried about potential competitors in order to maintain it.

BOARDS

Be a Customer of Your Board

The CEO is the customer in the board meeting, and there are three main things they need to get out of it. First, regular board meetings can act as a forcing function to make things happen in a company. This is why CEOs tell their teams that something needs to be ready "to present to the board." Board members actually hate to sit through presentations from the head of customer support or some other division. But if it's helpful for the CEO to have them, bring them in. Second, the board is the CEO's base of outside thinking and environmental knowledge. Using that knowledge is essential when making strategic decisions. Finally, the board should handle corporate governance when it comes to taking or minimizing risks, stock options, accounting, and legal practices. CEOs can't focus their time on those kinds of issues; they need to be able to get directives on them from their boards.

BUSINESS OPERATIONS

Build a Flawless Onboarding Process

If you're going to build up one process, make it the interview and onboarding process. If other processes aren't in place at the beginning, you can build them later and easily recover from whatever issues arise. If you fill your company with less than great people, though, that's going to be hard to recover from.

FOCUSING TIME & ENERGY

Understand Every Detail of Your Business

CEOs need to devote a huge amount of time to understanding their own businesses. When things are going well, that can be up to half of what they do. You're looking at product plans: where is the roadmap headed? You're talking to customers: what are they going to be looking for in the next quarter? You're talking to employees: how easy is it for them to get their job done? The rest if your time will be devoted to administrative duties and setting a clear vision for the company. For that to have real depth and color, you have to know your business.

HIRING

Don't Be Impressed by What You Don't Know

One of the mistakes people make when interviewing a potential hire is that they ask questions about something that person knows about, but that they themselves know nothing about. It's like interviewing a Japanese interpreter when you don't know Japanese. Anything they say will impress you because you have no way of knowing if their grammar is correct or if they even speak the language. Instead of falling into that trap, ask interviewees to school you in what you know: your business. The bar there is extremely high. First of all, you'll immediately know how well prepared they are for the interview. But more important, you think about your business all day, every day. If they're going to say something about it that impresses you, they'll have to be exceptionally smart.

HUMAN RESOURCES

Hire to Specific Tasks

It's great to hire people who have leadership qualities that you can scale up, but you can't prioritize ahead of your main concern: are they going to be world-class in their job *today*? When you bring someone into an organization, the only thing that matters is whether they can do the job you're hiring them to do in the next twelve months. If they can't ace that, it doesn't matter if they have the potential to scale. They'll end up being ostracized and sidelined by the time you get to that point.

LEADERSHIP

Being Consistent Isn't as Important as Being Right

Al Davis, the owner of the Oakland Raiders, once said that he was more worried about being right than about being consistent. When I saw that, I read it over and over again. It's absolutely true, and it's extremely difficult to live up to. Admitting that it's impossible to get out of a situation is often the right thing to do. If you insist on consistency, it will be impossible for you to adapt.

MARKET DEVELOPMENT

Bad Markets Always Beat Good Teams

If you invest in a bad market, you'll never get a good business out of it, no matter how big that market is. A bad market always beats a good team. You have to enter a good market, preferably one that's not too small. Google is a great example. They went after a really big, existing market, and they made it into a much bigger market with a great product. For them, it was really simple: the search results worked. They served the ones people used as opposed to the ones people didn't use. Good companies address big, robust markets with a winning product. Bad companies are missing one or both of those things.

PRODUCT DEVELOPMENT

Create a Culture of Innovation

The entrepreneur's main partner has to be the core inventor and innovator in the company. You have to know every detail of your product so you have the ability to question every assumption about it. In fact, you have to be willing to capsize the entire business based on a product vision. One of the things that has been so powerful about Mark Zuckerberg's leadership is his level of courage with respect to the product. He had the courage not to sell the company, the courage not to monetize early, the courage to blatantly change around the product. Those were all scary decisions, but Facebook wouldn't have killed MySpace if he hadn't made them.

TALENT

Build a Team That Nobody Else Can Get

In putting together a team, you can't only assess people relative to what you know. You need to ask if it's possible for *anybody* to bring in people who are better than your people. If it is, then you're going to have a problem.

BEN'S VISION FOR THE FUTURE

In 2009, Ben and his old partner, Marc Andreessen, cofounded Andreessen Horowitz, a venture-capital firm based in Silicon Valley. The firm holds financial stakes in some of the biggest Internet companies of the moment—Facebook, Twitter, and Skype—and counsels their executives into unprecedented growth. Networking and personal computing are said by some to be in their golden age already, but Horowitz and Andreessen see explosive growth coming that will drive innovation to unheard-of levels.

In the most popular post on his blog, Ben explained why he and Marc always prefer to back founding CEOs: "Founding CEOs naturally take a long view of their companies. The company is their life's work. Their emotional commitment exceeds their equity stake. Their goal from the start is to build something significant."

By the time *The Economist* profiled Andreessen Horowitz in late 2011, the pair had $1.2 billion under management, and that capital is overwhelmingly in favor of founders.

TONY HSIEH

FOUNDER:

LINKEXCHANGE

VENTURE FROGS

CEO:

ZAPPOS

INTRODUCING TONY HSIEH

In his recent memoir, *Delivering Happiness*, Tony Hsieh clearly lays out the key themes of his personal and professional life, especially when he describes the moment when Zappos' culture truly began to cohere. The major struggle the company faced in its early years was finding employees as committed to customer service as the executives were. After realizing that they weren't going to find them in California, Tony and his team decided to move somewhere with a much stronger culture of service. They considered many options, but ultimately chose Las Vegas. As Tony writes, "We had about ninety employees in San Francisco at the time, and I had thought maybe half of them would decide to uproot their lives and move with the company. A week later, I was pleasantly surprised to learn that seventy employees were willing to give Vegas a shot."

Employees who decided to make the move were making a major commitment to Zappos. "Probably the biggest benefit of moving to Vegas was that nobody had any friends outside of Zappos, so we were all sort of forced to hang out with each other outside the office." That proximity forced Tony to clearly define the culture he was building. He eventually settled on ten core values, but the last value is the most profound. It consists of only two words: "Be humble."

Tony is a humble leader with a strong commitment to his partners, his employees, and his customers. If past performance is the greatest predictor of future outcomes, then we should expect great things from Tony in the years to come. He's only in his mid-thirties, but with the founding of LinkExchange and his leadership of Zappos, he has had a huge career already. I have no doubt that he will continue to repeat his successes and learn from his failures. With genuine honesty and perspective, Tony knows that nobody has it all figured out.

TONY'S STORY

With the sale of LinkExchange to Microsoft, Tony Hsieh achieved major success very early in his career. His next move was to cofound Venture Frogs, a fund that invested in and incubated Internet companies. One of their investments was an online shoe retailer.

Tony Hsieh: Venture Frogs was invested in about twenty-seven different companies; Zappos just happened to be one of them. At the time, we were running an incubator and providing office services and so on. Zappos was one of the companies that moved into the incubator. I didn't go into it thinking, "I'm going to find a shoe company to invest in, and then I'm going to bring people along with me and try to make it work." I just started working more and more with them. Over the course of a year, I slowly got sucked into working with them full-time. [This is Tony's characteristic humility at work: he didn't just start working "full-time" at Zappos; he became the CEO of Zappos.] If it hadn't worked out, I wouldn't have become emotionally invested in the company.

Second-time entrepreneurs are sometimes reluctant to devote real time and energy to the hard work of building a new company, especially if they had a major success with their first venture. This was never Tony's problem.

Being successful is just about doing whatever it takes to get stuff done. In the early days of Zappos, we did everything. If we had 100 orders that needed to go out, everybody stayed late at night packing boxes and chipping in. That was true for all of us, not just me.

Creativity and persistence in solving problems would always characterize Tony's work at Zappos. In some cases, it was a simple matter of working through the next day's order. At other times, it involved major operational issues.

Many brands said we needed to have a physical store before we could sell their shoes. That wasn't part of our original business model, so we just turned our reception area into a shoe store, took a picture of our "shoe store," and sent it into the brands. That worked for some of them, but others were more diligent. Their reps would actually visit and see that it wasn't a real store. They were right, of course, the "store" probably sold one pair of shoes a day.

THE LINKEXCHANGE STORY

Tony and his partner, Sanjay Madan, founded LinkExchange in 1996 after graduating from Harvard University. Within a year, ads powered by LinkExchange were reaching nearly half of all Internet-enabled households. In late 1998, Microsoft purchased LinkExchange for $265 million. Tony was twenty-four.

THE ZAPPOS STORY

Tony Hsieh is not the founder of Zappos. When Nick Swinmurn founded the company in 1999, Tony was an early investor through his fund, Venture Frogs. He became CEO of the company the following year. Today, Zappos is the world's largest online shoe vendor. They have an inventory of more than five million shoes in 200,000 styles from 1,200 shoemakers, including Bruno Magli, Nike, and Ugg. On November 1, 2009, Amazon.com purchased Zappos for $1.2 billion. At the time, it was Amazon's largest acquisition.

To attract the brands we wanted, we had two options: start a real shoe store or find a real shoe store. Starting a real shoe store would have been a big pain, and we would still have to convince brands to sell to that store. We decided to find an old mom-and-pop store somewhere in the middle of nowhere that we could buy cheaply. That's how we ended up buying the shoe store in Willows, California. As it turned out, there was an abandoned department store across the street. We were expanding at the time, and we ended up turning that space into a two-story, 30,000-square-foot warehouse.

There was no way we could possibly have predicted how things would turn out. We were just looking at all of our options and trying to find creative ways of getting things done.

In the years that followed, Zappos experienced extraordinary growth, but it took an extremely risky and difficult path that could have ended very differently.

For a vivid example of the challenges the Zappos team faced, look up the chapter "Improvising Inventory" in Tony's book Delivering Happiness. *In 2002, Zappos decided to move their warehouse from Willows, California, to a spot near the UPS hub in Kentucky. Tony and his team packed five semis with 40,000 shoes before taking a "minivacation" to New Orleans. While on their trip, they got some bad news: one of the semis had overturned. The driver was fine, but the cargo wasn't. "The shoes are strewn all over the side of the highway," they were told. "I don't think we'll be able to recover any of them." In one shot, Zappos lost 20 percent of its inventory. Zappos overcame that challenge as well as others, but it was a clear reminder that there's no such thing as "overnight success."*

> ## "You sometimes feel very lonely as an entrepreneur."

You sometimes feel very lonely as an entrepreneur. Every time you fail at something, you wonder how all these other companies are doing it so effortlessly. But those ups and downs are part of every eventual success story. Very few entrepreneurs are successful in the first thing they try. From the outside, Zappos might seem like an overnight success. The truth is that we made a lot of mistakes along the way and learned a lot of lessons.

"The people in overly proud companies start believing their own press releases . . ."

**THE
TONY HSIEH
PLAYBOOK**

Be Humble

Just because you were once a great company doesn't guarantee that you always will be. Businesses that have gone from being great to going under or becoming irrelevant have often lost their sense of humility. That's step one of falling or failing. The people in overly proud companies start believing their own press releases and feeling like they can do no wrong. To help protect us against this, one of our core values at Zappos is being humble.

Embrace and Drive Change

Another core value at Zappos is to embrace and drive change. Never accept or be too comfortable with the status quo. Historically, the companies that get into trouble are the ones that aren't able to quickly respond and adapt to change. At Zappos, we are constantly evolving. If we want to stay ahead of our competition, we have to continually change and keep them guessing. As long as embracing constant change is a part of our culture, nobody will evolve as fast as we can.

Adopt a "MacGyver" Mentality

My favorite TV show growing up was *MacGyver*. He could combine duct tape with a pencil and a paperclip and make a sailboat out of it. He never had exactly what he needed, but he figured out how to make things happen. For me, that's what the entrepreneurial spirit is about. It's about being able to combine optimism and creativity, kind of with the faith that it's going to work out somehow in the end, only you don't know exactly how. So being an entrepreneur, I think, is really just about playing MacGyver with business.

BUSINESS OPERATIONS

Overcome Complexity with Acquisitions

We needed to have a physical shoe store in order to work with certain brands. An acquisition with a clear purpose helped us avoid the complexity of starting a real store and allowed us to quickly add fifteen to twenty new brands.

FAILURE

Don't Be Afraid to Fail Your Way to Success

So many people label themselves a "failure" when they fail at something. Instead, the entrepreneurial spirit is realizing that these failures are a necessary part of the path to wherever you're going to end up.

FOCUSING TIME & ENERGY

Prioritize Passion over Profits

Make sure you're passionate about whatever you do. It has to be something you'd be happy doing for ten years, even if you never made any money from it. The irony is that your passion will greatly *increase* the chances that you'll end up doing well. There are going to be hard times, and your passion will get you through them. It will also rub off on the other people in your company.

HIRING

Make Sure Early Hires Are Willing to Take on Any Role

Every company needs people with different skill sets and passions. But early on, everybody should be willing to wear ten different hats. They can't have the attitude that something isn't "their job" or "their responsibility." They have to have the MacGyver mentality and do whatever it takes to get the job done.

PRODUCT DEVELOPMENT

Prioritize Progress over Process

Stuff needs to get done, and you need to do whatever it takes to get things done. Sometimes you just don't have all the resources you would like, but you just have to fight through it; that's part of the process. You're going to have to cut some corners in the *process*, but you can't let that stall your *progress*.

TALENT

Avoid Top-Heavy Titles

Giving early managers and executives top-heavy titles inhibits growth. If your company grows and becomes successful, you are going to outgrow the capabilities of the people who were with you at the beginning. Chances are very small that your first ten people are going to be the ten VPs you want five or ten years down the line. In the beginning, be very stingy about giving away titles.

VISION & MISSION

Don't Let Your Vision Inhibit Change

Don't lock yourself into a specific business model when you start out, especially if you're going into a new industry. You just don't even know what you don't know. Because nothing ever turns out the way you expect it to, you have to be open-minded about the path your company takes. Don't get stuck on what you envisioned when the company first started.

WORKING FOR YOURSELF

Choose Partners You Enjoy Spending Time With

It's important to choose partners you would want to be around even if you weren't in business together. Would you go on a cross-country road trip with them? I would actually recommend taking a vacation with whoever you're going to be working with. When you're with somebody 24/7, it accelerates that process of acclimating to each other. This can help show you what working together is going to be like after six months or a year.

TONY'S VISION FOR THE FUTURE

Recently, Tony has shifted his focus from delivering footwear to "delivering happiness." This is the title of the book he wrote and then promoted on a cross-country bus tour. From Las Vegas to Chicago, from Boston to Miami and back to Portland and Seattle, Tony spread his message of delivering happiness one individual, employee, and company at a time. As ever, Tony wasn't content to do things the traditional way. The book's website didn't simply promote sales; it acted as the hub of a movement. Readers were encouraged to start clubs to build happiness at their workplaces or in their communities, and to share their stories on the *Delivering Happiness* site, on Facebook, or on Twitter.

Tony also achieved the high point of traditional publishing success: on June 22, 2010, *Delivering Happiness* reached the number-one spot on the *New York Times* Bestseller list.

CYRUS MASSOUMI

FOUNDER:

ZOCDOC

INTRODUCING CYRUS MASSOUMI

Cyrus Massoumi certainly isn't the first entrepreneur who's attempted to revolutionize an industry or, for that matter, to take a stab at revolutionizing healthcare. But most of his predecessors have tried to accomplish that transformation in a single step—one "killer app," one tweak to a service, one enterprise deal, and the largest sector in the U.S. economy has been remade. Obviously, this never works. But entrepreneurs, on the whole, are not a patient bunch. This is what sets Cyrus apart.

When Cyrus launched ZocDoc, he did so with the goal of remaking an entire industry. But his vision for ZocDoc isn't monthly or quarterly. It spans decades. He began with more efficient dental appointments in Manhattan and moved on from there, one specialty and one region at a time. His eventual goal is to create a comprehensive and transparent platform for consumer health care. I'm confident he'll do so.

CYRUS'S STORY

ZocDoc was an idea born of Cyrus's own medical emergency: a ruptured eardrum. At the time the rupture occurred, he was working as a consultant with McKinsey and Company and was on a business trip without access to his usual physician.

Cyrus Massoumi: I had great health insurance at the time I ruptured my eardrum. I was willing to go out-of-network, and I would have paid my doctor with cash because I knew that I would get reimbursed. And it *still* took me four days to find a doctor. That gave me an idea: I would create a network to connect people with doctors who were out of their insurance networks. The doctors would see the patients when they wanted to be seen because they were going to be paid so much more, and patients would see out-of-network doctors in cases where they cared most about convenience, or where there was an urgent need.

Early on, I realized that that system wasn't going to work. One of the first interviews I conducted to test the idea was with a guy who had made $20 million working at a hedge fund the previous year. And he insisted that he would never see a doctor out of his network. "But you made $20 million last year! Why wouldn't you book outside of your network?" He explained, "I don't want to deal with all of that paperwork. I just need to know whether a doctor accepts my insurance or not."

So, it was going to be essential to include insurance information in the first version of ZocDoc. Rather than being a specialized, out-of-network tool, it would be a general online medical-booking system.

While Cyrus's experience at McKinsey helped him quickly build an efficient organization, venture capitalists weren't interested in consultants. They wanted people who built things.

At our first meetings, people immediately turned my partners and me down. "You're consultants. You don't actually do anything." Of course, all of my cofounders and I had run companies in the past. But it didn't matter; they looked at our suits and saw consultants. So we went to the Gap, bought some jeans, and started wearing them to our meetings. The consulting issue never came up again.

THE ZOCDOC STORY

ZocDoc started in 2007 as a free service for booking appointments with doctors and dentists in New York City. Since then, it has expanded to nineteen major U.S. cities, offering millions of appointments at any given time with specialists in dozens of medical fields. More than a million patients use ZocDoc to find doctors every month. In 2010 and 2011, *Crain's New York Business* named ZocDoc the "Best Place to Work in New York City." ZocDoc's popular ratings and reviews system solicits feedback from every patient who books an appointment with the service. The reviews help other patients choose the best doctor to meet their needs.

Cyrus and his team rolled out ZocDoc very slowly and deliberately. The original tool allowed people to book dentist appointments in Manhattan. Despite his ultimate ambitions, Cyrus was convinced that the highly complex and fragmented nature of the health-care industry required patience.

"[S]olve your clients' number-one problem."

Focus is important in any business, but particularly in health care. There are very few truly scalable businesses in health care because there is so much fragmentation in the marketplace. Why? Because doctors are very smart, discerning people who want the product they want. They don't want to do things someone else's way. (A partner once told me that there are more than 1,400 different medical-practice-management EMR systems in doctors' offices.) As a result, hospital systems are never really scalable.

Of course, we couldn't customize ZocDoc for every physician. Instead, we decided to optimize for the lowest common denominator and ignore all the special cases. The reason we were able to succeed despite our unwillingness to customize was because we were meeting our customers' number-one need. Doctors obviously want to be more efficient with their time and make more money. That depends entirely on the number of patients that they see, and we've made that process significantly more efficient. As a result, we've been able to get doctors to adhere to the ZocDoc way of doing things and implement process changes in their office.

While Cyrus has been very deliberate in developing ZocDoc's products, his ultimate ambitions are anything but modest.

ZocDoc will be more than just online scheduling. We want to build a health-care platform. Ten years from now, I'm confident that you'll be able to go to a website that has all of your medical information, say that you want to see a doctor, have the option to video chat with that doctor, and book an appointment right then and there. As consumer-driven health care begins to grow, patients are going to want the ability to shop across doctors. Our goal is to make that transparency—which every patient wants—a simple and affordable reality.

THE CYRUS MASSOUMI PLAYBOOK

Start With the End User

A lot of entrepreneurs start executing on an idea without first making sure that it's connected to the end user. My first company failed because our products missed the mark; we didn't do the work of determining whether these were products people actually wanted to use. After that experience, I went to work for McKinsey doing exactly the kind of analysis needed to create ZocDoc. When I started the company, I applied those lessons. We implemented techniques such as rapid prototyping and hypothesis-based product development in order to rapidly collect customer feedback. So far, it's worked.

Solve a High-Priority Problem

You can't build a venture-backed business with venture-backed economics for something that's the tenth problem on a CEO's list. You can raise an organic business in that way, but you'll never achieve the rocketship growth that venture capitalists expect. To do that, you have to solve your clients' number-one problem. Salesforce.com is a great example: they solved a top-level CEO problem and it led to extraordinary growth. That won't happen if you're only delivering your clients' third or fourth need.

Hyperfocus

A lot of people have tried to "revolutionize" health care. It's an overly ambitious goal. Health care is the largest sector in the U.S. economy and it won't be transformed in a single step. Remain focused on one sector and one area at a time—you can't do multiple things in this sector at the same time and do them well. Don't do things outside of your realm without being extremely deliberate.

CYRUS'S BEST ADVICE

BUSINESS OPERATIONS

Split-Test Everything

Most startups do A/B testing. But we A/B test everything, even outside the Web: what we mail to doctors, how we recruit, the messages on our recruiting sites, the envelopes we might use for a particular purpose. We've literally tested everything in this business. Of course, I want to make as many correct decisions as possible. But if I make a bad decision and fail, I want to know *exactly* why I failed.

CULTURE

Divest Your Culture of Cliques

I'm very inclusive; I hate cliques. If I see too many employees from one department standing next to each other in our lunch areas, I go and ask them to move around. If we have a company function, I train our team to make sure that each individual person is invited. I learned that lesson in business school. I led my cluster there, and we had 95 percent of people showing up to our events. Other clusters had 20 or 30 percent showing up. The only difference was that I personally invited everybody.

FIRING

Have the Courage to Let Early Hires Go

In the early days of your company, when there are only ten or twenty people on your team, it feels like a small family. In that context, it's extremely difficult to fire people. Letting someone go takes a lot of courage. But, as many entrepreneurs will point out, those first people are extremely important; they set the tone of your entire company. Therefore, if someone isn't working in the early days, it can cause significant damage. It makes intuitive sense, of course, but it's hard to act on that knowledge. It takes a lot of courage to let one of your early employees go. But if they're not working out, you have to be willing to do it.

FOCUSING TIME & ENERGY

"Focusing" Means Different Things at Different Times

Every founder needs to make sure that his company keeps focused. But "keeping focus" means different things at different times. Early on, it involves the CEO literally making every yes/no decision. But once your organization becomes larger and more complex, you can't possibly make every edge-case decision. The best you can do is articulate a vision and make sure that everybody is on board with that vision. Within that context, your job is to build a team that can set their own priorities and make good choices within that vision. It's very different than the first 100 days.

HIRING

Use Consultants as Provisional Hires

There's always a certain amount of instability involved in a consulting contract. However, a two- to three-month engagement with a very specific deliverable is a great way to determine whether someone would be a valuable long-term hire. We've probably vetted consultants as potential hires about ten times, and five of those ten people have come on full-time.

SALES

Be Your Company's First Salesman

When we started ZocDoc, people didn't believe that doctors would pay money for our services—or that you could sell anything at all to doctors. We knew we had to prove our critics wrong, so we just kept banging our heads against the wall trying to figure out ways that we could sign up doctors. We had three different sales forces, but eventually I needed to become a salesperson myself. I was never a salesperson, but I had the will to make the company succeed. I went door to door. I got thrown out of three doctors' offices. Ultimately, I figured out how to sign doctors up; I signed our first fifty clients myself.

TALENT

Probe for Passion

Our intent is to build a big company, and we plan to be around for a long time. When we hire people, it's really important for us to determine how fanatical people are about the company. When we give offers, we don't give people a long time to decide. We don't want to put them into a high-pressure situation, but if they really want to join our team, it shouldn't take them long to make a decision. The right person is going to be very excited about ZocDoc. They should be able to make a decision very quickly.

VISION & MISSION

Keep Your Entire Company Aligned to the Core Mission

At ZocDoc, our goals aren't centered around money or valuations. I don't care about that. I measure success by customer response. One week last year, which was our best sales week to date, the thing I was most proud of was an email from a deaf customer who wrote to say that for the first time, he had access to health care without help. We get emails like that every five minutes, and that's what drives us. As long as everyone on my team shares the same values and works toward the same mission, I know we'll succeed.

CYRUS'S VISION FOR THE FUTURE

Cyrus is determined to stay focused and use ZocDoc to perfect one niche of the health-care industry.

"I'm careful not to overreach or allow myself to be pulled in too many directions. I think of running this business like playing a difficult chess match. In the original matches between Garry Kasparov and IBM's computer, Deep Blue, Kasparov won because he wasn't playing to win. He was playing to *tie*—to survive while he slowly removed his opponents' paths to victory. With ZocDoc, we're not playing to win and revolutionize the health-care system with one effort. We're playing to fix it bit by bit.

"We're trying to improve the accessibility of health care in America. We could just as well have been a nonprofit company. It just so happens that we have a business model to make money, which gives us more control of our destiny."

JIM MCCANN

FOUNDER:

1-800-FLOWERS.COM

INTRODUCING JIM MCCANN

Unlike many of the entrepreneurs in this book, retail florists seldom face "all-or-nothing" outcomes. The probability of bankruptcy is extremely low; the probability of a comfortable, middle-class life, quite high. By the early 1980s, Jim McCann had achieved exactly that. With fourteen Flora Plenty stores throughout New York City, he was face-to-face with ambition's greatest enemy: comfort.

Thirty years earlier, Jim was the oldest child in a struggling Queens family. As he put it in his perfectly titled memoir, Stop and Sell the Roses, *"I saw myself going down the same road my father traveled: hand-to-mouth, chasing down customers, dealing with checks that bounced as high as a four-story walk-up." Because he had known its opposite, Jim understood the value of comfort. He had a clear, visceral awareness of how much he had to lose. Nevertheless, he bet it all.*

In 1986, Jim purchased a failing Texas company called 800FLOWERS. He was confident that the 800-number was the disruptive technology of its time, and that making the brand identical with the number was brilliant marketing. To prove his thesis, he took a $17 million bet, risking everything he had built at Flora Plenty, and renamed his company 1-800-FLOWERS. The bet paid off. In 1993, the company had more than $100 million in sales.

By the time Jim brought 1-800-FLOWERS public in 1999, after a decade devoted to building the company, he might have gotten comfortable and stagnated. He didn't. That same year, he changed his company's name again to announce a new disruptive technology he had embraced. From now on, it would be 1-800-FLOWERS.COM.

In a radically fragmented marketplace that values lifestyle businesses, Jim wanted a category winner and he got it. There are more than 15,000 florists in the United States, and Jim is in the top position. More important, he has maintained that position for over twenty years. This is not luck. This is a brilliant businessman at work—one, moreover, who will never settle for comfort.

JIM'S STORY*

Jim began his career as a social worker in his hometown of Queens, New York. He was the manager of a church-run home for "wayward" boys in Rockaway, making a good salary for the time. It wasn't enough.

Jim McCann: I wanted more out of life. I wanted to make more. I wanted more stimulation than I was getting on the old nine-to-five. I wanted to work for myself. This made me a budding entrepreneur, but at that point I didn't have any comprehension of what an entrepreneur was.

Jim's first step toward entrepreneurship was to buy an existing business.

A retail store sounded like a good way to enter the business world. I had worked in retail stores in my neighborhood and noticed that the owners seemed to live well. One day, while satisfying my genetic requirement as a young Irish boy in Queens—working as a bartender in the first Friday's located on 1st Avenue in New York—I heard one of my customers mentioned possibly selling his flower shop located just across the street.

I liked the idea of flowers as a business. People are always getting married, having birthdays, graduating from high school, retiring, apologizing to girlfriends. Flowers and the customers for them are endlessly renewable resources.

Here was a retail business already up and running that I could buy. So I maxed my credit cards, borrowed from my family, and raised $10,000, which bought me Vic's shop at 1st Avenue and 62nd Street, an old but rapidly disappearing Irish-Italian neighborhood, where the likes of Jimmy Cagney and Whitey Ford had played stickball as kids.

I was an entrepreneur—and a successful one—but it took a long time before I believed my success was going to last. I was like some of the bankers and stockbrokers I know who never give up their taxi licenses—just in case.

Jim's instincts were correct. Over the next several years he used all his profits from the first store to open one new store per year, naming his new chain Flora Plenty.

Eventually, Jim reached the point where most entrepreneurial careers end: comfort.

THE 1-800-FLOWERS.COM STORY

Technically, Jim is not the original founder of 1-800-FLOWERS. He first got involved with the company that owned the phone number by fulfilling orders through his chain of Flora Plenty flower shops in New York. When their orders began dropping off, Jim did some research and sensed a key opportunity. He was right: Dallas-based 800FLOWERS was failing. Jim bought the company in 1986 and renamed it 1-800-FLOWERS. As he explains in *Stop and Sell the Roses*, "We inherited forty boxes of useless records and a phone number." He also inherited $7 million in outstanding debts.

Despite these early challenges, 1-800-FLOWERS became an incredible success. The company went public in 1999. Today, 1-800-FLOWERS has more than $700 million in annual revenues.

* Material for Jim's story is adapted from his memoir Stop and Sell the Roses: Lessons from Business & Life *(New York: Ballantine Books, 1999).*

Between the morning I plunked down $10,000 for my first store and the afternoon when I paid millions for 1-800-FLOWERS, the story is one of ten years of growth from a *small* small business to a *big* small business. If it had ended there, you wouldn't be reading this. Financially, I would have been very comfortable. By 1983, the year my brother Chris joined us full-time, we had grown to fourteen shops in the New York area and were, as far as I am aware, the only twenty-four-hour, full-service florist chain in the nation.

Comfort did not end Jim's career. Soon after his brother joined the business, Jim was going to risk it all on a much bigger bet.

I remember exactly where I was the first time I heard about 800FLOW-ERS. It was 7:14 on the morning of November 16, 1984. I had just showered and was shaving. I was at that critical part when you purse your lips and squinch them to one side as you try to bloodlessly trim your upper lip. I had the radio on and some fast-talking announcer was extolling the virtues of a nationwide florist service called 800FLOWERS.

I was stunned. A company whose name was the same as its phone number. What a concept! I got the hugest tingle I have ever felt in the presence of a brilliant business concept. I have a clear, physical memory of continuing to shave with my face all contorted while my image in the mirror did a double take and turned to the real me and said—"McCann, that is the greatest idea you have ever heard. Do something about it!"

I had to get in touch with 800FLOWERS. I wanted to be part of them.

Flora Plenty became a fulfilling florist for 800FLOWERS, but it didn't take Jim long to see that there were problems. "The ads disappeared. And then the orders started to decline." The original investors wanted new management and approached Jim. He was excited for the opportunity, but after two years of nego-tiations he was almost ready to move on. It was at that moment that an original investor in 1-800-FLOWERS suggested something much more ambitious than a change in management. If Jim wanted to buy the company, he would back him. In 1986, Jim became the new owner of 800FLOWERS.

I had buried myself in debt and I was going to have to climb out of it or sink. So within a week of becoming the proprietor of the far-flung, thoroughly debt-ridden, renamed 1-800-FLOWERS "empire," there I was on the phone at a makeshift desk of planks and packing crates, working the hold buttons. "Thank you for calling 1-800-FLOWERS; this is Jim speaking. How can we help you today?"

Within five years, Jim had paid the company's debts and assured its continued growth. "As silly as it might sound today," he told me, "an 800-number was the disruptive new technology of its time." Jim was also an early adopter of the next great disruptive technology: the Internet. Back when he wrote Stop and Sell the Roses *in 1998, he still needed convincing about its potential. He wrote then:*

An alarming thing happened on January 1, 1996. 1-800-FLOWERS was named the single most successful business application on the World Wide Web. I say "alarming" because after all the hype about the way the Internet is transforming our lives, to have our little company come in ahead of Microsoft and IBM tells you about how far the Web has to go before it begins remotely to fulfill the predictions we see in the television commercials.

The Web would fulfill the predictions, and Jim would respond by changing the company's name from 1-800-FLOWERS to 1-800-FLOWERS.com. He brought the company public in 1999.

THE
JIM MCCANN
PLAYBOOK

Focus on What's Important

We all work hard. We're all as busy as can be. When it doesn't seem like we could possibly get any busier, we do. But if you're not focused on the right things, you'll be the busiest guy on the way to the poor house. You have to focus on the right things in the right order, and you have to tolerate a lack of perfection. There will always be more tasks than time and more decisions than data. Your task is to determine what's really important: what do you *have* to do and do well? The challenge is the same whether you're running a startup or a multibillion dollar company that's been around for thirty-five years.

Being Poor Is Exhausting

The biggest mistake I made at the beginning was bootstrapping. Managing an underfunded startup is terribly exhausting. It zaps all of your energy. All of your focus is devoted to keeping the expenses under control, managing your payroll, or getting the next dollar. You're forced to spend a completely disproportionate amount of energy keeping the ship afloat rather than rowing it in the right direction. You have no other choice. My lack of knowledge and sophistication in the beginning caused me to waste a lot of time, energy, and resources on being poor. To avoid that route, get the funding you need.

Curate Your Superego

I'm a mimic. I mimic good ideas, and I mimic people who have characteristics that I like. I'm a mimic when it comes to attitude, so I try to surround myself with people who I can catch attitude from. It's similar to Freud's idea about the id, the ego, and the superego. The superego is your conscience, the voices in your head telling you what to do. Those voices come from the books you read or the people you encounter, personally and professionally. There are a dozen people in my life whose voices I want in my head, especially when I'm in the depths of a problem. They can help you step back, simplify things, and see the forest for the trees.

BUSINESS OPERATIONS

Privilege Internal Advisers over Consultants

We modified our compensation structure a few years ago, and we were about to hire a firm to help us do it. I mentioned this to one of our board members while we were having a glass of wine. He said, "I don't have anything against consulting firms, but I know your firm as well as anybody. Let me save you some time and money here." Then he pulled a pad out of his briefcase and redesigned our compensation structure in about twenty minutes. It was spot-on. We were about to spend $280,000 on a consulting engagement. Instead, he said, "You pick up the $28 check for the wine and we're done."

CULTURE

Cultivate Alumni

When we were a young company, I used to become upset whenever we lost somebody to another organization, but now I recognize that having a widespread alumni network is an advantage. The world is changing. People don't work at one place for a long time anymore. If somebody leaves on good terms, gives proper notice, and treats everyone with professionalism and integrity, we want them to be one of our "alumni." It's not formalized, but we have a very strong community of former employees all over the world in all kinds of companies.

CUSTOMER DEVELOPMENT

Harness the Power of Conversation

When you're in the retail business, everybody is a customer or a potential customer. That means you have to be ready for conversations with a wide variety of constituent audiences. It's a challenge, but it's also an opportunity to expand your opportunities. Ideas you hear in one area will help shape your thinking in another. It sharpens your focus, and helps you put a vocabulary to new areas of focus.

FAILURE

Gloss Over Nonfatal Errors

When somebody makes an error, you have to evaluate it in terms of their character, the context of their mistake, and their history at your company. Sometimes you'll determine that the error was fatal and they have to be let go. Otherwise, they can and should recover from it. In those situations, be honest and clear about what happened, but don't dwell on the failure. Gloss over it and move on.

LEADERSHIP

Create New Vocabularies

A key component of leadership is to define a situation and get others to embrace a new vocabulary. For instance, I've recently become involved with the organization Conscious Capitalism, which was cofounded by John Mackey of Whole Foods. The phrase "conscious capitalism" names a behavior that comes naturally to us. It adds more depth to the idea and helps us define the way we think, act, and do business. A new vocabulary gives everybody you interact with a set of tools to understand where you're going as an organization and how you define success.

MARKETING

Embrace Instant Identification

Your brand is defined by the initial reaction that people have when they hear your name. If you strapped somebody to a chair, gave him an injection of sodium pentothal and said, "1-800-FLOWERS!" or "Jim McCann!"—what would he respond? That's your brand. It's emotional, and it's the first unconscious reaction people have to your personal brand or your business brand. Everything you do—good, bad, and indifferent—affects it.

METRICS

Redefine Success

When you define success, you're painting a picture of the future. Sometimes that picture will be accurate. Other times, reality will intrude and force you to change it. A milestone might take longer to reach than you had originally expected, or the end goal might have to be different. Declare victory and define a new set of goals. I think our job as small-business leaders is to step back and do exactly that.

TALENT

Tailor Communication to Individual Goals

Every individual in an organization should have the tools and information they need to achieve their specific, clearly defined goals. It isn't your responsibility to make sure that each of your employees knows how the organization makes money. It's important that they know that you know how to do it. But all they have to know is that their job is to move the ball from here to there. All your employees achieving their goals will roll up into a colossal success for everyone. But if you spend all of your time trying to educate and teach and evangelize, you'll spend yourself poor in terms of energy and resources.

JIM'S VISION FOR THE FUTURE

Though Jim has been in the business of selling flowers since 1976, he's recently expanded into a new field. "Service-center leaders and managers from around the company were asking me when we were going to start offering fruit arrangements. Customers were asking for them every day." Though 1-800-FLOWERS didn't offer fruit arrangements, Jim was comfortable with the business. "When I ran my first flower shop thirty-five years ago, customers often asked for fruit baskets. A friend in catering taught me how to make them, and I put them together whenever customers asked."

After considering the possibility of acquiring an existing company, 1-800-FLOWERS.com launched their own offer, a new brand: FruitBouquets.com. Today, the service is only offered in a small number of locations, but Jim wants to bring it to all 35 million of his customers. "It's going to remake our company from the inside out. Ten years from now, I suspect that we'll be delivering a lot more food gifts than flower gifts.

STEPHEN & HEIDI MESSER

FOUNDERS:

LINKSHARE

INTRODUCING STEPHEN & HEIDI MESSER

For nearly a century, marketing worked in largely the same way: businesses would choose a demographic they wanted to target, identify a platform that served that demographic, and pay for space on that platform based on audience size. Since at least the 1920s, this model was the basis of nearly the entire media industry, from magazine ads to television commercials. As with so much else, the Internet radically disrupted it.

Pay-for-performance advertising is one of the lesser-known revolutions brought about by the Internet, but it's also one of the most significant. Rather than paying for eyeballs and hoping for sales, advertisers can use the Web to track customer behavior from the moment they see an ad to the moment they click on it and make a purchase. In other words, marketing costs can be directly tied to bottom-line revenues for the first time. Without this form of advertising, companies like Google couldn't exist. It is one of the pillars of the digital economy, and Stephen and Heidi Messer helped to create it. In particular, they were pioneers of online-affiliate and performance-based marketing.

When Stephen and Heidi founded LinkShare in 1996, major online advertising networks like Google AdWords didn't yet exist. (In fact, Google itself was still a couple of years away.) They were nearly alone in their recognition of this opportunity, and they had to endure years of being told that it was a foolish pipe dream. They weren't fazed. When Stephen and Heidi commit to an idea, their commitment is deep. They will work together for as long as it takes to build a lasting company, always avoiding the temptation to exit before seeing their vision through. The marketplace needs more founders like them.

There is, by the way, one thing that makes the Messers' story almost completely unique: it's one of the only sibling startup success stories that I know of.

STEPHEN & HEIDI'S STORY

Stephen and Heidi launched LinkShare in 1996 out of a studio apartment in New York City. The company had a part-time tech and a part-time marketer; Stephen and Heidi were the only full-time employees. These were the very early days of the consumer Internet, and the Messers were looking for an opportunity that nobody else had recognized.

Stephen & Heidi Messer: In the very beginning of the Internet, our goal was to find an area that we could disrupt. We were looking for a place where the reigning logic had historically been very successful, but the world around it had changed so that the logic didn't fit anymore.

When we started LinkShare, everyone was doing impression-based advertising. You paid depending on the number of people who saw your ad. That was the only way to work on television, radio, and magazines. John Wanamaker (who largely invented modern advertising) famously said, "Half the money I spend on advertising is wasted; the trouble is, I don't know which half." You had to pay for widespread advertising because you had no way of knowing which impressions led to sales and which didn't.

What nobody else realized was that the Internet solved that problem. On the Web, you could trace a decision-making process all the way down to a sale. That meant you could implement pay-for-performance advertising for the first time, which was what we did.

In attempting to create an entirely new marketplace, Stephen and Heidi constantly faced the criticism that their vision would never come to fruition.

Both of us quit really lucrative jobs to start LinkShare. People told us things like, "You're ruining your career!" or "You're ruining your life!" Those are actual quotes. Fast-forward a couple of years later. Then we started to hear, "You're the smartest people we ever met! You're brilliant!" And then the market crashed, and it was back to, "We knew this was going to happen!" And then the market came back . . .

At some point, you have to stop listening to what everybody has to say—both bad and good. Focus on what you're doing—that's the most powerful weapon against failure.

THE LINKSHARE STORY

While LinkShare is not well known outside the enterprise-marketing world, in the decade following its founding, two-thirds of Fortune 500 companies with affiliate advertising networks were signed on to be LinkShare clients.

For the first two years, LinkShare was self-funded. It needed to be, Stephen and Heidi were nearly alone in seeing the opportunity presented by quantifying the value of online advertising.

"We launched pay-for-performance marketing very early on because it was just more logical," Stephen said. "The rest of the world hadn't come to that conclusion because they thought, 'We've had thirty, forty, fifty years of buying this way, so we're doing a good job.' We thought that inertia might carry them forward, but the logic no longer supported their assumptions. We saw that as a very disruptive way of treating the world."

In 2005, the Japanese Web portal Rakuten Inc. acquired LinkShare for $425 million.

In the early days, LinkShare was staffed by a team of generalists who had to quickly adapt to the realities of a rapidly changing business. The structure of the business changed drastically as the company scaled.

Companies go through different stages. In the early days, you expect people to pick up projects and move with them, even if something doesn't fall directly into their role. At LinkShare, the early team did everything except vacuum the office (which happened to be our apartment).

As you transition from twenty employees to forty, you start having managers. Most likely, the jack-of-all-trades who took on a number of roles in a specific area like operations or finance will now have four or five employees. When you get closer to eighty employees you need to start hiring multiple managers. Now your managers are the jacks-of-all-trades, and employees have to become masters of one. That's where you start to encounter challenges. People who were your best employees in Year One become your worst employees when they have to start focusing very narrowly.

The focus that Stephen and Heidi expected of their employees also needed to be ingrained into their company.

Early on we decided what we were not going to do. We weren't a very big company, so there were certain roles that a company normally performs that we just couldn't do. For example, in the first years, we decided that we would not invest in customer support, period. We were a B2B technology company, we were digging a well that didn't exist and we had the best technology out there. It wasn't as if someone was going to do better customer support. We knew that if we did implement customer support, we would end up doing it poorly. Frankly, no customer support is better than bad customer support.

Despite the ups and downs of the late '90s and early 2000s, Stephen and Heidi were so committed to their idea that they resisted a pair of temptations many founders succumb to: spending too much money and sacrificing too much equity.

If your company is a successful investment for a VC, it's actually in their interest to get you to spend more money. It's counterintuitive, but it's the only way they are going to get larger equity stakes. Sometimes you do need to get out there and spend more, but you have to ask whether those expenditures are going to create the incremental value that increases equity for the entrepreneur and all the employees.

It's always easier to spend money than it is to save money. As your company grows, you'll have more and more constituents who come in and ask for more money to spend. If you're going to survive, you have to become more of the "no" person than is in your nature, because entrepreneurs, by their very natures, want to say yes.

Of course, there is an upshot to restricting costs and preserving equity: a lucrative exit.

If you asked most entrepreneurs whether they'd rather sell a company for $80 million or $150 million, they'd probably say $150 million. Then the second question is whether they'd rather own 100 percent of an $80 million company or a third of a $150 million company. That's the calculus you have to keep in mind when you're raising money.

It's a calculus that Stephen and Heidi mastered. When they sold LinkShare to Rakuten in 2005, they owned a significant stake in a $425 million company.

THE
STEPHEN & HEIDI MESSER
PLAYBOOK

Don't Flock to Watering Holes; Dig Wells

There are lots watering holes out there, but if all the sheep are running toward the same one, it's going to run out pretty fast. Good entrepreneurs are going to say, "It doesn't matter what everyone else thinks. Where are the sheep *not* going?" If you're a good entrepreneur, it's like being a shepherd. You're finding a place that people didn't know about and leading the herd there, instead of following everybody else.

Be Prepared to Work Through All the Phases of a Successful Startup

When you first start a business, you're spending 100 percent of your energy on something that you love: figuring out the business, getting people motivated, and understanding the market better than anyone else. Later, you're probably spending less time creating the new and more time doing what a corporation needs to be successful. Don't get caught up in loving the newness rather than the journey. The ability to scale and grow is much harder when you get beyond the stage of having only 30 employees and you know everyone's name. Embrace the challenges of running a 300-person company or a 3,000-person company.

Work with a Gritty, Honest Partner

Most people think it is lonely to found a startup, but having the best partner you can find and a person that complements your skill set is the key differentiator. It's hard to be naysayers and tell people where they're wrong, and you don't necessarily want to hear that you're wrong. It's nearly impossible to find somebody you can have that honest relationship with. But if you pick the right partner and that partner wants to stay through the whole venture, you'll end up in a great place. Picking a partner is like adopting a sibling or getting married. You want to pick someone for better or worse who you're not going to abandon, and who you won't worry is going to walk away when things get rocky. We were fortunate to be brother and sister, best friends, and good at very different things.

STEPHEN & HEIDI'S BEST ADVICE

FOCUSING TIME & ENERGY

Prioritize Tasks as "Air," "Water," and "Food"

Stephen: If you separate things into High, Medium, and Low priority, everything is obviously "High." So we came up with a new standard. All life survives on air, water, and food. You can live only minutes without air, days without water, and weeks without food. So we categorize all the high-priority things as what you need to do now, tomorrow, or in a few weeks. You're not going to live for long without food or water, but clearly air rises to the top. When you look at things as air, water, and food, you'd be amazed at how easy it is to focus.

HIRING

Hire Broad Generalists in the Beginning

Stephen: In the early days, everybody in the company is a jack-of-all-trades. Someone may be have been hired for accounting, but can do anything from technical integration to writing reports. That's broad, but it is broad in a narrow area. In the beginning, everyone should be prepared to do what's needed and make clear where they can serve as a jack-of-all-trades.

LEADERSHIP

Relinquish Control to Managers, but Be Ready to Take It Back

Heidi: It's scary the first time you walk by someone's desk and you don't know what they're working on. Once you have a strong infrastructure in place, it's about getting comfortable with the fact that there's stuff going on that you don't even know about, and that you have put in place good processes to hire trustworthy and competent people. On the flip side, when you see a department that you thought was really well run start to fall off a cliff, trust your gut and don't be afraid to do what's needed to fix it. You're not a corporation where politics and bureaucracy are relevant and that's a critical advantage.

METRICS

Year One Metrics Are Guesses

Stephen: In the first year of the business, whatever metrics you have are essentially estimations. You're using your best judgment, but plenty of logical guesses are wrong. After three years, your metrics get much more defined. Usually, once you have more data, they look much different than what you initially developed.

RAISING CAPITAL

Don't Mistake Raising Capital for Success

Stephen: Raising an inordinate amount of capital is often seen as a sign of success. The consequence of raising *too* much capital, however, is that the company has to be that many times bigger to get a return on that investment. Optimally, you're taking money to actually grow, rather than as a false indication that you're growing. Raising capital is not necessarily success; building the business is success.

TALENT

Find Employees Who Can Transition as You Scale.

Heidi: As you scale, it becomes necessary for people to become more specialized and more disciplined about what they're doing. Your best employee from zero to six months is often times your worst employee from six months to twelve months. Some people just can't make the transition from the "Wild West" to a less chaotic environment. One of your hardest tasks is finding people who are scalable, or finding new roles for people as your company grows.

VISION & MISSION

Don't Start a Company to Get Rich

Stephen: When I see entrepreneurs make money, I'm thrilled because I know that they worked hard for it and they deserve it. Yet those entrepreneurs didn't choose their career path in order to make a fortune. Given a startup's odds of failure, there are easier ways to make money. If you're starting your own venture, you have to have a desire to create something new and valuable and control your own destiny.

WORKING FOR YOURSELF

Don't Be a "Serial Entrepreneur"

Stephen: I think the title "serial entrepreneur" is an insult. If you're a serial entrepreneur, you don't care enough about your idea and you don't believe it's big enough to focus on. You're just playing craps: you're throwing a whole bunch of chips out on the table and hoping that something hits.

Heidi: If you found this watering hole that no one else knows about, those first two years require supreme self-confidence and faith. Everyone is telling you that it's a bad idea; that it doesn't exist; that it's not going to work. Unless you have this extreme conviction and almost total indifference to what everyone else around you is saying and thinking, you'll question yourself. Questioning yourself is the worst possible thing you can do once you come to the conclusion that this is a great opportunity.

STEPHEN & HEIDI'S VISION FOR THE FUTURE

The Messers have brought the same philosophy that made them such successful entrepreneurs to their work as angel investors. "We take the 'value-investing' approach to starting and investing in companies: when people run from an area that has strong fundamentals, we look and say, 'That's probably a good idea,'" Stephen said. Today, the Messers are at work on a new venture, Collective[i], a multi-tenant, high-volume decision support ASP that connects disparate data sources and automates data science, business intelligence, and knowledge sharing across sales, marketing, and general management functions, as well as continuing to focus on angel investments and launching companies in the United States and around the world.

ELON MUSK

FOUNDER:

PAYPAL

SPACEX

TESLA MOTORS

CHAIRMAN:

SOLARCITY

INTRODUCING ELON MUSK

Elon Musk's focus is clear, and it's nothing less than securing the future of humanity itself. At an early age, Elon identified three areas that he believed were particularly important to solving the world's most pressing challenges: the Internet, sustainable energy, and extending human life to other planets.

His first stop was the Internet, where he cofounded PayPal with an eye toward revolutionizing the financial industry. In his subsequent endeavors, Elon has pursued his visions passionately, even when it has meant risking every dollar he made after eBay acquired PayPal.

Today, Elon is supporting the creation of a renewable energy economy by installing solar panels on every home and by putting electric cars on every road. He's also working to build a reusable rocket, so that interplanetary travel will one day be as convenient and affordable as intercontinental travel.

Elon leads his businesses intuitively, perhaps because he is also their chief engineer, spending the majority of his time focused on development, design, and execution of the most outstanding products and services conceivable.

ELON'S STORY

Every entrepreneur wants to make a significant impact on the world, but Elon Musk might be the only one who seriously intends to make an impact in outer space.

Elon was born in South Africa, but after two years at a Canadian university he moved to the United States because "the U.S. is where great things are possible." He was also eager to avoid military service in what was then an apartheid state. (Never hesitant to speak his mind, Elon once asked a reporter, "Who wants to serve in a fascist army?") He earned degrees in business and physics at the University of Pennsylvania before moving on to Stanford's graduate program in applied physics. But after two days, Elon dropped out; the example of Netscape had convinced him to abandon grad school and become an Internet entrepreneur. His first venture was Zip2, an early online directory service.

Elon Musk: When I started the company, nobody was putting any money into the Internet. In fact, I wasn't quite sure if I'd be able to pay the rent. But as it turned out, the Internet was pretty huge.

Zip2 would be a success, but only after a very difficult start. In 1998, Elon convinced the company's board to drop out of a proposed merger with CitySearch at the last possible moment. One analyst compared the move to calling off a wedding after all the invitations had been sent out. Later that year, however, Elon's instincts paid off: Compaq acquired Zip2 for $307 million.

After Zip2, Elon took his first stab at transforming an entire industry: financial services.

I didn't have any experience in finance, so many people thought it was foolish for me to enter such an established field. But there is an extreme lack of innovation in these large industries. I saw it as an opportunity.

In 1999, Elon started X.com (later PayPal) to take advantage of that opportunity. As far as Elon was concerned, the opportunity created by PayPal's success was squandered. Rather than becoming a major financial institution, PayPal became "a glorified feature," a buy button. After his experiences with Zip2 and PayPal, Elon was determined to pursue his visions unencumbered.

I need to be protected against a private equity firm or hedge fund trying to force me to maximize profitability rather than affecting the future of humanity in a positive way. That's why I have to have a controlling stake, or close to one, in all of my ventures.

THE PAYPAL STORY

Elon started X.com in 1999 to take advantage of the stagnation of the financial industry. In 2000, X.com acquired Confinity. It would prove a lucrative move, but severed Elon's connection with the company. Because of disagreements about the direction of the company, Confinity cofounder Max Levchin and investor Peter Thiel pushed Elon out as CEO of X.com, which they renamed PayPal. The following year, eBay acquired the company for $1.5 billion.

THE SPACEX STORY

In 2010, Space Exploration Technologies (SpaceX) became the first private company to successfully send a spaceship into orbit and bring it back to Earth. That year, SpaceX also won a NASA contract to supply the International Space Station until the space shuttle's replacement becomes operative. In May 2012, its Dragon spacecraft became the first commercial vehicle in history to berth with the International Space Station.

Despite the enormous windfall he received from PayPal, Elon was still willing to take risks. Every company he's started since leaving PayPal has been in an industry riddled with failed attempts, including electric cars, renewable energy, and commercial space travel.

I wouldn't say that I'm pathologically optimistic. I always have optimism, but I'm realistic. It was not with the expectation of great success that I started Tesla or SpaceX. I think if you'd asked me at the beginning what I thought the odds of success were, I would have said, "Significantly lower than 50 percent." It's just that I thought they were important enough to do anyway.

In space travel especially, Elon is confident that he and his team have out-performed all predecessors.

At SpaceX, we're better than anybody in the industry. In fact, we're way better than anybody ever has been in our industry.

Recently, NASA recognized SpaceX's achievement by granting them an extremely lucrative contract. Nonetheless, if the company does not eventually create a fully reusable orbital rocket, Elon will consider it a failure.

One of the reasons for SpaceX's success is Elon's absolute commitment to creating an outstanding product. He spends the majority of his time at the company furthering that goal.

I have weekly meetings with each of the areas of expertise at SpaceX—the propulsion team, the structures team, avionics, the launch group—as well as the weekly general staff meeting. We'll also have period design reviews on new technology that we're developing. At a higher level, I set strategic objectives for the company and make sure that people meet those strategic objectives. But most of my time—60 to 65 percent—is spent in engineering, design, and execution of research and development. It's similar at Tesla.

The results at Tesla have been similar as well: outstanding products. The Tesla Roadster is an amazing vehicle, but only a preliminary step toward Elon's goal of producing high-quality, low-cost electric cars. If his previous ventures are any evidence, we should be seeing those quite soon.

THE TESLA MOTORS STORY

In 2008, Tesla Motors released the Roadster, an electric sports car that outperforms many Formula One competitors. Elon has his sights set on the production of midlevel electric cars that will eventually outnumber their internal combustion counterparts.

THE SOLARCITY STORY

SolarCity was founded in 2006 by brothers Peter and Lyndon Rive. (Their cousin Elon is an investor and the company's chairman.) In addition to designing energy systems, Solar-City is a pioneer of unique residential leasing programs for solar panels. SolarCity installed panels at eBay's North Campus in 2008. It was the largest commercial solar installation in the state. Yet, Elon's commitment to solar energy is so great that he has made it a philanthropic venture as well as an entrepreneurial one: in disaster areas, or in regions where SolarCity does not plan to expand commercial production, the Musk Foundation will install solar panels for free.

"[W]ishful thinking is one of the most profound human failings."

THE
ELON MUSK
PLAYBOOK

Impact the Future of Humanity

I've always tried to be involved in things that will impact the future of humanity and have a good effect on the world. I wasn't necessarily thinking about whether my ideas were the best way to make money. Of course, if your company goes out of business, you're not going to change the future of humanity at all. You have to be sensible and bring in at least as much cash as you spend. Otherwise, it's pointless.

Build Your Company Around a Great Product

I'm always surprised when people think they can make a great company without having a great product. The most important thing an entrepreneur can do is focus on making a great product or service. The only way to do so is by learning from the feedback loop of the market and constantly adjusting behavior. If I were to offer one piece of advice to entrepreneurs it would be to stay very close to the product and be hell-bent on making it as good as it can be. In other words: make your customers as happy as they can be. You're trying to get them to give you money, and the best way to do that is by giving them a product that they enjoy.

Never Engage in Wishful Thinking

I find it remarkable that I can explain the reality of a situation to people and still not change their point of view. The facts are very plain and the reasoning is very clear, but they still won't agree with the conclusion. It's crazy. Rather than learn from their experiences, they choose instead to engage in wishful thinking. Perhaps it's more comforting than reality. But I think that wishful thinking is one of the most profound human failings, the major reason that people adhere so strongly to wrong ideas. This doesn't mean that you can't be optimistic. You simply have to be realistic as well.

ELON'S BEST ADVICE

CULTURE

Don't Allow Jerks to Infect Your Team

If a manager is a jerk to the people who work for him, it's a huge demotivator. I once asked the factory technicians on the floor what they saw as the best value of unions. They said that if their boss was a jerk, they had no recourse, but the union gave them a recourse. So I made the rule, "There will be no jerks here." If one of your managers persists in being a jerk, fire him. It helps morale, and it's a great way to minimize people's tendency toward being jerks.

FOCUSING TIME & ENERGY

Business Is Easy: Focus on Products

My primary strengths are as a technologist and an engineering designer. Most of my time is spent in design and execution, and the rest on everything else. I also have skills on the business side, but that's much easier than the invention and design side.

FIRING

Make Sure People Know Why Somebody Was Fired

It's important to tell people why someone was fired. Otherwise, they may think that it was a random decision and not based on merit. That's tough, because you're potentially opening yourself up to a lawsuit in that situation, so you don't need to post this information on a billboard. However, people need to know why somebody is no longer with a company, and what action that person did that led to their departure. Then, employees who are doing their jobs will know that they're not in danger, while those exhibiting negative behaviors will curtail those behaviors.

HIRING

Avoid MBAs

As much as possible, avoid hiring MBAs. MBA programs don't teach people how to create companies. At my companies, our position is that we hire someone in spite of an MBA, not because of one.

HUMAN RESOURCES

Look Past Direct Managers to Assess Performance

When evaluating people, look past immediate supervisors. The feedback loop should also include a rigorous peer-review system. While relying on a single person might be arbitrary, we've found that the combination of the manager's report and the peer-review system provides a much more objective and accurate assessment.

LEADERSHIP

Run Your Company for as Long as You Reasonably Can

In the beginning, I thought I could focus on product development and hire somebody else to be the CEO. Now, I've come to the conclusion that I need to run the company as well as do the product stuff. Founders should run the company for as long as they reasonably can. You should only consider passing over the reins to somebody as good or better than you are at creating great products.

MARKET DEVELOPMENT

Prioritize Your Overall Market Above Your Short-Term Revenues

As a result of Tesla's actions, there's a much more rapid move to electrification in the auto industry. Not only are we developing our own electric cars, we're making it easier for other auto companies to do the same. Today, we're producing power train components for Daimler and Toyota. I don't care if I'm arming my competitors: I just want more electric cars on the road.

TALENT

Measure an Employee's Net Impact on the Team

You can't only look at what an individual employee gets done. You also have to look at how they've helped people around them get things done. An individual might be very, very skilled, but have personality traits that cause a reduction in the productivity of those around them. For instance, some people are great individual contributors, but they engage in the sort of political machinations that cause people to spin their wheels instead of moving forward. It's an easy thing to overlook if they're performing at the individual level, but you have to assess an employee's net impact on your entire company.

WORKING FOR YOURSELF

Work Remotely on Weekends

I have five children, so balancing work and life is tough. I used to go to the office every weekend, but I don't anymore. I still work every weekend, but I work by email and phone in those interstitial moments when the kids are playing amongst themselves. It's a good thing that there are devices like iPhones that give you an immediate ability to do short snippets of work. Otherwise, we'd be in deep trouble.

ELON'S VISION FOR THE FUTURE

In 2008, Elon wrote a column for *Esquire* claiming that there have been only "a half dozen genuinely important events in the four-billion-year saga of life on Earth," ranging from the origins of single-celled life to the advent of consciousness. Elon's goal is to add a seventh item to the list: interplanetary life. He considers the invention of a "fully reusable orbital rocket" (his ultimate goal at SpaceX) to be the key to that goal. Speaking with *Inc.* magazine, he claimed that this event would rank slightly above "the movement of animals from water to land" in importance.

There are two other inventions that Elon believes will change the world forever: "rapid, low-cost, perfect DNA sequencing" and "viable fusion." Elon believes both are achievable, but a long way off. Instead, he's focusing on reducing the emission of greenhouse gases by putting more electric cars on our roads and more solar panels on our rooftops. It's a testament to Elon's ambitions that he considers those goals to be a slight compromise.

JACQUELINE NOVOGRATZ

FOUNDER:
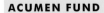
ACUMEN FUND

INTRODUCING JACQUELINE NOVOGRATZ

In the past ten years, Jacqueline Novogratz has brought moral leadership to a marketplace that is in desperate need of it: finance.

Philanthropy is a component of what Acumen Fund does, but it doesn't capture its essence. At the core of Jacqueline's work with Acumen is the notion of "patient capital," long-term investments in entrepreneurs and new businesses in impoverished regions, which fundamentally improve and save lives. Jacqueline learned early in her finance career that money could be about much more than acquisitiveness or greed. If properly directed and administered, capital can help human beings surmount the obstacles around them and prosper, to feel a sense of hope and pride. But what she is talking about has little to do with traditional charity.

Jacqueline started her career at Chase Manhattan Bank and she has brought that toughness to her nonprofit work. She's a disarmingly intense listener, but not the slightest bit bashful about stating her own views. She is committed to changing the traditional donor-grantee relationship. Acumen maintains a forthright, close connection to its donors, who it calls partners, and who all share Jacqueline's passion for creating a world beyond poverty.

I've known Jacqueline for many years, and I agree with her brother Michael when he says he realized long ago that his sister had to choose one of two paths. She could become the head of the United Nations or the World Bank or the IMF, or forge her own path. By building a new model with Acumen Fund, Jacqueline has unlocked the explosive potential of entrepreneurs the world over, from India to Pakistan to East and West Africa. She's clearly chosen to take a different track.

JACQUELINE'S STORY

Jacqueline Novogratz: Since I was a little girl, I've always had the sense that we're interconnected. I came from an immigrant background. My grandmother had a third-grade education and nine kids, three of whom died when they were little. The value of hard work equaling success—and the dignity that comes with it—was always a part of my upbringing.

Jacqueline's first foray into the work that would change her life began when she accepted a position at Chase Manhattan Bank that took her to forty countries on three continents.

I loved being a banker. I loved how numbers could tell a story, and how smart investment could transform ideas into jobs and sometimes things of beauty. What I didn't like was that poor people were not in the mix. The banks felt it was too expensive, too difficult, and too risky to lend to the poor. And low-income people themselves were often too frightened to even walk into the bank's doors.

I wanted to change that so, through a series of events, I took a job that led me to Rwanda.

While I was in Rwanda, I started the first microfinance bank in the country with several Rwandan women. I learned that a small group of people can indeed change the world. I also saw up close that charity alone would not solve problems of poverty. At a government-sponsored bakery I worked with in Kigali, I saw how charity created a culture of givers and takers, allowed a language that humiliated rather than dignified, and kept the women employees dependent on the goodwill of others.

After turning the bakery into a full-fledged business, we cornered the city's snack-food market and the women began earning two to three dollars a day, up from fifty cents. There was a total change—they began to see for the first time in their lives a correlation between the effort they put in and the income they earned. And I learned where business can play a role in giving people the tools they need to live lives of dignity and meaning.

THE ACUMEN FUND STORY

Acumen Fund is a nonprofit, venture-capital fund whose goal is to create a world beyond poverty. The Acumen model takes philanthropic capital and invests it as loans and equity in developing-world businesses that are tackling poverty in fundamental ways, including providing health care, water, housing, education, and other services to people in need.

Acumen calls the money they invest "patient capital" because they leave it in companies anywhere from seven to ten years, or more. Entrepreneurs in the developing world are creating new markets where there are often high levels of corruption, or where people face a sense of despair, so it takes time to establish trust in the outcome, as well as to build the systems that can sustain and scale over time.

As of 2012, Acumen has approved $78 million in seventy enterprises, creating new industries for low-income communities. They've supported 57,000 jobs and reached 90 million people.

After attending Stanford's Graduate School of Business, Jacqueline joined the Rockefeller Foundation, where she established the Next Generation Leadership program and the Philanthropy Workshop.

At Rockefeller, I would spend time in the archives learning about the history of the institution, its beginnings, and the power of philanthropy. It was an amazing time. The world was changing, and by the end of my decade there, the dot-com era was in full swing. With the tectonic shifts in technology and our growing interconnectedness as a world, we needed a new kind of institution, one that stood on the shoulders of the best of philanthropy, but utilized markets as a listening device. The missing ingredient was a kind of capital that held entrepreneurs accountable, but was patient enough to allow for experimentation and failure on the road to scale.

Jacqueline started Acumen Fund in 2001 with the support of the Rockefeller Foundation and other founding partners.

I began by talking to people about a third way, one that made investments using philanthropic capital. I so disliked the rubric of the "donor," and the dynamics that it often created, that I told my team we would ban the word. But people were confused by being called "investors" when they wouldn't get their money back. We needed to do things differently and try new approaches, even if some might fail.

In the early days, our success was in large part due to the willingness of two major foundations—the Rockefeller Foundation and the Cisco Foundation—to provide the startup capital and bet on this idea. The argument was "You've both been at the forefront of reinventing philanthropy, and I believe this is the next stage."

Then, we reached out to a group of core individuals to become founding partners. We created a partnership model right up front, saying "We don't just want your money—we want your brains, your connections—we want you to really be part of building this." We created a business plan, talked about it day and night, raised the money, and hired a small team that came together in April 2001 and began building.

Jacqueline, the Acumen team, and their partners were experienced in both business and philanthropy. What brought them to the next level was their willingness to look at the shifts underway in both sectors and integrate them into Acumen's model.

When you think about some of the institutions that are most sustainable, they are not large companies or corporations. Rather, they are the great universities, the political parties, religious institutions. When I think of the long-term sustainability of Acumen, I think of institutions that become so valued by a community that society decides it's in their

"We don't just want your money . . . we want you to really be a part of building this."

interest to help them flourish and bring them to the next level. One of the most critical building blocks of that vision is creating an institution that grows organically through strong local footprints. For Acumen Fund, this means establishing country offices with talented country directors and local teams. It also means cultivating local business leaders as advisers and partners who commit themselves to the success of each office by raising money, mentoring the team, and helping our investees scale to reach more low-income people.

Acumen's identity—business or philanthropy?—was tested early on.

Initially, there was a lot of pressure to make grants because no one had ever worked with a nonprofit that invested money. We understood the critical role that grants played, but we eventually saw that what businesses needed more was the discipline of investing. So we made the decision to make only equity investments and loans. We call these investments *patient capital*—commitments of $300,000 to $2 million combined with management assistance and expectation of payback or exit in roughly seven to ten years. We may only receive 80 or 90 percent of the money back, but through our investments we hope to achieve significant social impact and identify breakthrough business models that bring goods and services to low-income people for the first time.

For example, I think of Shaffi Mather, who decided to fix the broken ambulance system in India. In India, if you want to go to a hospital, you call a taxi. If you want to send someone to the morgue, that's when you call an ambulance. Shaffi decided there had to be a better way. He started with just 9 ambulances donated by friends and family, and everyone thought it was just a fool's errand. Today, with patient capital invested, hard work, and lots of bumps along the way, his company Ziqitza Health Care Limited now has 870 ambulances, 4,500 employees, and one million people served.

Change is possible—and it will take the best of both markets and philanthropy. It will take all of us—but if not us, who? If not now, when?

"[W]e hope to achieve significant social impact and identify breakthrough business models that bring goods and services to low-income people . . . "

THE
JACQUELINE NOVOGRATZ
PLAYBOOK

Identify What's Broken, but Seize the Possible

While it's important to recognize what is broken, it's much more important not to overemphasize it. Instead, focus on what you want to create. Seize the beauty, the possibility, and see the infinite potential of what's in front of you. Don't waste time talking about why things are broken; create a new model and a community of people who are willing to help you build it.

Create Founding Partners

Create a partnership model that is about much more than funding. In addition to being financial investors, your partners need to be, and in fact, likely *want to be*, fully invested in building the entire venture, from helping with strategy to working with team members on specific initiatives.

Be a Pillar of Society

Remember you are standing on strong shoulders. Daily, I'm astounded at how dependent we are on the work and ideas of so many who have come before. So walk with humility and a reverence for the human endeavor. Know it is your job to help take that forward in ways big and small.

JACQUELINE'S BEST ADVICE

BOARDS

Having the Right People Matters

Surround yourself with people who are different, who will speak the truth, who care as much as you do, not only about what you are doing but how you are doing it. Ensure diversity not because it is politically correct, but because it enables you to realize the mission more effectively.

BUSINESS OPERATIONS

Systems Matter

Systems matter, especially after the startup phase. We underestimate the importance of the COO and other senior managers in entrepreneurial organizations, while often placing too much emphasis on the "visionary." Without systems that work and without great execution, an idea can dissolve like snow in the sun.

CULTURE

Cultivate what You Honor

People make the culture, and the culture is what enables excellence, commitment, and, ultimately, the ability to create something beautiful and lasting. If you are in the long-term work of bringing about change, work with people you love being around. Make sure they are not only smart, passionate, committed, generous, and audacious, but also people who walk with humility, have a sense of humor, and reject the status quo.

CUSTOMER DEVELOPMENT

Build Lasting Relationships

Think in terms of relationships that will last forever. Commit to sharing failures as well as successes, and to learning on the edges. This isn't always comfortable, but if it comes from a place of values and a shared vision, then ultimately it will create a real community that is bound by something bigger than any single individual or even the entire group. We all crave this in our interconnected, but too often disconnected world.

DEPLOYING CAPITAL

Early-Stage Social Ventures Require Risk-Tolerant Capital

Like other ventures, early-stage social ventures require risk-tolerant capital that gives entrepreneurs room to fail and experiment with the business model. Our entrepreneurs are selling critical goods and services in markets that have never before had access to them, in environments that are often corrupt, in regions with poor infrastructure. Grants and philanthropically-backed financial support are needed to build and prepare these markets.

METRICS

Define Your Own Success Metrics

Just because traditional metrics may not apply to the new model you're creating, you can't simply say, "There are no failures. Everything is good!" That makes it too easy to avoid accountability. When traditional measures don't work, create your own and stick to them.

PUBLIC RELATIONS

Share Your Failures Openly

If you've created effective partnerships with your investors, your customers, and your public, they won't need to believe that you're perfect. People are serious when they say that they want to get involved and be part of the entire process. You need to respect that desire and commit to transparency. Share your failures as well as your successes. It isn't just about PR; it's about courage and humility.

VISION & MISSION

Dream Big and Just Start

Dream big, articulate dreams in as precise a way as possible, then just get started. Let the work teach you what you need to know.

JACQUELINE'S VISION FOR THE FUTURE

After its ten-year anniversary, Acumen is expanding its vision. The original idea was "to fix, even revolutionize, philanthropy." But it turned out that wasn't enough. There are parts of the philanthropic system that are broken, but there are also parts of the commercial system that are broken. We needed a third way. Beyond changing lives, we needed to invest in leaders. The goal now is to create models that do not involve handouts but offer real choice, real opportunity, a real sense of people making decisions in their own life's journey.

People are finally ready to look at this extraordinary thing, the human being. If we can only help him get rid of the challenges in front of him, he can solve his own problems. That is where dignity starts, and where the commitment to using patient capital is so important. Fixing not just Third World, but also First World, economies, "That's where this next chapter is taking us at Acumen."

HOSAIN RAHMAN

FOUNDER:

JAWBONE

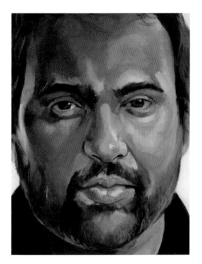

INTRODUCING HOSAIN RAHMAN

When Elvis Costello released his first album in 1977, everybody declared him an overnight success. But with fresh memories of the long preparation that went into building that success, Costello offered a correction: he was "an overnight success, after seven years." The exact same thing can be said about Hosain Rahman's company, Jawbone. Founded in 1999, the company became a sensation with the release of its first Bluetooth headset in late 2006. It was a seven-year overnight success.

Hosain has never forgotten the long run-up to the Jawbone's success, and he doesn't expect his future achievements to be any easier. He knows that category-defining products like his take a long time to build, and he remains as committed to the process as he is to the product.

The most impressive thing about Hosain's team is their ability to recognize the fundamental problem they are trying to solve. They originally came together in order to invent the first truly effective speech-recognition tool, but soon realized that you couldn't voice-activate mobile devices if you couldn't effectively talk to them.

The Jawbone headset finally made it possible to effectively communicate to a mobile phone—and it included HD audio to boot. Best of all, Hosain never tires of reminding us that this elegant device was the result of a nearly decade-long struggle; the triumph of the scrappy underdog who builds some of the most beautiful consumer products in the world.

HOSAIN'S STORY

Jawbone has released two major product lines: their flagship Bluetooth headset and the Jambox, a portable Bluetooth speaker. Both of them are category-breakers, and neither was part of the company's original vision. When Hosain launched the company in the late '90s, he set out to create the best speech-recognition-enabled mobile software in the marketplace.

Hosain Rahman: We started Jawbone in 1999, but had actually started working on the original idea in late 1996. At that time, Nokia had just released mass-market mobile phones differentiated on the basis of better user interface. Our goal was to make it possible to interact with these devices in an even more elegant way. The Nokia phones and original PalmPilot were fantastic devices, but based on text inputs. We thought that was pretty inefficient. If you're walking down the street using these devices, why couldn't you just talk to them?

Our original plan was to build a speech-recognition overlay into the operating systems so people could use their voice to control mobile devices. We took a step back and tried to understand what was preventing speech solutions from being deployed. Was there something that no one was paying attention to? Did there need to be some enabling technology, or an innovation at the computing level?

We discovered that the input signal for getting commands into the phones—the user's voice—was corrupted in the real world. Without a clear input signal, software solutions would be fatally flawed. In order to make speech recognition work in a live environment, there needed to be innovations around audio input and noise cancellation.

That was the insight that led us to start work on the Jawbone. We created the noise-cancellation technology to make speech recognition work and recognized it allowed people to talk effectively in places that they weren't able to do so before. Eventually, we decided to build our own consumer hardware as a means of deploying the technology and ensuring the best possible experience for the user. It was very hard in those days to raise money to build hardware, but we did that.

Hosain and his partners had no experience in the telecommunications space. In the early years of the company, they had not yet realized that this was one of their greatest competitive advantages.

THE JAWBONE STORY

Jawbone was founded in 1999 to tackle what was then an intriguing problem: integrating speech-recognition technology into mobile devices. "We thought mobile was the next big paradigm shift in computing, and that it would be perfect to interact with these devices in a totally seamless way, using voice." But before they could deploy effective speech-recognition software, Hosain and his team would need to solve a technology problem. Without an effective noise-cancellation technology, speech-recognition tools would be useless. They eventually released a hardware product as a means of getting their technology to market.

Jawbone introduced its innovative Bluetooth headsets, which incorporate Jawbone's revolutionary noise-cancellation technology, in late 2006. (With the Jambox, they've recently expanded into portable speakers.) In 2010, the Industrial Designers Society of America (IDSA) recognized the Jawbone as one of the greatest "Designs of the Decade."

When we decided to build hardware, we hired a few senior guys from the mobile and consumer electronics industry, but they turned out to be the wrong people. Because we weren't from any particular industry, we were free of biases and able to look at everything in a totally fresh way. As founders, we had no background in audio and no background in the headset business, and no background in consumer hardware. Zero. The few people on our team who did have that experience were the ones who told us not to do it. Luckily, we stayed unreasonable and pursued our vision because we were confident we could build something people loved.

Jawbone released their first Bluetooth headsets in late 2006, and they were resounding success. But rather than settle into being an accomplished provider of a single product, Hosain pushed his team to innovate in radically different fields.

As soon as we started to achieve dominant market share in our category, I gave every single person in our company a T-shirt that had "Underdog" printed right on the front. I wanted everyone to remember that we were always going to act like an underdog, just like we had when we were breaking into the market.

The success of the Jawbone wasn't an excuse to stagnate; it was an opportunity to expand. If the Jawbone hadn't been successful, would we have gone into the speaker business? No. Would we have gotten into health? Not even close. But the only reason that we were successful with the Jawbone was that we went through the struggle of tackling the really hard problems, sometimes down to the raw science of how the product was going to work in addressing real consumer needs.

As Hosain has implied, the next major release from Jawbone was the Jambox, a portable Bluetooth speaker.

The Jambox brought us back to the thesis that we had in 1997: the mobile phone was going to become the center of your life. It took several years for that to indeed happen, but today, the phone is not just a communication device. It's a complete media platform and hub for all video, music, and voice. We wanted to create a high-quality, portable product that unlocks the real media potential in a really delightful way.

When we started looking at the speaker space, we discovered some amazing innovations in acoustics that other products weren't yet taking advantage of. We incorporated them into a completely mobile speaker, and now many people use the Jambox not just on the go but at home, even if they have a full stereo system behind them. It's been completely disruptive.

Even within the company, many people thought we were crazy to go into the speaker business. Now, after less than a year, the Jambox is the number-one selling speaker in North America by unit volume and revenue.

While Hosain continues to pursue disruption and innovation despite his already extraordinary success, he doesn't do so out of a severe startup discipline. The early challenges are simply his favorite part of running a company and provide the foundation for a way of embracing change and new ideas that lead to the next great thing.

THE
HOSAIN RAHMAN
PLAYBOOK

Build to an "Experience Continuum"

At Jawbone, we don't have a traditional research-and-development division. We develop products by considering the full "experience continuum." We map out every single part of any particular product or daily experience, identify the friction points, and think of ways to resolve them. When we started, for instance, we had no intention of building hardware. The experience we wanted to create, however, ultimately demanded that we focus in that direction. That's been the number-one focus for us over time: what is the experience we want to deliver to people and how do we innovate and create solutions around that? Whether we're building something on our own, bringing it in from the outside, or waiting for it to be developed, it's all in the service of reducing friction in our customers' lives.

Focus On What Your Customers Care About

The number-one lesson that I learned through all our trials and tribulations at Jawbone is stay 100 percent focused on what users really care about. The question is the same whether it's a physical product or a nonphysical one: what threshold do you have to cross such that customers perceive value in your offer and continue to use it? If anything, the ease of coming to market has made that question all the more important. It's much simpler and more capital efficient to

release a product today, and amazing distribution networks like the Web, or Apple's app store, have made it easy to get a large footprint very quickly. All that means, though, is customers have an unprecedented number of options, so getting them to see the value of yours is that much harder.

Yesterday's Home Run Didn't Win Today's Game

Look at how quickly things change in the world around us. At the end of 2007, when Jawbone raised $30 million from Sequoia Capital, RIM was an $80 billion company. Today, they're at $5 billion. They clearly took their eye off the ball of what people care about. There are hundreds of examples of the same phenomena. You're always in that adversity matrix. My favorite saying is that yesterday's home run didn't win today's game; you're only as good as your next hit.

In every business, you will fall down and make mistakes. If they don't kill you, they will give you the valuable experience of getting kicked in the teeth and feeling blood slosh around in your mouth. Remember what that tasted like and use it to inform your next decision. If you become satisfied with success, you'll stop focusing on what's coming next or how to get better. That's the mistake that *will* kill you.

HOSAIN'S BEST ADVICE

CUSTOMER DEVELOPMENT

Build Goods That Have Higher Perceived Values Than Costs

The essential product-development model is very simple: sell products for more than you paid to make them. In order to do that, people have to perceive additional value in what you offer. They won't pay a premium on what you made unless you've addressed an important pain point that they have. When they are willing to pay that premium, you've reached a tipping point and you can start building a business around it.

FAILURE

Facilitate Innovation by Minimizing Risk

If everybody in your organization is afraid of failure, they will be too paranoid to take real risks and try something innovative. You have to encourage your employees to try things and risk failure. An important part of the founder's job is to create an organizational culture that can fail fast and change direction without taking the ship down. You need to make sure that failures can be contained. Give yourself the protection of multiple products that generate multiple streams of revenue.

FOCUSING TIME & ENERGY

Think Carefully About What You Won't Do

When you're small, you don't have the capital, time, or resources to go spinning off in a lot of different directions. You have to stay focused because you don't have the luxury to *not* be focused. As you scale, you can do a lot more things. Then, focus becomes even more important because it's a lot harder to achieve; you need to devote just as much of your decision-making calculus to what you're *not* going to be doing. Always determine where you have maximum leverage and opportunity and don't waste resources in other areas.

LEADERSHIP

Communicate the Logic of Your Decisions

When you start to scale an organization, the key is to communicate *how* you make decisions. What is the calculus that led you to a conclusion? When your team understands that logic, they can apply it to making decisions themselves. That degree of explicitness may feel aggressive, strange, or even risky at times, but it ultimately ends up solving more problems than it creates. Your team also needs to be more comfortable talking about problems than hiding them.

MARKET DEVELOPMENT

Scale into Market Demand

When we built a Bluetooth headset with noise cancellation, we were entering a highly developed marketplace where millions of simple Bluetooth headsets were already being sold. People were using mobile phones for more and more, and we had functionality that clearly resonated with people. Because we built a product that served a clear, unmet need in a large marketplace, it shifted category and we were able to achieve massive distribution and scale almost overnight. We topped and scaled into a latent market demand.

PRODUCT DEVELOPMENT

Everything Is a Prototype

Product development is never done. Everything is a prototype—a stepping stone to the next stage; but to say that everything is a prototype is not to say that you should ship beta stuff. You have to be absolutely committed to high quality, but remember it's just the beginning of what is possible. You are never done. All the elements have to be in place before you go to market with a product, but it should still be just one step in a broad and inexhaustible vision. It should also be good enough to get you to the next steps.

TALENT

Build a Team That Astounds You

Surrounding yourself with people who are exceptionally great at things, even better than you are, is an amazing experience. You have the opportunity to enable them to be their best. They should constantly astound you. That's how I measure my executives: how much do they astound me? What can they envision that I had never dreamed of? What can they do that I could never possibly do myself?

VISION & MISSION

There Is No Playbook

The most important play in the playbook is to remember that you're always rewriting your playbook. Even the plays you ran six months ago are totally dead today; the world is moving that fast. As soon as something gets to a stable place, it's time to destroy it and build the next thing. Launch a product, re-create a marketplace, and then throw it all away and start again. Stay fresh, stay innovative, and move quickly. Never take any plays for granted. Experience is about making sure you don't make the same mistakes. Make sure you are always making new mistakes.

HOSAIN'S VISION FOR THE FUTURE

Viewed narrowly, the Jawbone is the outstanding product in a long-existing category: the Bluetooth headset. But Hosain sees it as the first product in the next major marketplace: wearable technology. "Computing began in mainframes, went to desktop machines, then laptops, and now it's in all of our pockets. The next thing will be wearable devices that gather intelligence from your body, and open up new experiences."

At a TED Global presentation in July 2011, Jawbone announced a wearable wristband called Up, which will collect information from your body (such as sleeping patterns and movement) and communicate it to smartphone applications. "Health problems in this country are growing rapidly, and the mobile health opportunity is huge," Hosain says. Jawbone is prepared to seize that opportunity: in 2011, they raised $120 million in venture capital to support their move into the new market. It's more than they raised in the preceding eleven years combined.

ADEO RESSI

FOUNDER:

THEFUNDED.COM

THE FOUNDER INSTITUTE

INTRODUCING ADEO RESSI

Before Adeo Ressi left New York for San Francisco in 2007, he had already developed invaluable startup skills and relationships. Rather than leveraging them into another standalone venture, however, he pivoted from building companies to building entrepreneurs, which he's doing in unprecedented and unique ways via the Founder Institute. The Founder Institute is a provider of the kind of startup training that MBA programs fail to deliver, and that real visionaries like Adeo (and *Playbook* participant Steve Blank) are just beginning to define. Of the accepted founders, fewer than 50 percent make it to graduation—it's that tough. Adeo's other game-changing venture, TheFunded.com, also serves entrepreneurs by providing unbiased, firsthand information about VCs. As many of the participants in this book have commented, fundraising is the beginning of a crucial relationship in any founder's life and career. TheFunded.com is one of the only places they can go to decide, based on the accounts of others who have dealt with them, whether it's a relationship they want to engage in.

In 2010, Adeo caused a commotion when he told a Singapore audience that entrepreneurship couldn't be taught. He clarified his point later: only a small percentage of people are suited to the particular challenges of founding a startup, and their innate predispositions can be fostered and nurtured. In a sense, though, anybody who was surprised by his statement didn't understand that Adeo is a provocateur—passionate, supremely confident, boisterous, and loud. Only somebody like Adeo could have engineered the cloak-and-dagger secrecy around "Ted"—his original pseudonym as the founder of TheFunded.com.

ADEO'S STORY

Before he became a Bay Area incubator and catalyst, Adeo was a seven-time New York entrepreneur. His first company was Total New York, an early (1994!) advertiser-supported, online city guide, which was acquired, retitled AOL Digital City, and eventually sold for $675 million. Next, he founded Web development firm methodfive, which he sold in 2000 to Xceed for $88 million. Then came a consulting firm (Sophos Partners), followed by Game Trust, Inc., an e-commerce platform for online gaming that was acquired by RealNetworks, Inc. in 2007, after a protracted dispute that left Adeo wanting never again to be a CEO. He was so angry with the VC world that he vowed to find a way of holding VCs accountable in the future. The Funded.com—a discreet forum where founders and CEOs could discuss and rate VCs—was born out of that experience. TheFunded.com, which went live in early 2007, was at first a website composed of a group of founders Adeo knew personally, all of whom used pseudonyms to contribute their feedback on individual VCs. Adeo himself was also anonymous. There was a lot of suspense and drama around the project, with founders and VCs taking bets on who "Ted" might be and Adeo zealously guarding his identity. Adeo finally came out as "Ted" in a November 2007 article in Wired magazine, an unveiling he carefully orchestrated.

Adeo Ressi: When we first started, there were twenty-five of us—mostly my friends. The original idea was that you could only join if you were invited by one of the twenty-five, so we grew at a snail's pace. Then, one of the original members suggested that we let people apply. That happened on March 14, 2007. Within twenty-four hours, it appeared on TechCrunch and scaled very quickly. That day, we took in something like 1,000 membership applications.

The site has been a magnet for controversy, both because of its policies of allowing contributors to remain anonymous, as well as because it is the first time that the dirty little secrets of the venture-capital world were so publicly aired. But Adeo is confident that it has made a huge difference in terms of enabling founders to know what they're getting into with potential investors.

CEOs who contribute to TheFunded.com realize that if they bind together and help one another, the problems they face today will be alleviated in the future—both for them, because they will gain the collective wisdom of everyone else, and for the next guy who finds himself in their shoes. It's not the middle cases that get written up on TheFunded.com. It's the

---

THE THEFUNDED.COM AND FOUNDER INSTITUTE STORIES

Adeo had founded three startups and a venture-capital firm by 2007, when he shifted his focus to incubating the work of other entrepreneurs. He began with TheFunded.com. This private community of startup CEOs addresses a strange irony: the unprecedented transparency brought about by information technology had not yet extended to the secretive, insular world of IT venture capital. By creating a forum where more than 17,000 CEOs could rate and research VCs, Adeo has helped to change that.

Two years after launching TheFunded.com, Adeo created the Founder Institute, a mentorship program for high-potential entrepreneurs. Though he is an enthusiastic member of the Bay Area startup community, Adeo wants to "globalize Silicon Valley" and see its creativity replicated elsewhere.

boundary cases: the guys who did something really good or the guys who did something really bad.

TheFunded.com generates revenue through limited advertising, and through subscriptions sold to non-CEO members such as lawyers and consultants. But generating revenue is not Adeo's primary goal for the site.

The success metric for me is that I can go to a room and a couple of entrepreneurs come up to me and say, "Thanks to TheFunded, I was able to bring a new solar panel to market that will change the way that we live." That's the success metric I'm looking for.

Soon after revealing himself as Ted, Adeo also revealed plans to leave New York in search of greener pastures.

New York is a very unhealthy place to do most anything. It's very easy to get distracted by basic things: you try to go dinner with a friend and you end up with a belligerent cabdriver, a weird waiter, and the person next to you spilling a drink in your lap. It's a high-friction environment and it drives people to really bad behavior.

The average startup founder in New York, for instance, operates in a zero-sum game. If they defeat the opponent and win, then they're the victor. Everything becomes a small battle or a small war. In fact, this focus on "winning" is a big distraction. I'm happy to lose a hundred battles if I survive to the end, but no New Yorker thinks that way. If they lose a hundred battles, they're a 100-time loser. Winning the war is a plus-one. Net-net, they're still a 99-time loser.

He found a more congenial atmosphere in San Francisco. To be precise, he found it in Silicon Valley, which in Adeo's view is a community of startup entrepreneurs who are fostering and supporting one another rather than simply trying to defeat each another. In 2009, he launched the Founder Institute, a training program on steroids for startup entrepreneurs. In a few short years, it has helped incubate nearly five hundred companies on five continents, and trained hundreds of entrepreneurs via its bootcamp-like, four-month programs. In addition to leveraging the Bay Area's startup culture, Adeo was putting two of his greatest talents to use: an ability to gauge talent and an ability to catalyze ideas.

"I can walk into a room and gauge the talent level of everybody in it."

I can walk into a room and gauge the talent level of everybody in it. It's an innate scale. Everybody has a way of interacting with and thinking about the world, and I can spot it within a second of watching somebody. It's obvious to me. I'm also a really good catalyst. In fact, I might be the best catalyst that I've ever met. I can see people's potential and pull it out of them. With the Founder Institute, I've industrialized that talent.

THE
ADEO RESSI
PLAYBOOK

Apply the Strengths of Your Personality to the Deficits of the World

Success comes from applying the strengths of your personality to the deficits of the world. When you look at the world's greatest engineering challenges, space flight is probably number one. Automotive is up there, as is solar. If you have a great engineering mind, you should tackle the world's great engineering challenges. If you're a great catalyst and can see potential and pull it out of people, industrialize that.

Start with Multiple Ideas and Kill Them Off

Begin with a pantheon of related ideas and kill them off until you get to the best one. It's much easier to kill an idea when it's not yet a business, it's still just a project. The more ephemeral you keep it, the better.

Conserve Dollars in Every Way You Can

In the beginning stages, you just don't know if your idea will work. There's a long gestation period when you're not spending money while still validating your idea. But even after you prove the idea viable, conserve as much capital as possible until you prove conclusively that it will work. Starve the company until you prove that it can live, and then start feeding it a healthy diet. Hungry startups grow faster. Once you're persuaded it can survive, then start really putting money into it. When you decide to go out and raise a boatload of money, it should only be after you have done an enormous amount of research and work on a shoestring budget to validate your idea.

ADEO'S BEST ADVICE

CULTURE

Reward, Relieve, and Drive

Your entire culture needs to be directed toward getting things done. That has to be the primary goal of your organization. To maintain that drive, implement fun social rewards to vent the stress. Reward achievement, relieve stress, and drive the next achievement.

FAILURE

Make New Mistakes, Not Old Ones

Making the same mistake twice isn't a consequence of ignorance or bad luck. It's stupidity. After a founder makes a second fatal mistake, don't placate them by saying "This is your learning moment." Their learning moment should have been one mistake ago. Often, founders don't learn what they should because people refuse to be up front with them.

FIRING

Have Zero Tolerance for Mistakes

If an employee makes significant mistakes in the beginning, it will only get worse. You can't have any tolerance for mistakes. Implement a two-strike policy. If someone makes one mistake, let it slide. If they make a second, they're out.

HIRING

Everyone Has Potential

If you're a human being on the planet today, you have potential. Everyone has potential, and most of it remains untapped. The irony is that the great minds have more aggregate untapped potential than most other people. Just look at how much they've achieved, and they're probably only running at 30 percent. When you evaluate talent, it's pointless to ask if *they* have potential. The important question is whether *you* can tap it.

HUMAN RESOURCES

Leverage Social Science Testing

Don't rely entirely on your character judgment in hiring decisions. Social science tests such as the Myers-Briggs Type Indicator can supplement your hunches with far greater precision. If you want a real indication of a candidate's specific skills and intentions, there are a number of tools that can help you gauge it.

LEADERSHIP

Be Tough and Intellectually Honest

When you're intellectually honest with someone, you pull the best work out of them. In reality, you also have to be a little tough. If people fail or make mistakes, tell them directly. A person cannot grow without hearing the truth. That's not to say that you shouldn't recognize accomplishments, but that's not the same thing as patting people on the back and being polite. I actually don't think there's any point in being nice or supportive or accommodating or polite. It's a complete and utter waste of time.

WORKING FOR YOURSELF

Be Relentlessly Devoted to Your Idea

Being devoted to an idea goes beyond hours. Your whole person has to be devoted to solving a problem. If you are going to survive after the first year or two, it will only be because your devotion has led you to create something exceptional. This requires extreme attention to detail. You have to do anything and everything to make it happen.

ADEO'S VISION FOR THE FUTURE

Adeo talks about the Bay Area startup community with the passion of a convert, but his goal at the Founder Institute isn't only to incubate more Silicon Valley startups. As he explained to Anthony Ha at Deals & More, his goal is far more ambitious. "The vision of the whole institute is to launch 1,000 companies a year. I set out with a macroeconomic goal, which was to help get us out of recession and go back to innovation by forming hundreds of companies in different geographies. Of course, when you model it out, you have to assume failure. You have to assume that not everyone who applies will get in, and you have to assume some people who get in won't graduate, and you have to assume some people who graduate will fail. The model calls for maybe two companies out of fifty being wildly successful."

LINDA ROTTENBERG

FOUNDER:
ENDEAVOR GLOBAL

INTRODUCING LINDA ROTTENBERG

The vast majority of the entrepreneurs in this book, and a disproportionate number of the world's entrepreneurs, are based in the United States. Linda Rottenberg noticed this fact while living in Buenos Aires in the 1990s. But for her, this wasn't a passing observation. It was the beginning of a global opportunity. If you spend any time with Linda, you'll quickly be zapped by her electric personality and fearless approach to getting people to say yes. Linda is a gale-force wind— a warm one.

Linda cofounded Endeavor Global in order to catalyze "high-impact" entrepreneurship throughout the world. In doing so, she was targeting a market sector that had scarcely been defined up until then. She wasn't looking to provide aid to the world's poorest nations, or to make investments in highly developed venture markets. Endeavor set its sights on economies with up-and-coming middle classes, but where there was a clear lack of organized entrepreneurship behind the cultivation of new, high-growth businesses. Without local investment ecosystems, potential entrepreneurs couldn't get started. Endeavor was built to nurture a new class of local entrepreneurs, and to provide them with access to a global network for training and financing.

Today, Endeavor sponsors so-called High Impact Entrepreneurs throughout the world, with offices in fifteen countries. The success of the six hundred entrepreneurs Endeavor has "selected, mentored, and accelerated"—together they have produced 180,000 jobs and generated $5 billion in annual revenue—underscores how huge the potential for opportunity was in this area. That's what great startups do—they take previously unidentified opportunities and turn them into gold. With Endeavor, Linda has created something that is changing the world.

LINDA'S STORY

Linda Rottenberg graduated from Yale Law School and soon thereafter decided she had no interest in practicing law. She traveled to Latin America and fell in love with it. She settled in Buenos Aires, where she very quickly observed that there was no path to wealth creation for even the most talented local entrepreneurs. In fact there wasn't even a Spanish word for "entrepreneur" (the term emprendedor *had yet to take hold). Nearly all the wealth and capital in Argentina in the 1990s were held by huge companies and a few wealthy families. She wondered how to lay the groundwork for a Steve Jobs, or a Michael Dell, or a Walt Disney to emerge there.*

Linda founded Endeavor Global in response to this need. Because she was doing something radically new, she had to think outside the box when it came to procuring capital for the new venture.

Linda Rottenberg: We had a strategy, but we knew no private equity firm would touch us because, for trust reasons, we needed to be a nonprofit given what we were trying to accomplish. At first, we had every door shut in our faces because we weren't helping the poorest of the poor or the richest of the rich. We needed seed money.

One of the first people I contacted was Stephan Schmidheiny, a prominent Swiss investor and philanthropist with a passion for Latin America. Eventually, he came in; he offered us $200,000 up front and another $100,000 for every company that we could get financing for. He structured it as a twelve-month grant. Six months in, we told him that we needed more money. We'd launched in Chile; we needed to officially launch in Argentina, and I needed $200,000 more. His people told us that you couldn't rewrite the terms of our grant in the middle of the term. Nonprofits didn't operate that way. But we weren't modeling ourselves on nonprofits. We were modeling ourselves on the great IT startups that were emerging at that time, like Netscape.

Stephan agreed to provide more money, but on one condition: that we prove our model was market driven by finding local entrepreneurs to match his investment. He'd spent a lot of time in Latin America, and he knew how difficult this was going to be. He imparted this piece of wisdom: "I've lived all over Latin America and the only thing in shorter supply than entrepreneurship is philanthropy." He said, "Good luck!" and sent us on our way.

**THE
ENDEAVOR GLOBAL
STORY**

Endeavor is a global nonprofit founded in 1997 with the goal of enabling high-impact entrepreneurship in emerging economies. Through a rigorous screening process, Endeavor identifies entrepreneurs in countries throughout the world and provides mentoring and investment, resources their native countries often do not have the infrastructure to support.

To date, the company has selected just over 600 "high-impact" entrepreneurs from nearly 30,000 applicants. These individuals, in partnership with Endeavor, have created high-quality jobs in countries in the Americas, Africa, and the Middle East. More than 97 percent of the businesses Endeavor fostered are still in operation. Sixty-six percent of Endeavor entrepreneurs invest in other Endeavor companies. In the first two years after a startup engages with Endeavor, it will grow, on average, by 70 percent.

Linda didn't need luck because she had a lead. Eduardo Elstein had become famous for making George Soros the largest landowner in Argentina at the time, through investments he'd made on Soros's behalf. Peter Kellner, Endeavor's other founder, was able to land Linda a ten-minute interview with Eduardo.

Five minutes into the interview, he says "I get it. You want a meeting with George Soros. I'll see what I can do." And I said "No, Eduardo. I'm an entrepreneur; you're an entrepreneur. You're one of the only entrepreneurs in Argentina. This is an organization of entrepreneurs. I want your time, your passion, and $200,000." He signed a check on the spot, and became the chairman of the board. He calls it the best investment he's ever made.

The next time I walked into somebody's office, the price had gone up to $2 million.

With capital available in the countries her first entrepreneurs would be based in, it was time for Linda to return to the United States and seek board members for Endeavor. She decided to target Peter Brooke.

Peter Brooke was considered the founding father of international venture capital. When I heard that he was speaking at the Harvard Business School one day, I went to watch him. Unfortunately, I wasn't the only one there who wanted to speak with him after the talk. I needed another way to approach him, and I found it. I waited for him outside the men's bathroom and introduced myself when he came out. I said, "I'd like to come talk to you. You've been providing venture capital in emerging markets for longer than anybody else, and I'm just starting to enter those markets. I'd love to get some of your advice." He was startled, but he still asked who else was involved. On the spur of the moment, I said, "Bill Sahlman." "Sahlman's involved?" he said, with surprise. He handed me his card and said, "Come see me."

Bill Sahlman, who runs Entrepreneurial Finance at Harvard Business School, was one of my mentors, though at the time somewhat skeptical of Endeavor. After that chat with Peter Brooke, I marched up to Bill's office and told him, "Guess what? Peter Brooke is going to join our global advisory board. Will you co-chair?" It was not until three years later, when Peter and Bill were cohosting our tenth global advisory board meeting, that they realized that neither had ever actually said yes first.

With the money and the board talent they needed in place, Endeavor took off. They screened entrepreneurs in multiple countries, and many of the companies they catalyzed made an extremely high impact. Endeavor entrepreneurs in

Argentina have generated nearly $2 billion in revenues, and Chilean entrepreneurs have created more than 6,000 jobs.

Having screened potential entrepreneurs from all parts of the globe, Linda is uniquely qualified to see the universal traits of a winning entrepreneur and a winning startup idea.

It takes a year to become an Endeavor entrepreneur. You have to go through eight rounds of screening, culminating in an international selection process. Every decision needs to be unanimous.

After more than a decade of engaging in this process, I've come to realize that the most important traits in an entrepreneur are passion and controlled obstinance. I don't think all entrepreneurs need to be charismatic; not everybody is going to fall in love with you. But you have to give people a reason to support you and your business; you have to be obsessed with your vision. The other key is mentorship. That's where Endeavor comes in. The entrepreneurs who grow the fastest and biggest within Endeavor are the ones who gain a fierce advocate within our board—somebody who will fight for them when everybody else thinks they're going to fail.

THE
LINDA ROTTENBERG
PLAYBOOK

Crazy Is a Compliment

If you're not being called crazy, you're not thinking big enough. Something's wrong if they're not calling you crazy—maybe you're not doing something innovative enough. You should be thinking "I'm the next Steve Jobs," even when everyone's telling you to go jump in a lake.

Don't Push. Be Pulled

In the early days of a startup, you have to stalk potential investors. But eventually, you have to convert from being a stalker and pushing for your vision to being *pulled* into markets—and that point arrives faster than you'd think it would. Don't push your way into a new market; go in when you're pulled by people who are ultra-committed and will be local champions for your company or cause.

Minnovate

It's not only radical disruptions that lead to successful companies. It's small tweaks in products, distribution, or customer acquisition. Large companies perpetuate the belief that every change needs to be a radical innovation. It has to be a breakthrough. But our entrepreneurs often innovate in small iterations. They are agile. We call it "minnovation." Along with their vision of the big picture, they foster minidreams that are conquerable every year or every quarter or every day. Dream big but be able to break your dream down into manageable pieces.

BUSINESS OPERATIONS

Have One Clear Executor

When we enter a new market, it's much easier to find founding teams than founding individuals. In those cases, we need to make sure there are shareholder agreements—the lack of a shareholder agreement is one of the clearest predictors of long-term failure. There can be numerous partners, but there has to be one clear executor. It's a real challenge because it often involves making very difficult decisions, particularly with family-owned companies. I always say that Endeavor 101 should be "How To Fire Your Mother-in-Law Gracefully." If you can't make decisions like that, you won't be able to build a new company.

CUSTOMER DEVELOPMENT

Build Relationships

The majority of client acquisition occurs because customers trust your products, your brand, and your people. It is a process very costly in effort, energy, time, and money. Unless you make building relationships based on trust a core focus, all of that time, money, and energy will be wasted.

LEADERSHIP

Vulnerability Is an Asset

To be a great leader today, you have to focus on your family, too. When people see you doing that, they connect with you more, respect you more, and want to follow you more. Sometimes it's hard to accept that, because you want to appear self-sufficient. But there will be times when you'll have to tell your team, "I'm not always going to be available." They won't lose respect for you for that. They'll gain respect. Vulnerability is a real asset.

MARKET DEVELOPMENT

Markets Are More Similar Than Different

Our experience in numerous global markets has led me to a controversial conclusion: markets are more similar than they are different. We'll often hear businesses on the verge of expanding claim that what works in Brazil won't work in China or India or Latin America. We've found the opposite to be the case. What works in Argentina is probably going to work in South Africa. And it's probably going to work in Turkey. There obviously need to be adjustments to the local market, but they're not as drastic as one might imagine.

PRODUCT DEVELOPMENT

Break Big Problems into Small Pieces

It's important to have big ideas, but it's equally important to have the capability to break that big idea into many pieces. You need to sustain your business with incremental, quick wins. You can't spend your entire time striving for an intangible, ten-year-out goal.

RAISING CAPITAL

Stalking Is an Underrated Strategy

Stalking is an underrated startup strategy. You have no choice in the beginning but to insistently track down potential investors. If you stop at "Don't bother them! That would be rude!" you'll never get a yes. What's the worst that can happen? They'll say no.

TALENT

Allow Your Team to Override Your Opinions

You can't convince some of the top people in the world to devote a significant amount of time to your organization if you never allow them to override your opinions. Sometimes when you start, you think you'll be so persuasive that everyone you work with will submit to your vision. But that won't work if the people you are targeting are at the top of their fields. They aren't the top business leaders in their countries for nothing. They need to have a piece of psychic equity. Their voices need to matter.

VISION & MISSION

Define Yourself by Saying No

Saying no is as powerful as saying yes. Saying no to the wrong opportunities helps reinforce who you actually are.

LINDA'S VISION FOR THE FUTURE

Linda looks forward to a day when Endeavor doesn't need to sponsor more entrepreneurs in a given country, a point that will only arrive when entrepreneurs in all countries have the same opportunities as entrepreneurs in the United States.

"My Brazilian board and I were discussing the notion of a natural end to Endeavor's involvement in a country where the economy takes off. A boom in the overall economy, however, doesn't signal the arrival of the change we want to bring about. In the United States, every small-business owner thinks that they can be the next Mark Zuckerberg or Oprah Winfrey if they have a great idea. That day hasn't yet arrived yet in these markets. When every cabdriver in Argentina can dream about creating a Facebook or becoming a Ralph Lauren, then I'll be happy to say 'Job well done.'"

The day when Latin American, African, and Middle Eastern countries would produce as many new international businesses as the United States seemed infinitely distant in 1998. But thanks to all Endeavor's been able to accomplish, that day is getting closer all the time.

KEVIN RYAN

FOUNDER:
ALLEYCORP

CEO:
GILT GROUPE

INTRODUCING KEVIN RYAN

They say, "Once, you're lucky; twice, you're good." I'll add, "Four times, you're Kevin Ryan."

Kevin has an extraordinary talent for executing on ideas. He's not trying to invent a better mousetrap. He wants to find the inventor of a better mousetrap so he can produce it and market it and sell it. He built DoubleClick into a billion-dollar company, then created AlleyCorp as an incubator for multiple startups. He hoped AlleyCorp would produce one hit. As of this moment, it has produced at least three: Gilt Groupe, 10gen, and Business Insider.

With AlleyCorp, Kevin has designed a model of entrepreneurial reward that values execution as highly as ideas. Not only has it proven successful, but it better reflects the reality of company building. The startups that succeed are not just the ones with the best ideas. They're the ones who execute on their ideas most effectively. Despite this fact, the compensation structure at many startups favors those who initiate an idea over those who bring it to fruition. To an extent, Kevin was a victim of that structure as the CEO of DoubleClick, and he's built AlleyCorp to rectify the mistake. I would not be surprised if he's sparked a new trend that will allow more great ideas to survive all the way to market.

KEVIN'S STORY

Before he and business partner Dwight Merriman created the AlleyCorp net-work of companies, Kevin had nearly a decade of success with one of the great Internet stars: DoubleClick, an early application service provider with a focus on online display advertising. Kevin joined the company in 1996 and soon became CEO. Over the next nine years, he turned the company into the leader in its space, expertly helming it through various crises and the bursting of the dot-com bubble. In 2005, the private equity firm Hellman & Friedman LLC acquired DoubleClick for $1.1 billion and Kevin stepped down as CEO. The company was eventually sold to Google for more than $3 billion. But by that time, Kevin was already focused on launching a new group of businesses.

Kevin Ryan: Most people don't have the confidence to quit their jobs and start companies. They'd rather join something already established, with the security of a salary and where somebody else has the responsibility to set the vision. But, as I learned in retrospect, starting a company is where you get the payoff. As the tenth employee of DoubleClick, I ended up with something like 2.5 percent of the company. But if I had taken more risk and been involved in the first three months in a senior role, my stake might have been closer to 10 percent.

Kevin's experience with DoubleClick remained invaluable. It gave him the skills and track record he needed to found companies on his own, as well as the finan-cial resources to work on an early-stage startup. With AlleyCorp, Kevin made two unique and important decisions. First, he would distribute his risk by building numerous companies at the same time. Second, he would develop a model that valued execution equally with ideas.

Gilt, Business Insider, and 10gen are completely different. They don't even have the same revenue stream. The reason for this model is that I didn't take the risk of owning a single company. Starting from scratch is a really risky bet. I may have gotten lucky with DoubleClick, but I didn't want to spend four years building something only to find out that it didn't work.

I actually decided to start Gilt and Business Insider in the same month. When I told my wife, she said, "You have four companies already. Can't you just do one of them?" It was a reasonable point, but I was too committed to both ideas to let either go.

Kevin did not have experience in either the retail or publishing industries, but he understood that those industries were only superficially related to the ideas he was pursuing.

At Gilt, we started by getting six senior people together, and not one of us was a retailer by trade. I doubt that most people would have started that kind of company without having anybody who had purchased merchandise before, purchasing being the particular area that scares people in the retail business. I started to think that maybe we did need someone somewhere to actually pick out the clothes and accessories that we'd be selling on the site, but it became clear relatively quickly that that wasn't the business we were in.

Everybody on our senior team had an Internet background, and we were in the business of building a technology platform that happened to focus on a particular niche: high-end fashion and luxury items. The fact that none of us came from that niche was not a real problem. Look at Amazon, for instance, Jeff Bezos never claimed that he picked the books for you, or that you should care what Jeff Bezos reads. He created an environment where you can find great books.

Amazon doesn't curate at all, so Gilt is a little different in that respect. We do need people here who can choose great products. The essential problem is not purchasing, however, it's to make sure that the systems work—and the systems are incredibly complicated. Warehousing is complicated. The technology is complicated. The spikes in our usage and orders are higher than anybody else's spikes. We do incredible amounts of data manipulation. Like Amazon, we're essentially in the business of creating technology platforms. The curation is incidental.

Gilt is Kevin's most successful venture at AlleyCorp, but it is not the only major company in their network. While Kevin serves as CEO of Gilt, his partner Dwight Merriman serves as CEO of 10gen, which recently raised $20 million in additional funding. Business Insider, the business and entertainment site that Kevin launched in the same month as Gilt, achieved profitability in the fourth quarter of 2010. Though Kevin started a portfolio of companies in order to distribute his risk, the end result has been to compound his gains, because nearly all of them worked.

Our plan was always to run the six companies for three years, then pick one or two to focus on. We didn't expect most of them to make it. Then it turned out that most of them were successful. That was better than we'd expected.

"Don't start a company unless you're obsessed with an idea."

THE
KEVIN RYAN
PLAYBOOK

Execution Is More Important Than Ideas

Most people believe the myth that you can only succeed as an entre-preneur if you come up with a crazy idea that no one has ever thought of before. But three months after starting a business, however crazy you thought the idea was, it's not rare to find five other teams doing the same thing. To succeed, you need to leverage that three-month head start. You have to move faster than everybody else, and that's all about execution. Deciding whether you can execute in this way is the most important part of your idea selection.

Develop Obsessions

Don't start a company unless you're obsessed with an idea. The feel-ing behind it has to be "I have to start this company. I can't *not* start this company!" It's not based on deep research or focus groups. It's simply that the idea's rolled around in your head and you've come to a decision. There's no way to schedule this process, any more than you can tell someone, "I need you to have a girlfriend by April 15." If you meet her, you meet her. If you don't, you don't.

Get High Returns on Your Time

There was a point when it looked like Gilt was going to be enormous. At that time, I was still focused on the entire network of companies in AlleyCorp. It was clear, though, that I wasn't going to get the same return if I invested my time equally across all of those companies. ShopWiki, for instance, was worth $10 million and might have grown to $20 million if I did a lot of work. Gilt, on the other hand, was worth $100 million and may yet be worth a billion. Clearly, hours spent on Gilt were more valuable than hours spent on ShopWiki.

KEVIN'S BEST ADVICE

FOCUSING TIME & ENERGY

Don't Overinvest in Problem Areas

One of the fundamental mistakes that business managers make is that they focus all of their time on things that are going wrong. That is exactly what you shouldn't do. At best, you'll turn something that is going badly into something that is going only a little badly. It won't have a significant impact on your revenues or your profits, so stop spending time on those problem areas. Spend your time catalyzing your highest-growth areas.

HIRING

Seek Out Independent Thinkers

When I meet a new hire, I don't just want to hear that the person has been successful. I want to hear their questions and see if they're thinking independently. It's easy to forget that people in most companies have 90 percent of things decided for them in advance. They have very little control over their divisions, and they're working on products that have been around for several years. That experience won't prepare you for a startup career.

LEADERSHIP

Most Companies Aren't Mythical; They're Practical

A lot of attention is paid to entrepreneurs who, like Mark Zuckerberg and Bill Gates, dropped out of college to start companies. But that's not the right plan for the vast majority of companies. The right plan is to get ten years of experience working for a good company in the space you want to enter, and then go off and tackle it yourself. It's less extreme, less glamorous, more successful than anything else.

MARKET DEVELOPMENT

Get to Market

In the beginning, you have no way of knowing if you have the right design, or if it's going to work. There are a lot of things you don't know. You just have to get out the door and find out. When you're releasing a magazine or a TV show, everything has to be done perfectly right away. That's not true of technical businesses. You can push a tight timeline and just keep adapting.

TALENT

Force People to Make Fast Decisions

One of the hardest parts of a startup is bringing people in and forcing them to make quick decisions. Quite often, people will come to an Internet startup from a major brand because they want to be part of a business that moves faster. Then you find they're uncomfortable making decisions when they don't have a lot of information. In the beginning, people always asked, "Why are Gilt sales at noon?" The answer is that we had to pick a time, so we just picked it. We literally spent ten minutes on that decision. Now, there are hundreds of thousands of people who orient their schedules around our sales.

WORKING FOR YOURSELF

Make Personal Sacrifices

When you start a company, you have to make the conscious decision to cut back in certain areas of your life. In my case, there were things that I knew I couldn't compromise on. I exercise every day to stay in shape, and I take my children to school three days a week and spend time with them in the evenings. Those things couldn't go away. But I did have to find areas where I could cut back, like sporting events or dinner with friends. When I was in my twenties, I was everywhere—at the opera, at restaurants, watching Brazilian bands perform. I had to be willing to sacrifice that when I joined DoubleClick and started my own companies. You can do anything, but you can't do everything.

KEVIN'S VISION FOR THE FUTURE

As carefully as Kevin plans his businesses, he can still be surprised. The amazing growth of Gilt Groupe was one such surprise, while the perception that customers had of it in the marketplace was another. In an Abrams Research survey of experts in the luxury industry, Gilt wasn't simply described as a great supplier of luxury brands, but as a luxury brand itself. When Kevin and his team saw the results, they were ready to expand their offer beyond luxury apparel and discounted merchandise.

"The perception of Gilt in the marketplace was as a 'luxury brand' and not simply as a discount site. This was clearly a much bigger idea than I had realized. I never expected to be selling travel or other nonapparel items on Gilt, and I certainly hadn't thought of selling them at full price. But we realized that our customers wanted more from us, and we've started to provide it."

KIRILL SHEYNKMAN

FOUNDER:

STANFORD TECHNOLOGY GROUP

PLUMTREE SOFTWARE

ELASTRA CORPORATION

MANAGING DIRECTOR:

RTP VENTURES

INTRODUCING KIRILL SHEYNKMAN

At heart, Kirill Sheynkman is a technologist. But in his years of experience in Silicon Valley, he's come to realize that getting the technical details right requires ownership of the entire business and the entire roadmap. Though he loves coding and coming up with new, market-changing ideas, he's also up front about what for him is most important when it comes to evaluating a new idea or startup, and that is, can it be a commercial success? Product is at the core of the business—but is it something people will be willing to buy because it solves a tangible problem for them?

Kirill is a rational futurist: he has the chops to be thinking twenty years out, but he knows that entrepreneurs need to be grounded in the present. His passion is to take big bets on the future of technology, on companies whose markets, in many cases, don't even exist yet. Kirill tracks trends and finds markets where customer needs and technical capabilities are ready to intersect within the next two to five years. And when he finds those areas of confluence, he responds with practical business solutions that arrive on time.

For somebody with such a technical mind-set, Kirill never falls into the trap of building science projects. He recognizes the fact that products can't just produce satisfaction in the engineers who build them; they have to create value for the company's stakeholders. It's one of the hardest lessons for product-focused entrepreneurs to learn, and Kirill communicates that notion very effectively. But perhaps the most revealing piece of information about what makes Kirill tick is that he titles his blog Passionate Intensity.

KIRILL'S STORY

Kirill Sheynkman: There are only two things a software company does: build stuff and sell stuff. The rest (like everything below) is commentary.

I'm a three-time entrepreneur who has founded three companies in Silicon Valley. All of them were in the unpopular-in–New York field of enterprise software. I've recently started dabbling in venture capital, but I'm more of an entrepreneur than a VC.

Before he became an entrepreneur, Kirill worked as a sales consultant. But the job that intrigued him most was the product manager's.

The job consists of determining what customers need, understanding the sales team's concerns, and translating all of that into terms that engineering can build. It's the most important job at a company that is actually building things, rather than selling support on existing things. When I review résumés as a VC, I'm always looking for product managers. While a lot of people in software today neglect product management, I still think it's the best training ground for CEOs.

Kirill is a veteran of the pre-Web days of software development, and he brings the rigors of those days to his new ventures.

When I started my first company and became a CEO in 1993, software was a very different thing than it is today. The notion of software being sold in a box doesn't exist anymore, but that was still the reality in the early '90s. If you forgot something, it was very difficult to send out maintenance releases or patches. This forced companies into a rigid structure that is very different from what entrepreneurs are used to today. Of course, there are enormous advantages to being able to iterate quickly and make rapid changes. But there was a worthwhile discipline in being forced to get it right the first time.

While rapid iteration has its advantages, I'm less confident that outsourcing has been a positive development for software companies. Programming isn't just about meeting a spec; it's about solving intellectual challenges in elegant ways. When you outsource programming, you're herding a team toward meeting a spec as quickly (or as cheaply) as possible. But programmers aren't cattle. They should be members of your team who are really excited about solving problems.

THE STANFORD TECHNOLOGY GROUP, PLUMTREE SOFTWARE, AND ELASTRA CORPORATION STORIES

Stanford Technology Group was founded by Kirill in 1993, and the online analytical-processing technology they developed caused the company to be bought just two years later by IBM.

A year after the sale, Kirill founded Plumtree and spent over a decade releasing a slew of successful corporate portal-software solutions. BEA Systems acquired Plumtree, and was subsequently acquired by Oracle.

In 2007, Kirill saw that not only was cloud computing the future of information hosting, but the time had come to begin development of cloud products. Elastra grew its offerings for secure cloud-computing platforms. In 2010, he left Elastra to become a venture partner at Greycroft Partners. He has since become senior managing director for the U.S., New York–based division of RTP Ventures.

Throughout the '90s, Kirill assembled fantastic teams and solved some of the most complex problems he could identify.

"You don't necessarily need money when you start a company, but you do need to write some code."

At Stanford Technology Group, our immediate focus was on solving problems. We were building very sophisticated tools. At the time, there were databases, and there were analytic systems, and there were exchanges that were actually data sources as well. What did not exist was a product that unified all three and allowed you to query all of these sources to bring information together. My group developed an analytical technology that filled that purpose. The company became profitable and was acquired by Informix/IBM in 1995.

You don't necessarily need money when you start a company, but you do need to write some code. You need to actually get something working. If you're the kind of CEO who can do that yourself, that's great. If you're not, you need to find another person who can give you a rough start on your product development. It's perfectly legitimate to be the CEO who is all about acquiring the resources—from initial capital to a team to customers—needed to get a great new product out there. In fact, what I understood less well at the beginning of my career was that you had to be just as focused on leading a team as on developing a product.

With my second company, Plumtree, we were also doing something completely new: building corporate portals. It didn't even exist as a concept back then. We wrote white papers introducing the idea. Unlike existing portals, this was not about information. It was about getting work done. It was another success. We had an IPO and the company was eventually acquired.

In the past ten years, portals have started to become obsolete. In 2007, I saw that the next major approach businesses were going to take was cloud computing. (Oracle tried introducing this idea many years earlier, but it was premature at that time. The infrastructure wasn't there yet.) I decided to develop a cloud-computing platform with Elastra Corporation, which I founded and ran until leaving in 2010 to join Greycroft. I left Greycroft last year for RTP Ventures, where my focus is on venture capital and investment.

THE
KIRILL SHEYNKMAN
PLAYBOOK

Know Your Whole Revenue Model

In the past, revenue models were fairly simple: you give me a dollar and I'll give you this in return. It was about identifying a pain that people wanted relieved. Most important, they had to be willing to pay for that relief. The difference between science and engineering is that in engineering, there's an extra variable in every equation: a dollar sign. There's nothing wrong with being passionate about science or art, but that's not about business. There has to be quantifiable value and revenue.

Handcraft Your Company

To build an effective company, you need to spend time in the trenches. You don't necessarily have to write code yourself, but you should sit with the sales team and go on calls. Sit with the marketing team and brainstorm about messaging. Rather than thinking about your company as divided into autonomous departments, think of it as being composed of teams. And don't simply delegate tasks to those teams: participate in them.

Make Something Better, Faster, and More Efficient

It always comes down to doing more, or being able to do something faster. That's ultimately what entrepreneurship is about. It hasn't really changed, whether it was camel caravans in the Middle Ages or Federal Express jetliners today. It's still the same kind of math: if you can make something more efficient, selling it isn't difficult.

KIRILL'S BEST ADVICE

CULTURE

Keep Your Team in One Place

Avoid distributing your workforce. Everyone, and I mean everyone, should be in the same office. Many entrepreneurs advocate outsourcing, or having their sales and marketing in New York and their product development in San Francisco. That doesn't reflect the reality of startups. I've never seen a sales office that is just a sales office at a startup. Everybody should contribute beyond their narrow field. If you disperse your team, it will be much harder for them to do that.

FOCUSING TIME & ENERGY

Start with Function, Not Fundraising

You don't necessarily need piles of capital when you start a company, but you do need to actually get some unique process working that will execute a saleable task more efficiently than what is already available. There are two kinds of good CEOs: Those who can develop that process themselves and those who know how to identify someone who has and can build a company around that great idea.

HIRING

Don't Rush Hiring

VCs will often tell you to hire and hire quickly, but you shouldn't rush hiring in the early stages of a company. If you do, your job will quickly become running Human Resources and pure management, and you won't be able to focus on building great products and exploiting market opportunities.

LEADERSHIP

Don't Hire Leaders. Lead!

Don't delegate the job of leader. Hiring professional managers isn't a substitute for leading yourself. You can't expect team cohesion if you are not engaged in team leadership. You can't simply hire leaders; you have to be a leader yourself.

SALES

Don't Treat Startup Sales like Mainstream Sales

If you're one of three thousand salespeople at a large company, the only exciting thing is beating the other guys and being number one. But early-stage salespeople get their kicks when they hear a customer say, "Wow! This is exactly what I need!" There's an honest, genuine excitement in solving a client's problem. The actual transaction becomes a no-brainer.

In startups, salespeople are really business-development people. This is something that VCs often don't understand. They'll say, "Let's bring in this top-notch sales guy. He ran this and this and this." But then you meet with them, and they start asking about compensation plans, and what tier they're going to be in, and what territories they're going to cover. That's not what early-stage companies are about.

TALENT

Don't Neglect Quality Assurance

It's very difficult to find professional Quality Assurance organizations. A lot of people neglect that department, treating it as a place for low-level developers. But there are people who are passionate about quality. Find one, and they'll attract other people like them. It's a key hire.

WORKING FOR YOURSELF

Never Start a Company Alone

When someone first has an idea, she'll often try it out on people. "Look, I have a great idea for a business. What do you think?" Some of the feedback will be negative, some of it will be positive. But you should look for more than validation. You want to find someone else who can get as excited about the idea as you are. This is the person who's running crazy ideas by you all of the time. You don't want them going directly to the product team because you'll shoot half of the ideas down. But the other half could represent real opportunities. Given that ratio, you need to find somebody who's constantly generating ideas, and you need to listen to them.

KIRILL'S VISION FOR THE FUTURE

Kirill has switched from being an entrepreneur to a venture capitalist, but his entrepreneurial experience informs all of his decisions at RTP. He knows how to spot both successful products and people who will be able to see those products through to success.

Kirill is an analytical man. He also knows that passion is a key ingredient, and indeed something that an investor should factor heavily into his decision to support an entrepreneur: "What has unified all of my experiences is a true love for the product. You can't be successful if you don't love the product that you're building. It has to be interesting to you. There are lots and lots of things that you'll encounter in life that make you think, 'Well, this could be better, and this could be better, and this could be better.' But there are relatively few that passionately involve you and are intellectually engaging to you. Those are the problems you should tackle, and which will bring out your excitement and passion."

JEFF STEWART

FOUNDER:

MIMEO

URGENT CAREER

LENDDO

INTRODUCING JEFF STEWART

Jeff Stewart is a prolific idea-engine. He is passionate about finding opportunities and starting companies, but he balances that enthusiasm with a relentless search for reasons not to do something. He's an optimist, but not a wishful thinker. He insists on looking critically at lots of ideas at once, knowing that most of them won't make the cut. The ones that *do* have been tumbled around for a long time. The jagged edges that ruin so many other companies have been smoothed away. Once Jeff enters a marketplace, he knows the business inside and out.

Part of the reason for Jeff's success is his high level of self-awareness. He recognizes himself as a serial entrepreneur. At a given moment he might be building an online printing company (Mimeo, more than $80 million in revenues), a social credit scoring service (Lenddo), and an algorithmic tool for optimizing sales performance (Urgent Career). Jeff doesn't want to settle into the role of managing every detail at a single company. He wants to assemble an amazing team that grows meaningful companies that he'll be involved in for the rest of his life.

The role that amplifies Jeff's strengths is chairman of the board. It's a position he's already held at three companies. With the right team in place, the chairman role allows Jeff to carefully form his opinions, set high-level strategies, and pursue many things at once. He can also stay on the lookout for the next great opportunity.

JEFF'S STORY

Jeff Stewart: I always knew that I wanted to start companies. I love the idea of building something, the intellectual challenges associated with it. More than anything, I want to leave the world better off than it was before I started a company. Saving people $7.00 on sweaters, is that exciting? Or selling more blue sweaters than your competitors, is that exciting? No. Life's too short; I want to spend mine solving big problems.

Jeff's first company was Square Earth. With it, Jeff tackled one of the biggest problems of the mid-'90s: incorporating the Internet into day-to-day business.

In 1995, I realized that the World Wide Web was going to change everything, just like electricity, the combustion engine, and broadcast before it. It was going to change the entire landscape of how culture and business interacted, and I wanted to be a part of that.

My first company was called Square Earth. We tried a couple business models early on; we thought we would serve advertising firms, or publishers, or multinationals. You have to start broad early in a company, because you haven't yet figured out what out's there. But at some point, you have to say, "OK, what did we just learn?" There comes a moment when you need to focus. That means turning down business that doesn't fit with your high-level strategy. First, we dropped publishing as a target group. Eventually, we dropped agencies. Very quickly we settled in on helping large corporations with their Internet strategies.

The company grew organically over the course of three or four years. In 1998, we merged with a company called Proxicom, and we bought another company, Ibis, before going public. It eventually grew into a 1,200 person, $2 billion, e-commerce consulting company. Today, it's a part of Hearst Interactive.

Jeff's next venture has been his most successful venture to date: Mimeo.

Mimeo grew out of an idea I'd had back as a management consultant. I wanted to find a way for people to print professionally formatted documents right from their computers. At the time, 1992, it was a horrible idea, there still wasn't really an Internet, it would have had to use modems, and the digital printing technology wasn't there.

THE MIMEO STORY

Mimeo makes the execution of what used to be a frustrating business task simple. They offer the ability to have professional-quality printing delivered on demand. Since its founding in 1998, the company has won awards within their sector and within the broad landscape of American businesses. They are strategic partners with Hewlett-Packard, and count Goldman Sachs among their investors. If anyone thinks that the boom of conducting business online has reduced the demand for professional printing, Mimeo's continued prosperity would prove him incorrect. Over the past four years, Mimeo has achieved more than 50 percent revenue growth and opened two new printing facilities.

Six years later the world had changed. I was confident that it was a really good idea, but nevertheless I hired an analyst to spend the summer coming up with reasons why it wouldn't work. He soon came back and said, "This is tremendous. We need to move faster on this." People were starting to conduct commerce on the Internet; there was a much larger customer base, and paper wasn't going away. We raised $21 million and launched Mimeo in February 2000, and have been growing it ever since.

It took a forty-five-person team eighteen months to develop software for making it easier for people to produce hard-copy documents over the Internet. We set up a factory in Tennessee, near the FedEx hub. To this day, you can customize a document on your computer and have a professionally finished presentation in your hands as quickly as FedEx delivers. It's faster and cheaper than going to the local copy shop; we're saving people millions of hours by making our service available. That matters.

While my analyst came back with a positive report on the idea for Mimeo, not every idea you generate is going to work. For every company I've started, there are dozens that never got past the idea stage.

Jeff's next venture, which sought to aggregate online financial data, is one example of not every good idea panning out. What he and his partners had no way of knowing when they developed it was the rate at which that data would grow.

In 2003, I launched another company, Monitor110. This time, I went into the marketplace to figure out what people were looking for. I went out to large corporations and asked them, "What would you like to have?" I was talking with a senior executive at a Fortune 50 company when she told me that there was all this stuff going on the Internet and she knew it affected her company, but she didn't know how. She wished there was a way to monitor it.

I did some research, wrote some code, and went back to her with a system for monitoring the Internet in real time. She loved it. She thought all her peers at Fortune 1000 companies would need it. I asked her what she would pay for it. She said, "Oh, I would easily pay $1,000 a month; $12,000 a year."

You get more interested after you have a Fortune 50 company saying they would write you a check if you had the software. When I showed the software to some hedge fund friends, they said they also needed unique information. When I asked, "Well, would you pay $12,000 for it?" They replied, "Sure, we'd pay $12,000 a month, no questions asked." That's when we realized that we should develop the system for hedge funds.

Unfortunately, we had no idea that the amount of content online was about to grow exponentially. We spent $20 million on the first round of development and realized that we'd have to spend at least another $20 million to deal with the new volume of data. That didn't make sense economically, so we had to wind the company down. The need for the product was absolutely there, but the technical hurdle was insurmountable at a time before ubiquitous cloud computing.

There are dozens of other ideas we experimented with, and some of them involved truly incredible technologies. One idea we reviewed would have used semiconductors to accelerate the growth of produce. But when it becomes clear that you one of your key scientists would not be able to execute in a startup, you have to walk away—no matter how impressive the idea sounds.

THE
JEFF STEWART
PLAYBOOK

Don't Run with One Biased Idea

It's very hard to evaluate a single business idea. You have to compare it to other ideas. If you've only had one idea for starting a business, you probably have not thought enough. I believe in a Darwinian process: have lots of ideas and let them battle it out. Combine them, split them apart, reconfigure them.

When You Start a Company, It's Not Just About You

You're asking dozens or even hundreds of people to follow you; you're seeking millions and potentially hundreds of millions of dollars in investment. Therefore, you owe it to yourself and your partners to do the research and analyze the data. Even if there isn't data in your specific industry, you can draw on data from analogous ones. Once you do launch a business, you need to get feedback from the customer who's going to write you a check as early in the pocess as possible. That's the final test.

A Business Isn't One Big Invention; It's a Hundred Small Inventions

It's easy to think that a business is one idea or invention. Actually, it's hundreds of ideas and inventions that combine to create value for your customers. These can be ideas around pricing, around distribution, around marketing, manufacturing, and so on. It's really about combining these ideas to achieve a breakthrough. Just building a great product is not enough.

Avoid Stagnation

No entrepreneur needs to be told to avoid failure. You don't want to die, so you're going to do everything possible to figure out how to avoid that. The real danger is that you'll look back after five years have passed and say, "Wow, this is exactly where I was five years ago." Because stagnation is born of comfort and success rather than crisis, it can be easy to overlook. This makes it a much greater threat than failure.

JEFF'S BEST ADVICE

BUSINESS OPERATIONS

Don't Underestimate Small, Determined Teams

It is important to look broadly at all potential competitors, not just people who are currently in the market. Never underestimate a small, determined team as a potential competitor. To figure out who those teams might be, listen to your customers. It's not just people who are targeting a niche of your customer base, but people outside of your business who are serving your existing customers. You have to watch it all.

CULTURE

As the Company Grows, Shift from Generalists to Specialists

In the early stages of a company, when you're growing 10, 20 percent a month, nearly everybody needs to be able to do everything and be interchangeable. But as you grow, you need people who are going to focus on a specific area. At that stage, you can sometimes solve problems simply by changing a role or changing a responsibility. Earlier on, you can't do that because you just need everybody to be pointing in the same direction.

CUSTOMER DEVELOPMENT

Hire Salespeople Who Can Empathize with Your Clients

Drive is a key factor for sales, but so is empathy for the client. Salespeople need to be able to step into their clients' shoes and understand the problems they're facing, whether it's political pressures on a large complex sale, or a short-term emotional hang-up about a quick transaction. If a salesperson doesn't have that level of empathy, they're not going to be successful.

FIRING

Immediately Get Rid of People Who Don't Work

In a startup, things move very quickly. One piece of advice I consistently give is this: who you're in business with is more important than what you do. So when you realize you have the wrong person on the team, you need to address that right away. You owe it to people to let them go the moment you realize they're not going to work out. You're doing them a disservice keeping them any longer than that.

MARKET DEVELOPMENT

Turn Away the Wrong Customers

One of the hardest things for an entrepreneur to do is to turn business away for the sake of focus. When you're small, it's very easy to get excited every time somebody offers you money to do something. But successful companies pick a subsection of the market and focus on that. If business doesn't fit that focus, turn it away. You have to define what you say no to and focus on your market segment. You'll grow more slowly, but you'll become very good at your focus and start to grow very, very quickly.

SALES

Hire Salespeople Who Can Work with the Rhythm of Your Sales Cycle

Different salespeople work at different paces. Some of them thrive on the adrenaline high of selling something every week; others like the challenge of a nine-month sales cycle. But if you take the greatest week-to-week salesperson in the world and give him a nine-month cycle, he'll probably fail. You have to make sure that your sales team's pace matches your company's sales cycle.

TALENT

Overinvest in Talent

As the CEO, your single, most important job is getting great people. This is the one area where you should overinvest, overinterview, over-build the pipeline. It's a lot easier to manage exceptional people; in fact, exceptional people almost manage themselves. Valuable employees have a sense of urgency; they just don't want to leave until some-thing's taken care of. They have an intellectual curiosity about how the world works and empathy for the customer. If you get these types of great people and set the vision for your company, it is going to cover all sorts of unexpected things that are going to come up.

VISION & MISSION

Inculcate a Love of Technology

There are people who view technology simply as a cost, or as a thing you need just to get something done, like hiring an architect; you build a house, you have an architect, but then you're done. As long as your house is built, you don't care how it happened. Successful businesspeople need to have a different attitude. Your senior execu-tives need to care about technology and believe it can be used as a competitive advantage. Of course, there are businesses that don't operate that way. But in my experience, technology is crucial to the ongoing management and success of the company.

JEFF'S VISION FOR THE FUTURE

Jeff's combination of genius and pragmatism allows him to identify how vital new technologies can be applied to the fundamental issues of the marketplace. Most recently, he started a company called Lenddo, which seeks nothing less than to radically improve global consumer finance. It uses a consumer's social network to rank credit. He explains, "We're using microfinancing techniques, but instead of targeting the bottom of the pyramid in emerging markets, we're actually targeting the wired middle class.

"Essentially, we're reintroducing reputation-based lending, which is how lending worked in the 1920s and for literally hundreds of years before. But we're leveraging social media to make it possible for lend-ers to implement community-based lending at scale. We think this model can unlock the potential of the emerging-market middle class and empower the middle class to have more control over their lives." Jeff made sure to approach Lenddo the same way he has his other companies, and hired a team to give him rea-sons why he shouldn't start the company. "This time, they came back and said, 'This is much bigger than you even realize.' Given the fact that dozens of ideas fall flat for every one that works, it's very exciting to get a response like that."

JAY WALKER

FOUNDER:

WALKER DIGITAL

PRICELINE

INTRODUCING JAY WALKER

Visiting Jay Walker's Connecticut library is a mind-blowing experience. I expected it to contain the vast collection of books and artifacts that Jay has curated over the years. I was prepared to see objects like an original Edison phonograph (Thomas Edison may be the historical figure Jay most brings to mind). I wasn't prepared to see a *Sputnik*, but there it was.

At the center of the "Walker Library of the History of Human Imagination" is a small seating area—two armchairs and a couch. Enshrouded by the ideas around them, this is where Jay and his team often meet to do the thing that Walker Digital was built to do: solve problems.

Jay's driving passion is solving problems. He also invests considerable time and thought in a step that most people skip: defining *problems. Walker Digital uses a very sophisticated methodology for pulling apart and stripping away "false" problems before executing on solutions. It's a deliberative process very much at odds with the prevailing startup ethos, but it's one that every founder should pay close attention to.*

One such problem was: How can suppliers sell a limited amount of perishable inventory below retail price without disrupting retail price on all future inventory of the same product in the process? This is the same basic problem whether we're talking about dresses on a rack (fashions change), melons in a supermarket (food goes bad), or airline seats in the sky (planes take off). The odds are, the solution to this problem would have a sustainable component to it and a long-term sustainable business could be built around it. That's precisely the thinking behind Walker's brainchild, Priceline.com, which helped the travel business solve that very problem.

JAY'S STORY

The typical entrepreneurial approach runs something like "Fire! (Ready, Aim.)" Jay's is very different—more akin to "Aim, Aim, Ready, Fire." In 1994, Jay founded Walker Digital, a research-and-development lab with a focus on the interaction between large-scale digital networks and human behavior. Jay and his team begin by identifying the ecosystem or industry they want to work in. After defining a key problem inherent within that system, they begin exploring possible solutions. Typically, the team focuses on areas where human behavior intersects, or potentially could intersect, with large-scale digital networks such as the Internet in the '90s or cloud storage today.

Jay Walker: Ten years ago, we said, "Let's get involved in the gaming industry in China." We knew that the gaming industry there is going to be one hundred times bigger than the gaming industry anywhere else in the world, and that people who were willing to think through the problems of that industry were in a position to do very well financially. We spent many years in that industry, trying to understand its problems. It isn't terribly difficult if you spend time thinking.

Crucially, Jay did not start his work at Walker Digital Gaming by solving problems, but by trying to understand them. This is, for him, the essential first step.

Tell me the problem you're trying to solve. Say, "Here's who we are: we're the people who solve this problem." If you can't say that, it indicates that you actually don't know the problem yourself. In contrast, you don't want to define yourself with today's product. "We're Speaker Model A300. Tomorrow, we'll be Speaker Model A305, and then we'll be Speaker Model A410." You're not solving any problem; you're just a new speaker model.

This is true even in the highly tactical businesses that I've built. We'll often spend years trying to understand a problem. At Walker Digital Gaming, we've created a whole series of inventions related to the slot-machine business. And you might ask, "Invented slot machines? Isn't it just like colors and a few symbols?" No. The question of why people go to casinos, sit in front of faux computer terminals that make sounds and have reward systems associated with them—this is not a simple problem. If you can understand it more fully, you can fundamentally innovate along many dimensions. That's when people will look at what you've done and say, "Wow!"

THE PRICELINE STORY

Priceline is one of the many projects to emerge from Walker Digital, the research-and-development lab Jay founded in 1994. As he explained at a Harvard Business School Entrepreneurship Conference in 2001, the airline industry was suffering a "peak-and-load balance problem" in the late 1990s. "Peaks" manifested as overbooked flights; "nonpeaks" as undersold ones. Priceline solved the problem with their "Name Your Own Price" system and quickly became popular with travelers. The company went public in April 1999. It serves more than 35 million customers each year, has occupied the top spot on the S&P 500 as best-performing company, and has a market cap of $22 billion.

Jay was only directly involved with the running of Priceline for the first two years. Since then, he's shifted his focus to solving many other problems under the Walker Digital banner, patenting hundreds of inventions and taking the helm of TEDMED as the leader of a new ownership team.

The end result of Walker Digital's problem-definition phase is an extraordinary "periodic table," a concrete look at the problem from every angle. It is only after defining problems in this comprehensive way that Jay feels ready to take aim at a particular solution. When I visited Jay at his office, he showed me his "Periodic Table of Lottery Emotions and Behaviors."

Why do people play the lottery? "Feeling Important. Hope. Guilt. Fear. Determination. Territoriality. Sense of Entitlement." These are some of the "problems" that people have in relation to the lottery. If you wanted to create a sustainable business that solved problems for lottery players, you would need to understand how lottery players felt and thought. Otherwise, it's just luck.

The final step—one that only happens years after the Walker Digital team first approaches a problem—is to execute. ("Fire!") This is primarily the job of the CEO, a role that Jay has tended to avoid. He recognizes the distinction between thinking about a problem and building a solution. More important, he recognizes that his strengths and interests lie in the former.

We tend to conflate the CEO and the owner under the term "entrepreneur." In most startups, those roles are handled by the same person, who manages the capital as much as he manages the team. The owner and the CEO can be the same person, but the owner often has a very different set of needs. The CEO runs the railroad. He or she is air-traffic control, in the middle of every decision, while the owner is saying, "What are we doing here? Are we learning something, but we are so busy executing we're not noticing?" The owner has a *thinking* job. In my life, I've tried to get out of the CEO role as fast as I possibly could. It's almost impossible to be a CEO and an owner. People tend not to see that, but that's because they don't think about the structure of startups as a series of problems that have to be dealt with.

Jay has very aggressively outsourced execution. Rather than simply assigning others within Walker Digital to take on execution roles, Jay has partnered with major firms that are ready to execute on well-defined solutions. In gaming, Jay partnered with International Gaming Technology (IGT), which eventually bought nearly one hundred relevant patents from Walker Digital and ran with the ideas. This suits Jay. In recent years, he's moved on from gaming to focus on biomedical technology.

The brain is the final unexplored frontier. We know extremely little about it now. Our research in that area is very primitive. We have machines that look for increased blood flow to different parts, though we don't know what function blood flow actually plays. We actually still poke around and ask patients, "How does it feel when I do this? How does it feel when I do this?" We know next to nothing. I expect that will change drastically in the coming years.

THE
JAY WALKER
PLAYBOOK

Think

Thomas Edison used to have a sign in his laboratory that read, "There is no expedient to which a man will not go to avoid the labor of thinking." This is especially true in our culture, where solutions are worshipped and problem definition is not. We celebrate people who are action-oriented—immediate, quick, fast. People don't want to take out the playbook and say, "Let's spend time thinking about the plays here." It's like watching an athlete do something great while ignoring the thousands of hours of practice that went into it. If you simply move forward and make progress, you get the Sisyphean illusion that the rock is moving up the hill. But if you don't think, it's impossible to know whether you're really solving any problems.

Recognize the Complexity Inherent to All Human Problems

If you think problems are simple, think again. You are wrong. If the problems you're working on involve humans, they are complicated by definition. You find real humility in recognizing that. It's a Rubik's cube. There's a class of problems in biology—complex ecosystem problems. A company is an ecosystem. It needs to work on many deep levels to really click. The problem with an ecosystem is that it has unpredictable outputs for predictable inputs. It's not linear. An innovation-driven business is a human ecosystem. You can't "build" it based on fixed blueprints. You have to "grow" it organically, embracing a process of experimentation that leads to incremental, evolutionary change.

Talk to People Close Your Problem, and to Ones Who Are Far Away From It

To test the definition you've formed of a problem and the solution you've arrived at, talk to people who are close to that problem. Talk to real customers. Actively listen and look for clues that reinforce or deny what you think is true. Is the problem real or is it in your imagination? Most people will claim not to have a problem, "I don't need a microwave oven; the oven I have is perfectly fine." So you probe further, "What if I gave you a solution that boils water or defrosts food faster?" Most likely, they'll ask how much it costs. At the same time, don't be afraid to talk to people you *aren't* targeting. More often than not, you'll get real insights. People who live focusing on a problem often get into an echo chamber around a specific solution. To break out of that, talk broadly.

JAY'S BEST ADVICE

CULTURE

It's Not About People; It's About Solving Problems

Entrepreneurs often say, "It's all about the people." It's not. It's about solving problems. When you bring people into an organization, you do it in order to address a problem. You can bring in the best possible person, but it doesn't matter if they're working on the wrong problem or the wrong solution.

DEPLOYING CAPITAL

Treat Your Capital Supply like an Oxygen Supply

Money serves many different functions. It allows you to bounce back from failures. It buys you time when you need time. It gives you the ability to withstand adversity that comes out of nowhere. Managing money is complex, but there is one fundamental fact you have to keep in mind: if you run out of money, you're toast. Businesses don't fail for any other reason. It's like oxygen to a scuba diver, the oxygen gauge is the only one that really matters. Whatever else you do, you can't run out of cash.

HIRING

Hire People to Execute on Solutions, Not to Solve Problems

Don't hire people to solve problems. Fundamentally, you have to solve problems first, then hire people to execute against the solutions you've created. You can't say, "I have this problem in my marketing area, and I'm going to hire a really good marketer to solve it." That's not right. The correct approach is to say, "We're going to market this product through a series of television ads, supported with PR. We need to find somebody who really knows that world." You've already decided what the solution to your problem is going to be; now you have to find somebody to execute. That's the difference.

LEADERSHIP

Don't Run the Ball; Call Plays

The primary job of the CEO is to assemble a great team and keep that team on track. It's not about what the CEO does; nothing gets done on an individual basis. It's about what the core team does, and CEOs are team leaders. A good quarterback rarely runs the ball. What you really want them to do is call the right play in the right situation. That's what a good quarterback does, and that's what a good CEO should do.

MARKET DEVELOPMENT

Start with a Vision of Your Problem, Rather Than Assumptions About Your Market

Markets shift tides and change overnight, so you have to maintain a focus on a problem that needs to be solved. For example, Steve Jobs stepped back and said, "There needs to be a portable media device that's stripped down and simplified and has a layer of fun to it." But when the iPad was released, it came under a lot of irrelevant criticism. "This doesn't make sense. Where are the ports? It's missing this. It's missing that." Nobody said, "People need a portable media device that's simple and easy, and this isn't it." None of the criticism addressed the actual problem Jobs was solving. And he succeeded because he had a clear vision of a problem, rather than a superficial vision of the customer.

METRICS

Obsess over Revenues

In a startup, it's all about revenues. Revenues are your oxygen supply. Costs can be all over the place, but it doesn't matter if your revenues are sufficient and growing. That's why so many entrepreneurs are obsessed with customers: they're the revenue supply.

TALENT

Have an Internally Driven Team

Show me a success, and I'll show you people who are focused and disciplined. The world is filled with distractions. It's filled with a cacophony of chattering class critics who think they know more than you and an endless Twitter stream about everything. But real entrepreneurs aren't worried about the weather outside. They have a clear compass and they're internally driven.

WORKING FOR YOURSELF

Clinically Analyze Mistakes and Move On

You are going to be defeated many times, but you have to pick yourself up and move on. When you make a mistake, look back and say, "That error was mine, but I am not defined by my mistakes. You can always make a fresh start; next time I'll know better." Winners are people who just don't quit.

JAY'S VISION FOR THE FUTURE

As varied as Jay's career may seem, he has maintained a strict logic for the past three decades. "Every ten years, I have knowingly started a new chapter in my life. There was intellectual property, then online commerce, and now I'm spending a ten-year period in health and medicine."

Despite his numerous accomplishments, Jay has not yet launched the project that he believes will define his legacy. "I've always wanted to found a great university. I've given it a great deal of thought over the last twenty-five years, though I'm still a decade or two away from doing it." A half-century of preparation may seem excessive, but Jay proposes nothing less than the complete reinvention of a half-millennium-old institution. "The university was invented in Oxford around the year 1500. Around the year 2000, it's time to reinvent it."

BOARDS

Populate Your Board with "Dinosaurs"

In addition to entrepreneurs who leverage domain expertise, there are entrepreneurs whom I'd call "domain un-experts." They're the outsiders who see things and say, "This is stupid. How come they're not using X or Y to solve this problem?" As I've found out, there's often a very *good* reason why they're not using X or Y. You might be a genius, but you still have a lot to learn from people who've worked in a domain for decades. If your board of advisers doesn't include the dinosaurs that you're trying to kill, you're screwed.

Steve Blank
Founder: E.piphany

Build Boards That Break Things

I'm a big fan of breaking things; a lot of interesting cocktails come together in that way. You need people outside your organization who don't spend all their time telling you how great you are. (If you need that, have some applause go off when you open your office door and get it out of your system.) Your board should engage and disrupt your company; it shouldn't simply affirm it.

Lisa Gansky
Founder: Ofoto

Cultivate Outsider Perspectives

One way to keep yourself honest is by cultivating people who are willing to say, "This isn't working." They're the ones who are really going to advance your business. In fact, as painful as it is, every founder needs to have a board of directors. They're going to present a more dispassionate, colder point of view—an outsider's point of view. When you have a boss, they force you to think about the metrics of your business, rather than getting buried in all the other stuff. That's really important.

Eileen Gittins
Founder: Blurb

Ignore Your Board; Embrace Your Customer

Learn to ignore the board and to get your employees to ignore the board. If you always say, "We need to do this to make the board happy," you are sending the signal that your organization is about pleasing your board. It's not. The purpose of every business is to please its customers. Do that, and your board will be happy anyway.

Scott Heiferman
Founder: i-traffic, Fotolog, Meetup

Be a Customer of Your Board

The CEO is the customer in the board meeting, and there are three main things they need to get out of it. First, regular board meetings can act as a forcing function to make things happen in a company. This is why CEOs tell their teams that something needs to be ready "to present to the board." Board members actually hate to sit through presentations from the head of customer support or some other division. But if it's helpful for the CEO to have them, bring them in. Second, the board is the CEO's base of outside thinking and environmental knowledge. Using that knowledge is essential when making strategic decisions. Finally, the board should handle corporate governance when it comes to taking or minimizing risks, stock options, accounting, and legal practices. CEOs can't focus their time on those kinds of issues; they need to be able to get directives on them from their boards.

Ben Horowitz
Founder: Opsware

BUSINESS OPERATIONS

Engage the Whole Process

Founders have to be part of the whole startup process. You have to smell and taste and absorb and feel every part of it, and keep rearranging the pieces until you suddenly feel it go "Snap!" Do that, and you'll reach a point where you know that the elements are there so that if you go in this or that direction, it's actually going to work. Although some founders are very technology focused and others are much more marketing focused, I would argue that you need to embrace a broader view of the world.

Chris Anderson
Founder: Future Publishing

Outsource Business Operations and Focus on Your Core Mission

Business operations and logistics are extremely complicated, no matter what industry you are in. They can easily overwhelm you and your team. Luckily, there are third-party solutions for nearly every task you need to support your business. Use those and add value by focusing on your core competency.

Michael & Ellen Diamant
Founders: Skip Hop

Build a Flawless Onboarding Process

If you're going to build up one process, make it the interview and onboarding process. If other processes aren't in place at the beginning, you can build them later and easily recover from whatever issues arise. If you fill your company with less than great people, though, that's going to be hard to recover from.

Ben Horowitz
Founder: Opsware

Split-Test Everything

Most startups do A/B testing. But we A/B test everything, even outside the Web: what we mail to doctors, how we recruit, the messages on our recruiting sites, the envelopes we might use for a particular purpose. We've literally tested everything in this business. Of course, I want to make as many correct decisions as possible. But if I make a bad decision and fail, I want to know *exactly* why I failed.

Cyrus Massoumi
Founder: ZocDoc

Privilege Internal Advisers over Consultants

We modified our compensation structure a few years ago, and we were about to hire a firm to help us do it. I mentioned this to one of our board members while we were having a glass of wine. He said, "I don't have anything against consulting firms, but I know your firm as well as anybody. Let me save you some time and money here." Then he pulled a pad out of his briefcase and redesigned our compensation structure in about twenty minutes. It was spot-on. We were about to spend $280,000 on a consulting engagement. Instead, he said, "You pick up the $28 check for the wine and we're done."

Jim McCann
Founder: 1-800-FLOWERS.com

Systems Matter

Systems matter, especially after the startup phase. We underestimate the importance of the COO and other senior managers in an entrepreneurial organizations, while often placing too much emphasis on the "visionary." Without systems that work, and without great execution, an idea can dissolve like snow in the sun.

Jacqueline Novogratz
Founder: Acumen Fund

CULTURE

Include a Combination of Optimists and Pessimists in Your Management Team

One of the challenges of being a CEO is that you have to be the most optimistic person in the company and the most pessimistic person in the company at the same time. You celebrate when things go well, but you also worry that things are never going to be so good again. That same balance needs to inform your executive team. It should include people who are paranoid and others who are native optimists. The pessimism part especially has to be baked into your company's operating system.

Matt Blumberg
Founder: Return Path

Don't Underestimate the Value of Ambient Learning

I no longer believe in the wisdom of having remote product development or remote employees. Especially in the early research-and-development phase, you need a small group of people rapidly cycling through iterations of your idea. That team needs to meet in a single place, overhear each other's conversations, and develop the same set of rhythms. Until you try remote development and fail, you simply can't understand how important ambient learning is.

Chris Dixon
Founder: SiteAdvisor, Founder Collective, Hunch

Form a "Molecule" with Your First Ten Hires

When you start a company, it's tempting to hire a team of people who have worked together before and finish each other's sentences. It's important to introduce different voices and approaches, though you don't want to end up with a team that looks like a mutant Mr. Potato Head. Your first ten hires should form a molecule. The team will be composed of different elements, but it will cohere.

Lisa Gansky
Founder: Ofoto

Build Power Through Relationships

The best employees and volunteers aren't necessarily the ones who are most gung-ho, but the ones who are mostly tightly wound into the social fabric of your organization. Political campaigns have to ask volunteers to wake up at six in the morning and go knock on strangers' doors. When the alarm clock goes off, it's easy to remind yourself that the candidate doesn't really know whether or not you're showing up. But the buddy who's picking you up does know. There is power in those relationships. That's a core part of any successful organization's culture.

Joe Green
Founder: Causes

Be Aware of Your Organization's Politics

One of the most central items in a company's culture is holding each other accountable to its principles, and that stems from the people who have power. Executives and founders often say, "There are no politics in my organization." That's idiotic. By definition, politics is what happens around people who have power. If you're sitting in a powerful seat and you don't see the politics, you're not seeing what is actually going on around you.

Reid Hoffman
Founder: LinkedIn

As the Company Grows, Shift from Generalists to Specialists

In the early stages of a company, when you're growing 10, 20 percent a month, nearly everybody needs to be able to do everything and be interchangeable. But as you grow, you need people who are going to focus on a specific area. At that stage, you can sometimes solve problems simply by changing a role or changing a responsibility. Earlier on, you can't do that because you just need everybody to be pointing in the same direction.

Jeff Stewart
Founder: Mimeo, Urgent Career, Lenddo

CUSTOMER DEVELOPMENT

Understand Your Audience's Interests

Even if you have an audience that's passionately committed to your offer, it can easily go away. A lot of things might bring that about: arrogance, technological shifts, or someone else coming along with a better proposition. Consider what happened to the magazine business when the Internet came along. Suddenly, people who were passionately committed to video-game magazines started to get their information online. It was there, on demand, for free, and their passion for the video-game magazines leaked away. To avoid being surprised by those shifts, you have to constantly pay attention to your community's center of interest and adapt your product to keep it.

Chris Anderson
Founder: Future Publishing

Crank the Pump

If you look at our growth curve over the last eleven years, it's not a step function. It's a pretty clean hockey stick. That gives the impression that our site has a life of its own, but my job is to *not* think that and to keep cranking the pump. In fact, we could even scientifically demonstrate the need to actively build growth because our virality coefficient is a lot less than one: every ten donors who support a project on our site bring in between one and three additional donors. But if you're using a true virality coefficient greater than one, like Hotmail-standard, then even some great companies don't qualify for having a life of their own yet.

Charles Best
Founder: DonorsChoose.org

No Business Plan Survives First Contact with Customers

The minute someone uses *business plan* and *startup* in the same sentence, I know they don't get it. In a large corporation, business plans make a lot of sense. You write them for the second, third, fourth, or *n*th product. There are a lot of knowns in a large corporation. That's not true in a startup. You're dealing with a marketplace that has never encountered an offer like yours. No startup business plan survives first contact with customers.

Steve Blank
Founder: E.piphany

Track the Evolution of Your Customers' Needs

Fred Smith of FedEx once said, "I thought I was in the business of transporting goods; it turns out, I was in the business of peace of mind." His customers needed to know exactly where their packages were at each particular moment, twenty-four hours a day. Their question wasn't, "Will I get it overnight?" but rather, "At what exact time will it arrive?" The key is understanding that evolution of customer desires by constantly taking yourself back to the moment when things were new and unexpected.

Chip Conley
Founder: Joie de Vivre Hospitality

Build Goods That Have Higher Perceived Values Than Costs

The essential product-development model is very simple: sell products for more than you paid to make them. In order to do that, people have to perceive additional value in what you offer. They won't pay a premium on what you made unless you've addressed an important pain point that they have. When they are willing to pay that premium, you've reached a tipping point and you can start building a business around it.

Hosain Rahman
Founder: Jawbone

DEPLOYING CAPITAL

Be Frugal, Personally and Professionally

In startups, every penny counts: you can't squander money when you don't have a lot of it. You'll still make mistakes, but the learning experiences won't be as costly if you're doing things as cheaply as possible. I'm very hard on my staff about costs. I insist that we spend as little money as possible, and it sometimes drives them crazy. But I hold myself to the exact same standards. I don't have a fancy car, take taxis everywhere, or go out for expensive dinners. I model the behavior that I expect. Frugality has to be a pervasive value.

Robin Chase
Founder: Zipcar

Be Respectful with Your Investors' Money

If you invest $100,000 of your own money in something and it goes belly up, at least you've only lost your own money. But when Jeff Bezos or Fidelity invests in MFG.com—that's *Jeff's* money I'm putting at risk. That's money that belongs to Fidelity's investors. Those people are counting on me, and it's a very heavy weight to bear.

Mitch Free
Founder: MFG.com

Run Lean

Nonprofits don't need a lot. They need talent and conviction, which are free as long as you are diligent in hiring the right people. One designer can handle the entire brand, and your people can learn to solve their own small IT problems. At a nonprofit, everyone understands that the money spent on shallow conveniences of other businesses goes to other, better places.

Scott Harrison
Founder: charity: water

Early-Stage Social Ventures Require Risk-Tolerant Capital

Like other ventures, early-stage social ventures require risk-tolerant capital that gives entrepreneurs room to fail and experiment with the business model. Our entrepreneurs are selling critical goods and services in markets that have never before had access to them, in environments that are often corrupt, in regions with poor infrastructure. Grants and philanthropically-backed financial support are needed to build and prepare these markets.

Jacqueline Novogratz
Founder: Acumen Fund

Treat Your Capital Supply like an Oxygen Supply

Money serves many different functions. It allows you to bounce back from failures. It buys you time when you need time. It gives you the ability to withstand adversity that comes out of nowhere. Managing money is complex, but there is one fundamental fact you have to keep in mind: if you run out of money, you're toast. Businesses don't fail for any other reason. It's like oxygen to a scuba diver, the oxygen gauge is the only one that really matters. Whatever else you do, you can't run out of cash.

Jay Walker
Founder: Walker Digital, Priceline

FAILURE

Don't Be Afraid to Fail

When I was growing up, my dad would encourage my brother and me to fail. We would be sitting at the dinner table and he would ask, "So, what did you guys fail at this week?" If we didn't have something to contribute, he would be disappointed. When I did fail at something, he'd high-five me. What I didn't realize at the time was that he was completely reframing my definition of failure at a young age. To me, *failure* means not trying; failure isn't the outcome. If I have to look at myself in the mirror and say, "I didn't try that because I was scared," that is failure.

Sara Blakely
Founder: Spanx

Conduct Brutal Postmortems

Postmortems are incredibly valuable tools for exploring how mistakes occurred and how they can be prevented in the future. At Open Market, every time we lost a customer account or had a flawed product release, we would get all the constituents in the room and do a brutally honest postmortem. It's an incredibly powerful and valuable way of probing experiences and really learning from them. It's OK to make a mistake, but don't let the same mistake happen twice or, God forbid, allow *the same team* to make the same mistake twice.

Jeff Bussgang
Founder: Open Market, Upromise, Flybridge Capital Partners

Gloss Over Nonfatal Errors

When somebody makes an error, you have to evaluate it in terms of their character, the context of their mistake, and their history at your company. Sometimes you'll determine that the error was fatal and they have to be let go. Otherwise, they can and should recover from it. In those situations, be honest and clear about what happened, but don't dwell on the failure. Gloss over it and move on.

Jim McCann
Founder: 1-800-FLOWERS.com

FIRING

Fire People When They Lose Faith in Your Ideas

When people lose faith in the idea, you have to let them go, because they start to undermine it for everyone else. Sometimes they will hide the fact that they've lost faith, because, of course, they've got expenses and responsibilities and they don't want to be out looking for another job. But superficial commitment is not necessarily going to get you where you need to go.

Rodney Brooks
Founder: iRobot, Heartland Roboticso

Cut Twice as Deep as You Want To

When you have to make cuts, go twice as deep as you want to. Some people try to cut "just the right amount," but you never know that amount for sure. (Invariably, it's higher than you think.) If you make the very hard-nosed decision to cut twice as deep once, you won't have to go through the trauma of a second round.

Marc Cenedella
Founder: TheLadders

Accept the Need for Judicious Firing

I had a colleague at Yahoo! who had a fantastic team. I asked him how he did it. He said, "Judicious firing is often part of the program around here." I have been in the unfortunate position of firing people who have been passed around: people who've moved from group to group, but people will not fire them. Employees like this can be poisonous to an organization.

Caterina Fake
Founder: Flickr, Hunch, Findery

Ineffective Team Members Cause More Harm Than Terminations

Whenever I've waited too long to fire someone, my excuse has always been that it would harm morale. "If we lose this person, the team's gonna be destroyed." The obvious truth is that the rest of the team already knows when somebody needs to go. In fact, they'll think you're an idiot if you don't make a move. As CEOs, we're often insulated from this obvious truth.

Eileen Gittins
Founder: Blurb

Make Sure People Know Why Somebody Was Fired

It's important to tell people why someone was fired. Otherwise, they may think that it was a random decision and not based on merit. That's tough, because you're potentially opening yourself up to a lawsuit in that situation, so you don't need to post this information on a billboard. However, people need to know why somebody is no longer with a company, and what action that person did that led to their departure. Then, employees who are doing their jobs will know that they're not in danger, while those exhibiting negative behaviors will curtail those behaviors.

Elon Musk
Founder: PayPal, SpaceX, Tesla Motors

THE
BEST ADVICE

FOCUSING TIME & ENERGY

Address Problems That Nobody Else Can Solve

I learned an important coaching lesson from a peer who took me aside and said, "You need to hang back and let your people come up with the solutions themselves. If you don't, you're going to get sucked into their problems as opposed to focusing on things that are really going to move the needle." If you're obsessed with problems that other people should be dealing with, you're not using your time well.

Jeff Bussgang
Founder: Open Market, Upromise, Flybridge Capital Partners

Allocate Time to Milestones

Hundreds of factors go into making a startup successful. Should you spend an hour coding, an hour talking to sources of capital, an hour marketing, or an hour convincing an NYU freshman to be an unpaid intern? There's no spreadsheet you can run that against; it's all relying on intuition. To decide, you need to be clear about the critical path you're taking to your next milestone and which steps you need to get you there.

Marc Cenedella
Founder: TheLadders

Triage Problems

Early in a startup, you won't have enough people to delegate the fires to. One of the mistakes that smart people frequently make is to integrate priorities, i.e., focus on Priority One *and* Priority Two, while also having an eye on Priorities Three, Four, and Five. That's absolutely the wrong way to do it. The key thing is to not be distracted by the fact that there may be other fatal fires you need to get to. Solve the biggest problems first, then stop and evaluate the rest.

Reid Hoffman
Founder: LinkedIn

Prioritize Tasks as "Air," "Water," and "Food"

If you separate things into High, Medium, and Low priority, everything is obviously "High." So we came up with a new standard. All life survives on air, water, and food. You can live only minutes without air, days without water, and weeks without food. So we categorize all the high-priority things as what you need to do now, tomorrow, or in a few weeks. You're not going to live for long without food or water, but clearly air rises to the top. When you look at things as air, water, and food, you'd be amazed at how easy it is to focus.

Stephen Messer
Founder: LinkShare

Think Carefully About What You Won't Do

When you're small, you don't have the capital, time, or resources to go spinning off in a lot of different directions. You have to stay focused because you don't have the luxury to *not* be focused. As you scale, you can do a lot more things. Then, focus becomes even more important because it's a lot harder to achieve; you need to devote just as much of your decision-making calculus to what you're *not* going to be doing. Always determine where you have maximum leverage and opportunity and don't waste resources in other areas.

Hosain Rahman
Founder: Jawbone

Don't Overinvest in Problem Areas

One of the fundamental mistakes that business managers make is that they focus all of their time on things that are going wrong. That is exactly what you shouldn't do. At best, you'll turn something that is going badly into something that is going only a little badly. It won't have a significant impact on your revenues or your profits, so stop spending time on those problem areas. Spend your time catalyzing your highest-growth areas.

Kevin Ryan
Founder: AlleyCorp

Trust Instinct over Credentials

Never hire someone if you have a twinkling in your gut telling you it's the wrong decision. Something in their background or résumé suggests that they're "The Right Guy," but you have a feeling that they're wrong. Go with your gut.

Marc Cenedella
Founder: TheLadders

Avoid False Positives

The most expensive hiring mistake is a false positive. False negatives are a bummer, but if you pass on a hire only to realize two months later that it was a mistake, at least it's not a very expensive mistake. On the other hand, if you hire someone who is wrong for the role or who doesn't fit into your company, it could be a huge deal to fix.

Lisa Gansky
Founder: Ofoto

Don't Try to Solve Every Problem with a Hire

I learned an important lesson from Marti Morfitt, the former CEO of CNS (the company that makes the Breathe-Right strips you see athletes wearing on the bridge of their noses). There is almost always a better option than taking on another full-time employee. The key word is *almost*. Growing businesses definitely need to hire, but the very best of them do so very carefully, with a strong focus on finding people who share their core values.

Tom Gardner
Founder: The Motley Fool

Don't Be Impressed by What You Don't Know

One of the mistakes people make when interviewing a potential hire is that they ask questions about something that person knows about, but that they themselves know nothing about. It's like interviewing a Japanese interpreter when you don't know Japanese. Anything they say will impress you because you have no way of knowing if their grammar is correct or if they even speak the language. Instead of falling into that trap, ask interviewees to school you in what you know: your business. The bar there is extremely high. First of all, you'll immediately know how well prepared they are for the interview. But more important, you think about your business all day, every day. If they're going to say something about it that impresses you, they'll have to be exceptionally smart.

Ben Horowitz
Founder: Opsware

Make Sure Early Hires Are Willing to Take on Any Role

Every company needs people with different skill sets and passions. But early on, everybody should be willing to wear ten different hats. They can't have the attitude that something isn't "their job" or "their responsibility." They have to have the MacGyver mentality and do whatever it takes to get the job done.

Tony Hsieh
Founder: LinkExchange, Venture Frogs

Avoid MBAs

As much as possible, avoid hiring MBAs. MBA programs don't teach people how to create companies. At my companies, our position is that we hire someone in spite of their having an MBA, not because of one.

Elon Musk
Founder: PayPal, SpaceX, Tesla Motors

THE
BEST ADVICE

LEADERSHIP

Don't Make Big Decisions at a Time of Weakness

When you're under extreme stress, you'll be tempted to say, "We'll have to close this whole thing down" or "We'll have to make this big gamble." But you're not mentally equipped to make smart decisions when you're feeling weak and beaten up. The right strategy is to get through it; get yourself to a place, psychologically, where you have some perspective and make the big decisions when you're strong.

Chris Anderson
Founder: Future Publishing

Be Radically Transparent, but Appreciate the Limits of Transparency

People do their best work when you trust them and give them all of the information they need to make good decisions. Moreover, most people will go beyond the scope of their own jobs when they have information about what's going on around them. To encourage that level of trust and engagement, be radically transparent, but also mindful of what people can and cannot handle. (You want your company to be aware of dangers, but not freaked out by them. You want your executive team to be aware *and* freaked out.) Ultimately, there are very few things that you *shouldn't* be transparent about.

Matt Blumberg
Founder: Return Path

Set Direction and Step Aside

If you really are a great CEO, you should wake up in the morning and have nothing to do. That would mean that you have set a clear vision, assembled a great team you could trust to move that vision forward, and given them the flexibility to operate. Of course, you'll never achieve that level of perfection, but you should organize with that goal in mind.

Steve Case
Founder: America Online (AOL)

Never Allow Your Anxiety to Infect Your Company

As the leader of a team or company, you will always have to deal with anxieties. You cannot let those anxieties spread out past you, the decision maker who can deal with them. You need to protect your employees from them, even if you cannot deal with them immediately.

Caterina Fake
Founder: Flickr, Hunch, Findery

Being Consistent Isn't as Important as Being Right

Al Davis, the owner of the Oakland Raiders, once said that he was more worried about being right than about being consistent. When I saw that, I read it over and over again. It's absolutely true, and it's extremely difficult to live up to. Admitting that it's impossible to get out of a situation is often the right thing to do. If you insist on consistency, it will be impossible for you to adapt.

Ben Horowitz
Founder: Opsware

Communicate the Logic of Your Decisions

When you start to scale an organization, the key is to communicate *how* you make decisions. What is the calculus that led you to a conclusion? When your team understands that logic, they can apply it to making decisions themselves. That degree of explicitness may feel aggressive, strange, or even risky at times, but it ultimately ends up solving more problems than it creates. Your team needs to be more comfortable talking about problems than hiding them.

Hosain Rahman
Founder: Jawbone

MARKET DEVELOPMENT

Make Investment Decisions Within a Market Context

Consider an executive who decides to target 15 percent of the PDA market. The marketing head will say, "I need a $15 million budget." The head of manufacturing will say, "I need to build three factories in China." Those are huge investments, but they might be worthwhile. Fifteen percent of the PDA marketplace is hundreds of millions of dollars. Twenty years earlier, it would have been absurd. The budgets would have been the same, but 15 percent of a nonexistent marketplace is "zero." A decision that would amount to burning loads of money in one era would be considered using it effectively in another. The only thing that changes is the market context.

Steve Blank
Founder: E.piphany

Consider Market Dynamics Alongside Market Size

It's tempting to look at an industry and say, "Boy, that could be a really big market." But the airline industry is a really big market, and the net profitability of that industry is negative. It's not just how big the market opportunity is. You need to know whether the dynamics in that market could yield a profitable and valuable company.

Jeff Bussgang
Founder: Open Market, Upromise, Flybridge Capital Partners

Be Your Own Competitor

Creating an organization of provocateurs means creating an organization that contains its own competition. You need people who are open to failure and willing to rewrite the industry rules if they feel that the marketplace is moving in a different direction. If those ideas aren't being generated within your organization, they're being generated outside of it. I'd rather compete with myself than with someone else in the marketplace.

Chip Conley
Founder: Joie de Vivre Hospitality

Create New Categories, Not New Businesses

What gets me excited is looking for ways to create new categories, as opposed to just building a particular business. Instead of just adding a new piece to the environment, new categories reframe the entire ecosystem. Think about the moment when the existing ideas or businesses or products in your category came to be and fundamentally shook things up. That's where the opportunities to effect real change are.

Lisa Gansky
Founder: Ofoto

Bad Markets Always Beat Good Teams

If you invest in a bad market, you'll never get a good business out of it, no matter how big that market is. A bad market always beats a good team. You have to enter a good market, preferably one that's not too small. Google is a great example. They went after a really big, existing market, and they made it into a much bigger market with a great product. For them, it was really simple: the search results worked. They served the ones people used as opposed to the ones people didn't use. Good company address big, robust markets with a winning product. Bad companies are missing one or both of those things.

Ben Horowitz
Founder: Opsware

Markets Are More Similar Than Different

Our experience in numerous global markets has led me to a controversial conclusion: markets are more similar than they are different. We'll often hear businesses on the verge of expanding claim that what works in Brazil won't work in China or India or Latin America. We've found the opposite to be the case. What works in Argentina is probably going to work in South Africa. And it's probably going to work in Turkey. There obviously need to be adjustments to the local market, but they're not as drastic as one might imagine.

Linda Rottenberg
Founder: Endeavor Global

Define Your Brand in Eight Words or Less

You need to be sure that the people your product is targeting are able to "get" it very quickly. If you can't define your brand in three to eight words, you're doomed. For instance, we had the idea in 1998 of launching a new magazine for business in the Internet age. It was exciting and we got good feedback, but I just didn't have the right name for it. Then, I was talking about it with [Amazon founder] Jeff Bezos at TED, throwing out ideas like *Business 2000* or *New Business*. He came up with *Business 2.0*, and in a flash, I knew that was exactly right.

Chris Anderson
Founder: Future Publishing

Engage in Guerrilla Marketing

It's not only about having a unique message, but presenting it in a unique way. You should always look for alternative ways to connect with people. Guerrilla marketing campaigns can be very effective, and they allow you to discover fun and interactive ways to introduce people to your brand.

Seth Goldman
Founder: Honest Tea

Target Customers Who Signal Their Interest

When we first launched Causes on Facebook, we overestimated how easy it would be to get random people to organize. There's a lot of hand-holding involved. At every stage you have to say, "Now do this. Now do this. Now do this." Over time, we've realized that many of the best organizers on the platform are existing nonprofits or people who work for them. We've ended up devoting much more time and energy to targeting that demographic and helping them be successful.

Joe Green
Founder: Causes

Take the Risk of Clearly Defining Your Product

The only way to really scale is by taking bets that might reduce your opportunity. This is especially true of your branding and marketing. People have the tendency to say, "I want to define my product as the best in the marketplace." You have to eschew that kind of vagueness viciously. Of course, when you say, "This is who I am," some customers will respond, "Nope. Not interested." But if you don't make those sorts of bold statements, you can never really learn whether people want what you're offering.

Reid Hoffman
Founder: LinkedIn

Embrace Instant Identification

Your brand is defined by the initial reaction that people have when they hear your name. If you strapped somebody to a chair, gave him an injection of sodium pentothal and said, "1-800-FLOWERS!" or "Jim McCann!"—what would he respond? That's your brand. It's emotional, and it's the first unconscious reaction people have to your personal brand or your business brand. Everything you do—good, bad, and indifferent—affects it.

Jim McCann
Founder: 1-800-FLOWERS.com

METRICS

Track Nonprofit Performance with For-Profit Precision

Nonprofits should be every bit as data driven, technologically agile, and performance minded as for-profit companies. DonorsChoose .org is not the first nonprofit to feel that way; Teach for America has been a pioneer in that respect, and there are many others for us to learn from. A major turning point in our organization was to begin operating, thinking, and performing more like a consumer Web company than a traditional nonprofit.

Charles Best
Founder: DonorsChoose.org

Identify Metrics That Test Your Hypotheses

Startup founders can't focus on income statements, balance sheets, cash flow—all of the metrics that fuel large corporations. When you don't have revenue, those metrics are irrelevant. You need to identify the metrics that test the hypothesis your business is built to prove. If you're in a Web business, it might be the number of clicks, the number of page views, the number of sign-ups or form submissions. After optimizing those metrics for a time, you need to determine whether they're the right ones. When you start, you don't even know what your metrics should be.

Steve Blank
Founder: E.piphany

Know When You're Being Boiled

Every consultant tells the story of the frog in the pot of boiling water: change the temperature gradually enough and the frog stays in the water until it dies. As CEO, you have to learn to smell smoke and realize there's fire. Otherwise, you'll get to a point where you've been soaking in boiling water and you're too limp to climb out.

Matt Blumberg
Founder: Return Path

Avoid Vanity Metrics

A lot of businesses focus on vanity metrics: comScore numbers, number of downloads, number of total users. For the most part, those are false, misleading signals. If you're building a software application, for instance, the number of downloads doesn't matter for the most part. You need to know who your active users are. Which subgroups are you reaching and which are you failing to reach? How can you improve reach in the demographics where you're missing your targets? Unfortunately, there are times when vanity metrics can become a self-fulfilling prophecy. The press sees great numbers and talks you up, and that can lead to its own sort of success. Don't plan for those scenarios. Optimize the metrics that really matter.

Chris Dixon
Founder: SiteAdvisor, Founder Collective, Hunch

Don't Micro-Optimize Yourself into Oblivion

With the proliferation of tracking tools and A/B testing, there is an extraordinary amount of data available to startup founders. Yet if you overreact to immediate feedback, you'll micro-optimize yourself into oblivion. You can't be *completely* oblivious to feedback, but you also have to be willing to trust your gut. Constantly adapting to every minor variation in your metrics will prevent you from ever making big bets. Visionaries are forced to set goals and strategy without perfect information.

Joe Green
Founder: Causes

Obsess over Revenues

In a startup, it's all about revenues. Revenues are your oxygen supply. Costs can be all over the place, but it doesn't matter if your revenues are sufficient and growing. That's why so many entrepreneurs are obsessed with customers: they're the revenue supply.

Jay Walker
Founder: Walker Digital, Priceline

PRODUCT DEVELOPMENT

Don't Make It Cheaper; Make It Better

I broke into an industry that was completely money-focused. Nobody was paying attention to women and thinking about how these undergarments felt, or how they fit. All the competition was just trying to make these commodities cheaper and cheaper, thinking that was the way to go. All of a sudden, I show up and charge more for one pair than anybody can comprehend, and women lined up in droves to buy them. I think I left the industry in shock, but I really believed that we needed to make it better, not cheaper.

Sara Blakely
Founder: Spanx

Start with a Target Market and Price, Then Build Backward

A lot of people get into the manufacturing business and think they can start by designing a product and figuring out the target and price later. They calculate the costs, double it wholesale, double it retail, and assume the consumer is going to pay for it—whatever it is. That's not going to work. Part of the challenge is bringing the product in at a realistic price that your customers can afford. You have to start with your buyer and price, and build backward from there.

Michael & Ellen Diamant
Founders: Skip Hop

Decode Problems Yourself

Every time I've gotten lazy and relied on somebody else to decode problems for me, I've run into problems. You have to apply yourself and find the mechanisms that drive your business with your own hands. Later on, you can teach managers the formulas you discover; but if it's your company, you need to be the one to blaze the trails.

Marc Eckō
Founder: Marc Eckō Enterprises

If You're Not Embarrassed by Your First Release, You Waited Too Long

One common piece of advice entrepreneurs get, and one of the worst, is your product has to be perfect before you launch. In technology, this is a holdover from when customers bought a piece of software at a store and installed it on their machines. If they didn't like it, they'd pull it off their machines and you'd be dead. That's not true with the Internet. There are lots of ways to get back to your customers. Products no longer have to be "perfect" right away.

Reid Hoffman
Founder: LinkedIn

Prioritize Progress over Process

Stuff needs to get done, and you need to do whatever it takes to get things done. Sometimes you just don't have all the resources you would like, but you just have to fight through it; that's part of the process. You're going to have to cut some corners in the *process*, but you can't let that stall your *progress*.

Tony Hsieh
Founder: LinkExchange, Venture Frogs

Everything Is a Prototype

Product development is never done. Everything is a prototype—a stepping stone to the next stage; but to say that everything is a prototype is not to say that you should ship beta stuff. You have to be absolutely committed to high quality, but remember it's just the beginning of what is possible. You are never done. All the elements have to be in place before you go to market with a product, but it should still be just one step in a broad and inexhaustible vision. It should also be good enough to get you to the next steps.

Hosain Rahman
Founder: Jawbone

PUBLIC RELATIONS

Be Your Own Publicist

When I first started out, I debated spending a bunch of money on a PR company to promote Spanx. Then I imagined myself as the person on the other end of the phone. If I were at the *Wall Street Journal* or *People* magazine, what would be more impressive: getting a call from someone who represents fifteen products or getting a call from someone who's passionately telling me about something she invented? I promoted Spanx myself, along with friends who liked the product, and it was much more effective.

Sara Blakely
Founder: Spanx

Never Make the Same Pitch Twice

No two pitches for your company should sound alike. You should always try new material and see what sticks with the audience you're addressing; you have to try things on for size. When you go to the store, you try on six blazers before you settle on the one you like. Defining your business is complex; a continual process of discovery is critical.

Matt Blumberg
Founder: Return Path

Clarify Your Vision Out Loud

I talk; I write; I give interviews. The more times I do it, the better I get and my staff always overhears the conversation. It teaches them how to think about the company, the values we share, the stories we think are important—even what we think is funny. I try to manifest openness and honesty in how I treat my peers, how I treat customers, and how I approach the market. By modeling these things, I set expectations for everybody else.

Robin Chase
Founder: Zipcar

Disclose Everything You Would Want to Know Yourself

Being transparent is about going beyond the rules of the game. Rather than asking what you *have* to disclose, ask what someone would *want* to know before buying your product. What you are *required* to tell your customers is irrelevant. It's really about what they would want to know if they knew to ask.

Jeffrey Hollender
Founder: Seventh Generation, American Sustainable Business Council

Share Your Failures Openly

If you've created effective partnerships with your investors, your customers, and your public, they won't need to believe that you're perfect. People are serious when they say that they want to get involved and be part of the entire process. You need to respect that desire and commit to transparency. Share your failures as well as your successes. It isn't just about PR; it's about courage and humility.

Jacqueline Novogratz
Founder: Acumen Fund

Pick a Valuation and a Closing Date, and Stick to Them

When you're raising angel money, pick a valuation, pick a closing date, and stick to them. There's always a range for angel funding. At the time I was raising money, the range was $3 million to $5 million, so I picked $4 million. If you don't pick a closing date, things will drag on and on. People will be in and then they'll be out, but suddenly they'll be back in, come the day you choose.

Marc Cenedella
Founder: TheLadders

Offer Friends and Family the Opportunity to Grow with You

A lot of people are rightfully scared to ask their friends and family for money. But if you really believe in your idea and think it's a money-maker, you'd be doing them a disservice if you didn't offer them first dibs. If you feel uncomfortable offering a great opportunity to your friends and family, it means you don't actually believe in your business.

Michael & Ellen Diamant
Founders: Skip Hop

Raise "Patient" Capital

Founders too often view raising capital as a transaction, when it is actually a very deep relationship. They think of money as money, when there is actually smart money, dumb money, high-integrity money, and low-integrity money. Most important, there is patient money and impatient money. If you raise money from your rich uncle to pursue a dream, he'll probably be very patient and leave you alone. Whereas if you raise money from professional institutional investors, they'll invariably fire you within two years. It is critical to know how patient your capital is.

Chris Dixon
Founder: SiteAdvisor, Founder Collective, Hunch

Don't Raise Capital for Validation

Too often, entrepreneurs are looking for validation as much as they're looking for capital. When you're putting yourself out there and sticking your neck out for an idea, a lot of people are telling you you're an idiot. And yet, someone is going to write a check and invest in you. That's so validating. But you have to ask yourself: what do I really need capital for? Funding is not the best way to be patted on the head and made to feel good. You want to build a great product or a great service that the people really need and love, and everything else is a means to that end.

Scott Heiferman
Founder: i-traffic, Fotolog, Meetup

Vet Investors like Potential Employees

Before taking money, interview three CEOs who have been recipients of money from the same person. Find out what it's really like to have them as a board member and an investor. Vet your investors the way an HR department vets potential employees. This is a much more significant decision. Think about the whole person outside of the context of how big a check they can write.

Jeffrey Hollender
Founder: Seventh Generation, American Sustainable Business Council

Don't Mistake Raising Capital for Success

Raising an inordinate amount of capital is often seen as a sign of success. The consequence of raising *too* much capital, however, is that the company has to be that many times bigger to get a return on that investment. Optimally, you're taking money to actually grow, rather than as a false indication that you're growing. Raising capital is not necessarily success; building the business is success.

Stephen Messer
Founder: LinkShare

SALES

Create Self-Serve Tools

If you've created a new market or reinvented an existing one, you'll find yourself with an open field and a clear value proposition. In those situations, you won't need a sales team. The best software companies, Dropbox for instance, don't have salespeople. They have self-serve products that are clearly valuable.

Kevin Efrusy
Founder: IronPlanet, Corio

Be a Tenacious Salesman

You have to constantly be pitching, pitching, pitching. Telling your story. Saying, "Here's my vision. Here's what I want to do with my organization." Almost everyone says no, but you can't allow that to frustrate you. Eventually, someone will say, "Here's $25,000." And then you pitch again.

Scott Harrison
Founder: charity: water

Be Your Company's First Salesman

When we started ZocDoc, people didn't believe that doctors would pay money for our services—or that you could sell anything at all to doctors. We knew we had to prove our critics wrong, so we just kept banging our heads against the wall trying to figure out ways that we could sign up doctors. We had three different sales forces, but eventually I needed to become a salesperson myself. I was never a salesperson, but I had the will to make the company succeed. I went door to door. I got thrown out of three doctors' offices. Ultimately, I figured out how to sign doctors up; I signed our first fifty clients myself.

Cyrus Massoumi
Founder: ZocDoc

Don't Treat Startup Sales like Mainstream Sales

If you're one of three thousand salespeople at a large company, the only exciting thing is beating the other guys and being number one. But early-stage salespeople get their kicks when they hear a customer say, "Wow! This is exactly what I need!" There's an honest, genuine excitement in solving a client's problem. The actual transaction becomes a no-brainer.

In startups, salespeople are really business-development people. This is something that VCs often don't understand. They'll say, "Let's bring in this top-notch sales guy. He ran this and this and this." But then you meet with them, and they start asking about compensation plans, and what tier they're going to be in, and what territories they're going to cover. That's not what early-stage companies are about.

Kirill Sheynkman
Founder: Stanford Technology Group, Plumtree Software,
Elastra Corporation

Hire Salespeople Who Can Work with the Rhythm of Your Sales Cycle

Different salespeople work at different paces. Some of them thrive on the adrenaline high of selling something every week; others like the challenge of a nine-month sales cycle. But if you take the greatest week-to-week salesperson in the world and give him a nine-month cycle, he'll probably fail. You have to make sure that your sales team's pace matches your company's sales cycle.

Jeff Stewart
Founder: Mimeo, Urgent Career, Lenddo

Hire Your Weaknesses

Like most entrepreneurs, I couldn't afford to hire anybody else when I first launched the product. I was the inventor, I had $5,000, and that was it; I had to be every department. But after two years, I could afford to hire people into roles that I didn't enjoy. In particular, I gave a ton of power and strength to my CEO, Laurie Ann Goldman, who's been with me for nine years. She's a strategic leader. Most important, she's *consistent*. To be an effective manager on a day-to-day basis, you have to be consistent. I'm more of a creative person. I recognize that about myself, which is why I hired my weaknesses early on. I think if most founders don't relinquish some control, then we hold back the development of our companies.

Sara Blakely
Founder: Spanx

Don't Collect Outstanding Individuals; Field a Great Team

You want people who are very flexible in their thinking and can survive in an atmosphere of change. You also need to field the best overall team. People who can get work done together effectively are "functional experts," and these are more valuable than "rock stars." They're not self-promoters. They're members of a group that puts the business first and has an understanding of people, the market, internal dependencies, and the broader implications of any and all decisions.

Matt Blumberg
Founder: Return Path

Promote Employees Who Contribute Beyond Their Immediate Jobs

There are certain employees who can't help contributing all over. Of course, some people are bubbling over with lousy ideas, but sometimes someone bubbles over and *helps* in many different areas. When that happens, you clearly know that you want to develop that person further because they get what you're trying to do and will move heaven and earth to make it happen. Wander around the cubicles now and then. Look for people who see the bigger picture beyond their particular team and contribute across a broad spectrum. They're the ones that you want to raise higher and higher up in your organization.

Rodney Brooks
Founder: iRobot, Heartland Robotics

Meet Your Immediate Needs

Young entrepreneurs often want to hire a core group of people who will stay together forever. But the reality is that, in the first days of your business, you aren't in a position to attract the financial officer or the operations person you'll need in a year or two. You have to realistically ask, "What's essential for *right now*?" The answer to that question is going to be different one or two or five years out. People who join the team early in a company's life can't take it personally when there needs to be a change.

Lisa Gansky
Founder: Ofoto

Empower Your Employees

You want employees to care about the long-term performance of the company, so you should give them as much control over their part in the business as you can, including giving them ownership of their P&L. Stock options are a very direct way of making them feel invested in the future of the company, and a good way to retain them. But, more important, hire people who are passionate about your core mission and make it clear that they can have a direct impact on moving it forward. There's a real satisfaction to building something that you believe in; employees should share in that satisfaction.

Seth Goldman
Founder: Honest Tea

Vision is a Team Thing

Everyone knows that hiring the right people is critical to an organization's success. But you won't get the best out of them unless you let them help shape your vision. All the best strategic decisions at TED over the last ten years have emerged as a result of animated conversations with the amazing people who work with me. Ideas are not lightbulbs that switch on out of nowhere. They come when creative people spark off each other. You have to give that process every chance. You not only get better ideas that way, you also get buy-in.

Chris Anderson
Founder: Future Publishing

Purpose Is Central to Motivation

The motivation for founding a company should be the fun of constructing and building something, and the feeling that you're making an impact. For me, the goal is to help kids from low-income families get the materials and experiences they need for a great education. Making a social impact in the world is a metric of personal worth that is as important, or more important, than the money you've made.

Charles Best
Founder: DonorsChoose.org

Never Hold "Immutable" Principles

A lot of entrepreneurs fail because they'll hold something in their minds as an immutable principle. The idea that your values should never change in the face of data is nonsensical. You have to recognize failure wherever it happens and look it straight on. When the evidence says that you're wrong, you have to be willing to relinquish even your most deeply held beliefs.

Robin Chase
Founder: Zipcar

Align Revenue and Impact

When we started Causes, we tried to build a business that was focused on both revenue and impact. That double bottom line doesn't work unless those two things are fully aligned. If you focus half your time driving revenues and half your time making an impact, you won't do either well. You have to find a business model that accomplishes both goals at once.

Joe Green
Founder: Causes

Don't Let Your Vision Inhibit Change

Don't lock yourself into a specific business model when you start out, especially if you're going into a new industry. You just don't even know what you don't know. Because nothing ever turns out the way you expect it to, you have to be open-minded about the path your company takes. Don't get stuck on what you envisioned when the company first started.

Tony Hsieh
Founder: LinkExchange, Venture Frogs

Don't Start a Company to Get Rich

When I see entrepreneurs make money, I'm thrilled because I know that they worked hard for it and they deserve it. Yet those entrepreneurs didn't choose their career path in order to make a fortune. Given a startup's odds of failure, there are easier ways to make money. If you're starting your own venture, you have to have a desire to create something new and valuable and control your own destiny.

Stephen Messer
Founder: LinkShare

WORKING FOR YOURSELF

Money Is a Magnifying Glass

Money makes you more of who you already are. If you are a jerk, it will make you a bigger jerk; if you're insecure, you become even more insecure; if you are generous, you become even more generous; if you are nice, you become even nicer. Making money is like holding up a magnifying glass to who you are, personally and professionally. It creates a lot of energy and power, and it's up to you to use that in a really good way.

Sara Blakely
Founder: Spanx

Don't Overestimate the Risks or Upsides of Entrepreneurship

People overestimate the likelihood that you will go broke as an entrepreneur, but on the other hand, they don't recognize how unlikely it is that you will become a billionaire. Bill Gates is the richest man in the world because he executed everything perfectly. He flipped fifty heads in a row. That almost certainly won't be any other entrepreneur's experience. It's also extremely unlikely that they will fail so completely that they won't be able live reasonably well.

Chris Dixon
Founder: SiteAdvisor, Founder Collective, Hunch

Don't Let Academic Models Take the Place of Lived Experience

Entrepreneurs often think that there is a formula for running a business: measure this, check that box, and you're done. But it never looks like that on the ground. It's messy, but it has to happen organically; that's heuristics. Academic types are really scared of that; they want to believe it's just Xs and Os. But you can't always learn everything in school. Sometimes your philosophy develops from your interaction with the world.

Marc Eckō
Founder: Marc Eckō Enterprises

Be Relentlessly Devoted to Your Idea

Being devoted to an idea goes beyond hours. Your whole person has to be devoted to solving a problem. If you are going to survive after the first year or two, it will only be because your devotion has led you to create something exceptional. This requires extreme attention to detail. You have to do anything and everything to make it happen.

Adeo Ressi
Founder: TheFunded.com, The Founder Institute

Make Personal Sacrifices

When you start a company, you have to make the conscious decision to cut back in certain areas of your life. In my case, there were things that I knew I couldn't compromise on. I exercise every day to stay in shape, and I take my children to school three days a week and spend time with them in the evenings. Those things couldn't go away. But I did have to find areas where I could cut back, like sporting events or dinner with friends. When I was in my twenties, I was everywhere—at the opera, at restaurants, watching Brazilian bands perform. I had to be willing to sacrifice that when I joined DoubleClick and started my own companies. You can do anything, but you can't do everything.

Kevin Ryan
Founder: AlleyCorp

Clinically Analyze Mistakes and Move On

You are going to be defeated many times, but you have to pick yourself up and move on. When you make a mistake, look back and say, "That error was mine, but I am not defined by my mistakes. You can always make a fresh start; next time I'll know better." Winners are people who just don't quit.

Jay Walker
Founder: Walker Digital, Priceline

INDEX

A

ACCEL PARTNERS 112, 113

ACUMEN FUND 220-27

ALLEYCORP 246, 247

AMAZON 191, 248

AMERICAN SUSTAINABLE BUSINESS COUNCIL 178

ANDERSON, CHRIS 20-25, 271, 273, 279, 281, 288

ANDREESSEN, MARC 103, 184, 185-87, 189

ANDREESSEN HOROWITZ 184, 189

AOL (AMERICA ONLINE) 45, 62-67, 131, 136, 137, 138, 139

B

BEST, CHARLES 26-31, 273, 282, 288

BEZOS, JEFF 24, 54, 128, 248

BLAKELY, SARA 32-37, 275, 283, 284, 287, 289

BLANK, STEVE 38-43, 154, 234, 270, 273, 280, 282

BLUMBERG, MATT 44-49, 272, 279, 282, 284, 287

BLURB 142-47

BONDS, BARRY 111

BRIN, SERGEY 114

BROOKE, PETER 242

BROOKS, RODNEY 50-55, 276, 287

BUFFETT, WARREN 140

BUSINESS INSIDER 246, 247, 248

BUSSGANG, JEFF 56-61, 275, 277, 280

C

CASE, STEVE 62-67, 279

CAUSES 154-59

CENEDELLA, MARC 68-73, 112, 276, 277, 278, 285

CHARITY: WATER 160-65

CHASE, ROBIN 74-79, 274, 284, 288

COLBERT, STEPHEN 28-29, 30

COLLECTIVE[I] 213

COMMONWISE 183

COMPAQ 215

COMPLEX MEDIA 107, 109, 111

CONLEY, CHIP 80-85, 154, 273, 280

CONSCIOUS CAPITALISM 206

CONTAINER STORE 139

CORIO 112, 113

D

DACHIS, JEFF 86-91

DACHIS GROUP 86, 88, 91

DANIELSON, ANTJE 75

DIAMANT, MICHAEL AND ELLEN 92-99, 271, 283, 285

DIXON, CHRIS 13, 100-105, 119, 123, 272, 282, 285, 289

DONORSCHOOSE.ORG 26-31

DOUBLECLICK 246, 247, 251

DRUCKER, PETER 85

E

EASTMAN KODAK 131, 132-33, 135, 142, 143

EBAY 114, 119, 214, 215, 216

ECKŌ, MARC 106-11, 283, 289

EFRUSY, KEVIN 112-17, 286

ELASTRA CORPORATION 252, 253, 255

ELSTEIN, EDUARDO 242

EMAIL CHANGE OF ADDRESS (ECOA) 45-46

ENDEAVOR GLOBAL 240-45

E.PIPHANY 38, 39

ETSY 114, 118

EVERGREEN COOPERATIVES 183

F

FACEBOOK 104, 112, 113, 154, 155, 156-57, 189

FAKE, CATERINA 101, 102, 105, 118-23, 276, 279

FEDEX 84, 260

FLICKR 118, 119-20, 121, 123

FLYBRIDGE CAPITAL 56, 58-59, 61

FOTOLOG 166, 168

FOUNDER COLLECTIVE 100, 101, 102, 118, 120

FOUNDER INSTITUTE 234, 235, 236-37, 239

FOURSQUARE 100

FREE, MITCH 124-29, 274

FRUITBOUQUETS.COM 207

FUTURE PUBLISHING 20, 22

G

GANSKY, LISA 130-35, 270, 272, 278, 280, 287

GARDNER, TOM AND DAVE 136-41, 278

GATES, BILL 105, 156, 250

GILT GROUPE 246, 247-49, 250, 251

GITTINS, EILEEN 142-47, 270, 276

GLADWELL, MALCOLM 11, 137

GNN (GLOBAL NETWORK NAVIGATOR) 130, 131

GOLDMAN, SETH 148-53, 281, 287

GOOGLE 113, 114, 187, 208, 247

GREEN, JOE 154-59, 272, 281, 282, 288

GROUPON 114

H

HARRISON, SCOTT 160-65, 274, 286

HASTINGS, REED 81, 114

HEARTLAND ROBOTICS 50, 52

HEIFERMAN, SCOTT 166-71, 270, 285

HEWLETT-PACKARD 185, 187, 259

HOFFMAN, REID 172-77, 272, 277, 281, 283

HOLLENDER, JEFFREY 178-83, 284, 285

HONEST TEA 148-53

HOROWITZ, BEN 19, 184-89, 270, 271, 278, 279, 280

HOTJOBS 69, 70

HSIEH, TONY 170, 190-95, 278, 283, 288

HUNCH 100, 101, 102, 105, 118, 119, 121, 123

I

IBM 112, 201, 253, 254
ICLIPS 92, 93
IROBOT 50-52
IRONPLANET 112, 113
I-TRAFFIC 166, 167, 168

J

JAWBONE 228-33
JOBS, STEVE 81, 113-14, 268
JOIE DE VIVRE 80-83
JONES, PAUL TUDOR 162

K

KANARICK, CRAIG 87
KELLNER, PETER 242
KIMPTON, BILL 81

L

LENDDO 258, 263
LINKEDIN 116, 172-77
LINKEXCHANGE 190, 191
LINKSHARE 208-11
LOUDCLOUD 184, 185-86

M

MARC ECKŌ ENTERPRISES 106-11
MASSOUMI, CYRUS 196-201, 271, 286
MATHER, SHAFFI 224
MCCANN, JIM 202-7, 271, 275, 281, 284
MEETUP 166-69, 171
MERRIMAN, DWIGHT 247, 248
MESSER, STEPHEN AND HEIDI 208-13, 277, 285,288
MFG.COM 124-29
MICROSOFT 87, 116, 191
MIMEO 258, 259-60
MONITOR110 260-61
THE MOTLEY FOOL 136-41
MUSK, ELON 214-19, 276, 278
MYSPACE 104, 189

N

NALEBUFF, BARRY 149
NETFLIX 81, 114
NETSCAPE 87, 139, 185, 215, 241
NOVOGRATZ, JACQUELINE 220-27, 271, 274, 284

O

OBAMA, BARACK 67, 129, 156
OFOTO 130-35
1-800-FLOWERS.COM 202-7
OPEN MARKET 56, 57, 58, 60, 61
OPSWARE 184-89

P

PAGE, LARRY 113, 114, 187
PARKER, SEAN 156
PAYPAL 214, 215-16
PERSONIFY 142, 143
PLUMTREE SOFTWARE 252, 253, 254
PRICELINE 264-65

R

RAHMAN, HOSAIN 228-33, 273, 277, 279, 283
RAZORFISH 86-88, 91
RESSI, ADEO 234-39, 289
RETHINK ROBOTICS 52-53, 55
RETURN PATH 44-49
REVOLUTION 62, 65
ROBIN HOOD FOUNDATION 162
ROTTENBERG, LINDA 240-45, 280
RTP VENTURES 252, 255, 257
RYAN, KEVIN 246-51, 277, 289

S

SAHLMAN, BILL 242
SALESFORCE.COM 199
SALSA 142, 143
SAPLING FOUNDATION 21, 22
SCHMIDHEINY, STEPHAN 241
SCHRAGER, IAN 81
SEVENTH GENERATION 178-82
SHEYNKMAN, KIRILL 252-57, 286
SHUTTERFLY 131
SITEADVISOR 100-103
SKIP HOP 92-99
SMITH, FRED 84
SOLARCITY 214, 216
SOROS, GEORGE 242
SOUTHWEST AIRLINES 82
SPACEX 214, 215, 219
SPANX 32-37
SQUARE EARTH 259
STANFORD TECHNOLOGY GROUP 252, 253, 254
STEWART, JEFF 258-63, 272, 286
SWINMURN, NICK 191

T

TED TALKS 20-23, 25, 233
10GEN 246, 247, 248
TESLA MOTORS 214, 216, 218
THEFUNDED.COM 234, 235-36
THELADDERS 68-73
THIEL, PETER 187, 215
TIME WARNER 64, 87, 179
TINDELL, KIP 139
TWITTER 119, 121

U

UPROMISE 56, 57-58, 61
URGENT CAREER 258

V

VENTURE FROGS 191

W

WALKER, JAY 264-69, 274, 282, 289
WALKER DIGITAL 264-67
WINFREY, OPRAH 28, 33, 35

X

X.COM 215

Y

YAHOO 69, 119, 120, 122

Z

ZAPPOS 190-95
ZIP2 215
ZIPCAR 65, 74-79
ZIQITZA HEALTH CARE LIMITED 224
ZOCDOC 196-201
ZUCKERBERG, MARK 113, 154, 155, 189, 250

ACKNOWLEDGMENTS

I want to thank my parents, Virelle and Steve Kidder, who have inspired all their four children to set goals at every stage of life, and to always take risks and reinvent ourselves. They are people who "let their life speak"—I am lucky to have them as friends and as a powerful model of marriage. My sincere thanks and respect to the Chronicle Books team, particularly Christine Carswell, who placed a brave bet on this idea after only one lunch together. The Chronicle team includes some of the last, truly artistic publishers—a rare group with vibrant imaginations and a startup spirit. I would also like to thank my agent, Joy Tutela, who is as smart as she is lovely; she is Audrey Hepburn with a velvet hammer.

It's not recommended that you write a book while building a startup. That's why I am not the primary author of *The Startup Playbook*. Instead, this entire work was born out of the notes from, and videos of, one-on-one interviews with the entrepreneurs whom I so deeply admire. The full credit of authorship goes to my coauthor, Hanny Hindi, and my Chronicle editor, Leigh Haber. Hanny completely assembled the book from the hieroglyphs of my notes, and demonstrated a supernatural patience in constructing the core content. My friend and long-time collaborator of now six books, Leigh, reconstructed and refined the book you are now holding in your hands. It would not exist without her efforts. Helena Holgersson-Shorter valiantly helped take it over the finish line. I also specifically want to thank several wise counselors: Roger Fransecky, my uncle, who started my entrepreneurial engine; and my metro-maven in New York, Sunny Bates, who was enormously generous and trusting in helping to create this book. I also offer my deepest gratitude to my first investor, friend, and now coinvestor in our own fund, Marty Schoffstall, who has been with me through every startup.

It's worthwhile to overcommunicate how grateful I am to the entrepreneurs who shared their time, wisdom, and experiences. You are all extraordinary in so many profoundly unique ways. I am certain the power of your ideas will intersect with the burning drive of so many entrepreneurs in incalculable ways. I know this gift to them will be returned to you.

Finally, I am profoundly grateful for my entire team, investors, and board at Clickable. I should list everyone by name, as everyone deserves credit for authoring and perfecting our Clickable playbook, but the list would be in the hundreds at this point. However, my appreciation of you goes beyond a list and beyond words, as it has been your tens of thousands of hours that have allowed us to make this journey together and realize the goal of giving birth to a company. I simply want to thank you for your belief in our efforts and in our common purpose, and for your unwavering drive to achieve it. I am humbled and awed by your profound dedication to our outcome, and our friendships will last a lifetime.

"I love this book. It's like having a virtual advisory board of some of the best entrepreneurs in the world. You will discover valuable insights or a good idea on every page to add to your own playbook."

—Brian O'Kelley
   Founder, AppNexus

"The world needs more entrepreneurs. By taking the hard part of building a business so seriously, this book should help more people get to the fun part—success. David Kidder brings both a writer's mind and a startup veteran's urgency to an entertaining and useful trip inside the minds of today's most successful creators of organizations— both for profit and for purpose."

—David Kirkpatrick
   Founder, host, and CEO, Techonomy Media; author of *The Facebook Effect*

"'I wish I had this idea' is my highest praise. It is truly unique. Kidder is one of the rare people who could pull this astounding volume of talent and wisdom together. This is driven by his generosity, judgment, and connectedness. The power of the content in this book is that it has been created by an experienced insider, not an intrigued outsider. This is David's special mastery, and the book is a gift."

—Andreas Weigend
   Professor, University of California, Berkeley, Stanford University, and Tsinghua University; former chief scientist, Amazon

"From technological entrepreneurs to social entrepreneurs, The Startup Playbook features important tips from top American innovators that will change the way you think about your job, your business, and maybe even your industry."

—Alexis Maybank
   Cofounder and chief strategy officer, Gilt Groupe

"David Kidder is a master at getting people to reveal themselves. These are all entrepreneurs I have heard from before, but David somehow got them to expose things about themselves—and to distill lessons from their experiences—that no one else has been able to do."

—Laurel Touby
   Founder, www.mediabistro.com

"Bravo! David Kidder's latest book is a gift to aspiring entrepreneurs. His interviews with our era's most successful startup players reveal what we need to know about turning dreams into businesses that last. Readers will benefit from the Playbook's practical advice and the inspiration in every story."

—Wenda Harris Millard
   President and COO, MediaLink; former co-CEO, Martha Stewart Living; former chief marketing officer, Yahoo!

"David has done it again! The Startup Playbook is a glorious mix of easily accessible, super-condensed information and elegantly distilled wisdom from some of the most successful disruptors of our generation. A great read full of everything you need to be inspired to start up your own business."

—Sunny Bates
   Founder, Sunny Bates Associates and Redthread

"David Kidder writes from experience and passion about what it means to succeed from startup to successful enterprise. Whether old company or new, big or small, Kidder reminds us of the entrepreneurial spirit that can propel many great companies and nations."

—Beth Comstock
   Senior vice president and chief marketing officer, GE